Creating the
South Carolina
State House

Creating the
South Carolina
State House

John M. Bryan

UNIVERSITY OF SOUTH CAROLINA PRESS

© 1999 University of South Carolina

Published in Columbia, South Carolina, by the
University of South Carolina Press

Manufactured in Canada

03   02   01   00   99   5   4   3   2   1

Library of Congress Cataloging-in-Publication Data

Bryan, John Morrill.
    Creating the South Carolina State House / John M. Bryan.
      p.   cm.
    Includes bibliographical references and index.
    ISBN 1-57003-291-2 (cloth)
    1. South Carolina State House (Columbia, S.C.)   2. Public
buildings—South Carolina—Columbia—Conservation and restoration.
3. Columbia (S.C.)—Buildings, structures, etc.   I. Title.
NA4413.C68 B78   1999
725'.11'0975771—dc21   98-40220

Contents

List of Illustrations   vii
Preface   xiii
Acknowledgments   xv

Chapter One: A False Start   1

John L. Manning and Milford Plantation   1
The First State House in Columbia   4
Archival Storage and the Need for New State Offices   10
Starting the Present, or Second, State House in Columbia   13
Peter Hjalmar Hammarskold   14
John Rudolph Niernsee   18
George Edward Walker   19
Walker vs. Niernsce   25
Dome vs. Tower: The Origins of the Controversy   28

Chapter Two: Getting Started   31

John R. Niernsee   32
Niernsee's Plan in Its National Context   36
Problems to Overcome   45
Henry Kirke Brown, Principal Sculptor   47
Architecture, Ornament, and Symbolic Meaning   51
Construction of the New State House during the Civil War   56
Major John R. Niernsee and the War Effort   57
The War Draws Near   59
John R. Niernsee and the Defense of the City   63

Chapter Three: The Hiatus   68

Niernsee Returns to Baltimore   74

Reconstruction   78
The Dual Government and the End of Reconstruction   85

Chapter Four: Substantial Completion   94

J . Crawford Neilson   94
Francis (Frank) McHenry Niernsee   102
John Quitman Marshall and the Campaign to Complete the State
    House   111
Frank Pierce Milburn, Architect of the Completion of the State
    House   115
The State of South Carolina vs. McIlvain, Milburn, et al.   120

Chapter Five: Defining the Grounds   124

Frederick W. Ruckstull and the Major Sculptural Monuments   125
The State House as Civic Center   132
Proposals to Enlarge the State House   141
The State Office Building   145

Chapter Six: The Renovation of 1992–1998   150

Notes   174
Selected Bibliography   195
Index   200

Illustrations

John L. Manning   1

Milford Plantation, detail   3

Corinthian Capital   3

Charleston Hotel, 1865   5

Milford Plantation   5

The first State House in Columbia   7

"Map of Columbia, surveyed by Arthur and Moore," circa 1850   8

"The First Map of the City of Columbia . . . from the Survey Ordered 1786,"   8

Site plan, location of State Houses   9

The first State House in Columbia, one dollar bill, Bank of South Carolina, 1862   10

The first State House in Columbia, principal floor plan, 1839   11

Fireproof building, flawed wall   18

John Rudolph Niernsee, circa 1870   19

U.S. Custom House, Charleston, circa 1850   20

Another view of the U.S. Custom House, Charleston, circa 1850   21

Footprint of the first State House, 1854   24

Calvert Street Station, Baltimore   33

Train shed roof structure, Baltimore   33

Tennessee State Capitol cupola   38

Model of tower of Tennessee State Capitol   38

Tennessee State Capitol, circa 1850   39

Palmetto Monument, circa 1902   41

Palmetto Monument, 1995   42

New State House north elevation on Confederate ten dollar bill, 1863   43

New State House north elevation, circa 1860   43

"New State House Depicted at Columbia," 1861   44

Henry Kirke Brown, circa 1860   47

Model for house pediment of U.S. Capitol, 1855   48

Columbia studio, Henry Kirke Brown, 1861   50

Model for north pediment of South Carolina State House   52

Model of central figure for north pediment, 1860–1861   52

Model of right wing of north pediment, 1860–1861   53

Model of left wing of north pediment, 1860–1861   53

George McDuffie, circa 1860   53

Robert Y. Hayne, circa 1860   53

Reconnaissance map of Congaree River, 1862   58

Reconnaissance map of Santee River, 1862   58

"Sherman's Army Entering Columbia," 1865   65

"Raising the Stars and Stripes over the [Old] Capitol," 1865   70

"13th Iowa Regiment . . . Raising the Stars and Stripes above the [New] State House," 1865   71

"Columbia after the Fire," 1865   72

"Columbia . . . Portion of the Burnt District," 1865   72

Main Street looking north from State House, 1865   72

New State House, south facade, 1865   76

New State House with temporary roof, circa 1870   77

New State House with roof by Frank Niernsee, circa 1890   77

New State House, north facade, 1896   82

Muldoon Monument Co. advertisement, 1900   83

Landscape plan, 1878   86

"Bird's Eye View of the City of Columbia," detail, 1872   87

"Map of Columbia . . . and Its Suburbs," detail, 1895   89

Pilaster, west side of north portico, 1997   99

Design of cast iron bracket for balcony in hall, circa 1890   106

Metal work, circa 1890   106

Library, 1995   108

Library stairs, 1995   109

Tennessee State Capitol library balcony, circa 1940   110

Tennessee State Capitol library, circa 1940   111

Design for electroliers on main stairs, circa 1890   111

Design of principal stairway in cast and wrought iron, circa 1890   112

Lobby stairway, 1995   112

Elevation with dome, circa 1900   114

Frank Pierce Milburn, 1906   115

Mecklenburg County Court House, 1901   116

Wythe County Court House, 1901   116

Bourbon County Court House, 1901   116

Lowndes County Court House, 1901   117

Abbeville, Georgia, Court House, 1901   117

South Carolina State House, 1901   117

"Steel Frame of Dome Completion of South Carolina Capitol Building," circa 1900   118

Dome structure, 1995   118

"Elevation of Main Street Facade, Completion of South Carolina State House," circa 1900   120

Frederick Wellington Ruckstull in his studio, circa 1900   125

General Hartranft   126

Statue of Wade Hampton, crated, 1906   127

Statue of Wade Hampton, 1906   127

Admiral Dewey Triumphal Arch, 1899   128

Gloria Victis, 1903   128

South Carolina Women of the Confederacy, 1910   129

Revolutionary partisan generals, 1913   131

"Suggested System of Inner and Outer Parks and Reservation and Connecting Roads and Driveways," Kelsey and Guild, 1905   133

"Proposed Park Areas," Kelsey and Guild, 1905   133

"Civic Center for the Grouping of Columbia's Future Public Buildings," Kelsey and Guild, 1905   134

"Alternative Plan for Civic Center," Kelsey and Guild, 1905   134

North elevation, Stevens and Wilkinson, 1995   135

Plaster model, A. W. Todd, 1911   136

Section, Stevens and Wilkinson, 1995   136

Section, Stevens and Wilkinson, 1995   136

North elevation, A. W. Todd, 1911   137

Plan, A. W. Todd, 1911   137

Plan, A. W. Todd, 1911   137

North elevation, A. W. Todd, 1911   138

Plan, A. W. Todd, 1911   138

Elevation, A. W. Todd, 1911   139

Plan, A. W. Todd, 1911   139

Elevation, C. C. Wilson, 1916   140

North elevation, W. Baker, 1946   140

End elevation, W. Baker, 1946   141

Plan, W. Baker, 1946   142

North elevation with proposed wings, Stevens and Wilkinson, 1992   142

State Office (Calhoun) Building, H. Tatum, 1927   145

Site plan, Stevens and Wilkinson, circa 1995   149

Seismic treatment of foundation, 1997   154

Excavation and installation of seismic beam and isolators, 1996   155

Excavation and installation of seismic beam and isolators, 1996   155

Excavation and installation of seismic beam and isolators, 1996   155

Civil War cannon balls found during excavations, 1997   156

Fragment of granite baluster found during excavation, 1997   156

Fragment of marble ornament found during excavation, 1997   156

Wrought iron lock and key found during excavation, 1997   157

Interior during renovation, boxed ornament, first floor corridor, 1996   157

Interior during renovation, House Chamber, 1997   158

Interior during renovation, Senate Chamber, 1997   159

Restoration of dome, 1997   160

Exterior view of finished dome, 1998   161

State House lobby, 1998   162

State House lobby from balcony, 1998   163

Hallway with boxed ornaments, 1998   164

Senate Chamber rostrum with painting of John C. Calhoun, 1998   165

View of the House Chamber, 1998   166–167

State House Library, 1998   168

Capitol lobby dome, 1998   169

Illustrations

North facade of State House with Confederate Monument, 1998   170

South facade of State House, 1998   171

Oblique view of south facade, 1998   172

South portico, east view, 1998   173

Preface

The State House is the most evocative building in South Carolina. Its creation spanned half a century with most of the work being done in three campaigns. Construction began in 1854, and the exterior walls were almost finished—but the building had no roof or interior walls or floors—when the Civil War brought the project to a halt. Little was done during the 1870s, but a temporary roof and interior allowed the building to be used by the Reconstruction government. Throughout the 1880s a second effort was made to finish the interior and landscape the grounds. A final burst of activity began in 1900 and focused on the principal exterior features, the porticos, and dome. It was declared substantially complete in 1903.

Several recurring patterns characterize the work. First, the site has always been viewed as symbolic. Antebellum planters, for example, who initiated the building wanted it to portray the legitimacy of their version of states rights—as late as 1901 the rumor persisted that some hoped they were creating a capitol for a future confederacy.[1] At the turn of the century a series of monuments were installed reflecting reverence for the Lost Cause. More recently, the confederate battle flag, an inflammatory, multifaceted symbol, was displayed in the House of Representatives (1938), then in the Senate Chamber (1956), and "in observance of the centennial" of secession was raised on the roof along with the state and national flags in 1962. The following year a resolution was passed "to have the Confederate flag flown on the flagpole on top of the State House."[2] Throughout the current renovation a public debate has swirled around the appropriateness and meaning of the display of the confederate battle flag. Whatever the outcome of the controversy, its intensity is a testament to the continued symbolic importance of the site.

Funding has rarely been adequate. Legislative frugality often slowed construction and adversely affected design decisions. Nevertheless, those responsible have usually tried to maintain high standards of design and craftsmanship. Much of the critical work has been done by people from out of state, and the search for the lowest bidder, or for skills unavailable in South Carolina, led to the participation of John Rudolph Niernsee, an architect from Baltimore; Edward Otto Schwagerl, a landscape architect from Philadelphia; Henry Kirke Brown and Frederick Wellington Ruckstull, sculptors from New York;

and Harlan P. Kelsey and Irving T. Guild, landscape architects from Boston. Understanding their contributions puts the State House in a national context; consequently, the significance of their work and ideas forms a major part of the story that follows.

Two more themes are noteworthy. First, in every generation since the 1880s, there have been proposals to expand the State House, for the growth of government and the advent of indoor plumbing, electricity, and heating quickly made the original building inadequate. Nonetheless, from 1885 to the present, proponents of change have been repeatedly defeated by a deep-seated reverence for the historic design and a resistance to the cost of additions. Finally, tracing the development of the State House, we see the architectural profession evolve in South Carolina and are reminded of many people whose contributions, by and large, have been forgotten.

All history is ultimately local, and local history is ultimately personal. Whenever possible the story that follows is based on diaries, letters, and contemporaneous documents by those who created the building and grounds. A glimpse of the people should make the site more meaningful and help us feel more at home.

Acknowledgments

This book is a by-product of the 1995–1998 renovation of the State House. The archival research took place as construction was revealing the historic fabric and excavations were unearthing artifacts; consequently, the writing was exciting. I am especially grateful to the State House Committee, which sponsored the research as part of their work. Senators serving on the committee have included J. Yancy McGill, Kingstree; William H. O'Dell, Ware Shoals; Kay Patterson, Columbia; Harvey S. Peeler, Jr., Gaffney; Holly Cork, Hilton Head; Hugh K. Leatherman, Florence; W. Greg Ryberg, Aiken; and J. Verne Smith of Greer, who has served as chairman. Members from the House of Representatives have included William D. Boan, Heath Springs; Rex F. Rice, Easley; Marion P. Carnell, Ware Shoals; Jerry N. Govan, Jr., Orangeburg; Harry M. Hallman, Jr., Mt. Pleasant; Jean L. Harris, Cheraw; Irene K. Rudnick, Aiken; and Annette Young-Brickell, Summerville. The day-to-day work of the committee has been done by Frank Caggiano, clerk of the Senate; Rick Kelly, General Services; and Sandra McKinney, clerk of the House. Their guidance and assistance has been invaluable.

Daniel Bilderback, project manager for the University of South Carolina Department of History invited me to participate in the project. Working with him has been a joy. In addition to handling all administrative details, he created a photographic record of the renovation and managed the retrieval of artifacts. Mr. Bilderback also retained the research assistants, Roger Christman and Daniel Vivian, whose efforts are reflected on every page. Roger Christman focused on records in the South Carolina Department of Archives and History, and Daniel Vivian ranged across nineteenth- and twentieth-century published and unpublished sources. We met each week to discuss the work. I learned from them and am grateful.

Staff members at several institutions made significant contributions. At the South Carolina Department of Archives and History Steve Tuttle, Paul Begley, Marion Chandler, Dr. Charles Lesser, Patrick McCawley, and Wade Dorsey helped us in a variety of ways. Dr. Rodger Stroup, now director of archives, provided critical guidance at the outset of the project when he was assistant director of the South Carolina State Museum. At the South Caroliniana Library of the University of South Carolina, Daniel Vivian and I want to especially acknowledge the assistance of Beth Bilderback, Henry

Fulmer, Laura M. Costello, Allen Stokes, Ann B. Troyer, Robin Copp, Mae Jones, and Thelma M. Hayes.

Beyond South Carolina, I am grateful to research personnel at the Library of Congress, especially Marilyn Ibach, Jennifer Brathovde, and Frederick Bauman; the Archives of American Art of the Smithsonian Institution; and the Maryland Historical Society. Lois Beattie of the Institute Archives of the Massachusetts Institute of Technology, Tony Wrenn of the archives of the American Institute of Architects, Phil Lapsansky of the Library Company of Philadelphia, Bruce Laverty of the Philadelphia Athenaeum, Catha Rambush of the Catalog of Landscape Records at Wave Hill, and Joyce Connolly of the Frederick Law Olmsted National Historic Site were especially helpful. Professor Jeffrey Karl Ochsner, University of Washington, and David A. Rash of Seattle provided information on the landscape architect Edward O. Schwagerl.

As the work progressed, conversations with a number of people were fruitful and stimulating. Especially memorable suggestions were made by E. Cecil Mills, manager of construction and planning for the state. Mike Frick and Wayne Redfern, project architects for Stevens and Wilkinson, and Rob Bryan, architect and site representative for the South Carolina Department of Construction and Planning, each offered important insights as did Joseph O. Rogers III, manager-architect for the state, and Jimmie Lewis of Caddell Construction. Harry Shealy graciously arranged a memorable tour of the Vauclus and Graniteville (now Avondale) Mills. Conversations with Harvey Teal, Harry McDowell, and Phil Grose, all well versed in local history, clarified several points. Lindsay Smith, another amateur, pointed out the unpublished landscape plan of 1878. I always looked forward to discussing the project with John Hammond Moore whose recent history of Columbia and Richland County has set a new benchmark in the field.

Beyond research, Hunter Clarkson of Alt Lee, Inc., has done the archival and architectural photography. His craftsmanship, patience, and generosity have been inspirational. At the University Press, Catherine Fry, director, and Fred Kameny, editor in chief, handled the contractual arrangements. The book has benefited from editing by Alex Moore and the sensitive design work of Carleton Giles. Also within the university, Pat Hatcher, Sponsored Research, arranged the external contracts with a grace that made it seem simple. Lester Lefton, dean of the College of Liberal Arts, and Bradford Collins, interim chair, Department of Art, also provided support at critical moments. During the final throes of the project the forbearance and competent assistance of Mana Hewitt and June Robinson kept me sane. Finally, a special note of thanks is due the SCANA Corporation; they supported the research as a gesture honoring Mr. Lawrence M. Gressette's love for and service to South Carolina.

Most of all, I am grateful to Martha, whose love and patience have been central to all my enthusiasms since we were fourteen.

Creating the
South Carolina
State House

Chapter One

A False Start

John L. Manning and Milford Plantation

The site and character of the present South Carolina State House were strongly influenced by Governor John L. Manning (1816–1889).[1] His taste and intentions provided an intangible—but nonetheless formative—foundation. On November 29, 1853, following the custom of the day, his private secretary read his inaugural address to the legislature.[2] Manning's agenda included railroad development, the establishment of free schools, and support for the construction of a new State House. His activism stemmed from a sense of well-being based upon prosperous agricultural conditions within the state and his own background as a well-educated, wealthy planter.[3] Manning and his secretary, John P. Richardson, were cousins; they were the current representatives of a political dynasty. If one counts in-laws and cousins as family, seven members of J. L. Manning's family, including himself, served as governors of South Carolina between 1802 and 1919, and three of them served two terms apiece.[4]

JOHN L. MANNING, ATTRIBUTED TO WILLIAM HARRISON SCARBOROUGH. COURTESY OF ELLEN MANNING BUTTS

With these connections came wealth. J. L. Manning was confirmed by the census of 1860 as the richest planter in the state, having $1,256,000 in real property, $890,000 in personal property, and owning 648 slaves.[5] Older legislators, looking for personal motives behind the proposal for a new State House, may have recalled that the new governor's father had participated in the Internal Improvements Program of 1819–1830. During the elder Manning's administration, eleven courthouses, nine jails, the Insane Asylum and the Charleston County Fireproof Office were all either completed or under construction. The aim of that program had been to bring governmental services to the people; it had been ambitious and in many judicial districts—the present-day counties of Greenville, York, Spartanburg, Charleston, Williamsburg, Georgetown, Marion, Lancaster, Williamsburg, Union, Horry, Edgefield, Chesterfield, Kersaw, Darlington, Orangeburg, and Newberry—buildings designed by, or based upon, the designs of Robert Mills (1781–1855) provided a concrete symbol and focal point of governmental services at the county level. Mills, a South Carolinian, had studied architecture under James Hoban, designer of the White House; Benjamin H. Latrobe, a distinguished English-trained architect and engineer; and Thomas Jefferson, who made his famous architectural library available to Mills. After practicing in Philadelphia and Baltimore, Mills returned to South Carolina in 1820 and spent a decade promoting a new level of sophistication in both functional planning and fireproof construction. Equally important for Manning and the future State House, Mills, who considered himself the first native-born American to train specifically for an architectural career, demonstrated the advantages of employing professionals instead of relying on local contractors for design and supervision.[6]

Whether or not J. L. Manning was moved by his father's support for public buildings, his own home demonstrated an interest in architecture which foreshadowed his approach to the new State House. He married Susan Frances Hampton in 1838, and the next year they began Milford in Clarendon County. It was said to be the finest Greek Revival residence in the state.[7] Situated on high ground above the Wateree River, the mansion was a testament to cultural sophistication. Milford's design and craftsmanship, outbuildings, and furnishings all signified that the Mannings had assimilated the international cultural trappings as well as the agricultural techniques of the lowcountry planters. In short, Milford demonstrated that in architectural matters Manning's horizon was not limited by the hills of the Piedmont.

There were no distinguished architects based in upcountry South Carolina in 1839; therefore, Manning called upon Nathaniel F. Potter (1807–1874) of Providence, Rhode Island, who was in Charleston directing the reconstruction of the Charleston Hotel.[8] The hotel's facade was dominated by a 150' long, two-story colonnade of Corinthian columns: Manning wanted something equally grand, something more ambitious than anything that had been built in the Piedmont.

The specifications show that Potter drew decorative details from Minard Lafever's *Beauties of Modern Architecture,* an architectural pattern book published in New York.[9] Potter wrote,

> Colonnade to be composed of six Corinthian columns, the style to be used is that of the monument of Lysicratus, the bases of the columns to be of granite, the shafts of bricks & the capitals of Wood. . . . The whole exterior of the house to be plastered [and scored to resemble stone] . . . the whole body of the House to be straw colored and all the trimmings white. . . . The drawing room to be finished with sliding and folding doors (as per plate No. 7 in Lafevers modern Architecture 1835). . . . All the doors and window in the hall and dining room & Library to be finished as per plate 19 in Lafever. . . . All the doors of the second story to be finished as pr plate on 14 with no 19 cornice. . . . Front entrance to be as p/ plate no 13. . . .[10]

MILFORD PLANTATION, DETAIL. HISTORIC AMERICAN BUILDINGS SURVEY, COURTESY OF THE LIBRARY OF CONGRESS

The elegance of the interior details was matched by the Mannings' art and furniture, and like the mansion, its furnishings demonstrated that the Mannings' cultural view was not circumscribed by the boundaries of the state.

Furniture for Milford was purchased from Duncan Phyfe and Brothers in New York. An active patron of the arts, Manning discussed paintings for the house with Henry Inman, a New York portrait painter; he also consulted the miniaturist Thomas S. Cummings, and James DeVeaux, a Charleston-born painter who studied painting in France and Italy and made copies of famous works for Manning and Wade Hampton.[11] Manning also purchased art from Count Joseph Guiseppe Binda, a New York art dealer and husband of the granddaughter of Thomas Sumter. (Binda was a colorful international figure. When Manning dealt with him in 1838–1839, he was American Consul to Leghorn, Italy; shortly thereafter, while still an American Consul, he became a spy employed by the French against his Italian hosts.)[12] Statues bought from Binda were purported to be Roman antiques from the collection of a Cardinal Bomvisi. In 1865, when Manning tried to sell his collection "in consequence of the disastrous effects of the late war" he wrote that he had "procured in more prosperous times" paintings and sculpture "to be preserved as heirlooms in my family." Among the paintings at Milford acquired from Binda, Manning said "two were from the collection of the late Count de Survilleurs, Joseph Bonaparte, from his collection at his residence at Badentown, N. Jersey, which he had brought with him to this country when he left Spain . . . they were originally in the Palace of the Escurial. . . ."[13]

Everything in Manning's collection was not genuine. Nonetheless, the mansion and collection represented the use of wealth to gather artifacts to express and perpetuate social standing. Taken as a whole, Milford set the Mannings apart from all but a handful of their upcountry peers in a concrete and visible way. When Manning, as

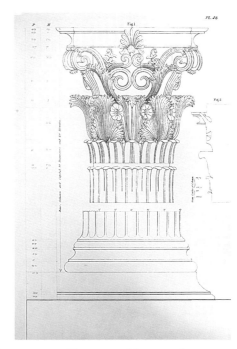

CORINTHIAN CAPITAL. MINARD LAFEVER, *BEAUTIES OF MODERN ARCHITECTURE,* 1839, PL. 43

governor, became involved in the design and construction of a new State House, it seemed natural to him to look for the best designers and craftsmen beyond the borders of the state.

The First State House in Columbia

In contrast to the new State House promoted by Manning, the original State House in Columbia was a simple building, built quickly and cheaply in a frontier setting. The earliest view of the first State House in Columbia is a watercolor done c. 1801 by John Drayton as a frontispiece for his *View of South Carolina*. Although Drayton's image has been called conjectural, it is undoubtedly based on his own observation. Contemporary descriptions all suggest Drayton's image is accurate. To record his travels, he often did watercolors in the eighteenth-century English topographical tradition. He intended "A View of Statesburg, 1791," a "View of William Reid's Farm and the Mountains," "Mr. Dunlap's Farm Catawba River, 1790," and the "View of the State House, Columbia, 1794" to be illustrations in his *View of South Carolina,* but noted that he was prevented from doing so by the cost of engraving.[14]

Drayton's illustration of the old State House shows the south end and east side of the building viewed from the southeast and looking north along the axis of the present-day Main Street. Structurally, the State House was similar to the typical residence of the upcountry leadership. It had a brick raised basement or ground floor which contained a number of offices. The floor in the raised basement was slightly below the level of the ground; consequently, the initial wooden flooring soon rotted and had to be replaced with square brick pavers in 1799. The lower portion of the building left much to be desired as office space, and occupants requested improvements including plastering the brick walls, white washing the ceiling, installing adequate shelving, providing locks for the window shutters and doors, a litany of complaints that continued well into the nineteenth century. Above the raised basement the body of the building was made of wood. It had porticoes on the east and west facades, and both porticoes had wooden stairs on each side that gave access to the legislative halls.

There are no interior views or detailed narrative descriptions of the inside of the building, but a fairly precise image can be pieced together from legislative records, c. 1790–1840. Using reports, resolutions, and petitions like pieces of a large, evolving puzzle, we can visualize the State House: it was unfinished when the General Assembly convened there on January 4, 1790 and was constantly being repaired and altered over the next twenty-five years as the government settled into Columbia.

This first-in-Columbia State House stood on the southeast corner of the block then bounded by Richardson, Gervais, Assembly, and Senate streets. Its grounds were surrounded by a wooden fence, which seems to have been in continual need of repair. The main gate opened onto Richardson Street and the main entry of the State House was the central, or eastern, portico. There was a well and an outhouse on the grounds as well as a small wooden dwelling used by the caretaker, but other than that, no landscaping and no sculpture. People who had business with the State Bank, the Comptroller, the Surveyor General, Solicitor, or the District Court of Equity for Orangeburg, Camden, or Cheraw used the door beneath the portico because their offices were in the raised basement. This door entered a central hall which bisected the lower story and contained a stairway to the main floor above.

Climbing the stairs brought the visitor into an entry hall wide enough to be called a lobby. Like the central hall below, the lobby-hall on the main floor bisected the building east to west. The lobby-hall was crossed by a hall running north-south down the center of the building, and this hallway gave access to the House on the northern end and the Senate on the southern end. Both legislative halls had adjacent committee rooms. There was a small, crowded library next to the Senate on the west side of the building. In 1790 there were no interior moldings, and the principal feature in the House and the Senate must have been the large palladian windows which marked the north and south elevations. The House and Senate had

CHARLESTON HOTEL, 1865. COURTESY OF THE LIBRARY OF CONGRESS

MILFORD PLANTATION. HISTORIC AMERICAN BUILDINGS SURVEY, COURTESY OF THE LIBRARY OF CONGRESS

ceilings high enough (c. 12 feet to 15 feet) to permit the later addition of galleries; both had white-washed, plaster walls and blue satin drapes behind the mahogany chairs of the presiding officers.

Both outside and inside, the State House was initially spartan and severe, but during the first decade of use its appearance became steadily more finished as the exterior was painted, shutters added to the raised basement windows, fanlights installed above the entries and railings added to the steps and porticoes. Inside, doors were added to the offices and committee rooms; lamps hung in the hallways; and baseboards and moldings fitted in the legislative halls. Initially there was no plumbing; coal was purchased, which suggests that cast iron stoves were used to heat the building.

The creation of a new state capital is a well-worn story and need not be repeated here.[15] The move from Charleston to Columbia is typically understood as an attempt to resolve tensions between the upcountry and the lowcountry; however, in a broader context it should also be viewed as part of a national trend, for between 1776 and 1812 eleven state capitals were relocated inland. Like Columbia, most of them were reestablished on navigable water in central locations.[16] To encourage a sense of stability and cohesion among the states, George Washington toured the new capitals; his visit was the first notable event in Columbia's history.

On May 23, 1791, Washington arrived in Columbia as part of his tour of the southern states. (He had toured the northern states in 1789 and 1790.) Celebrations marked his visits; these balls, toasts, and speeches were meant to encourage popular identification with the new federal government. Traveling on horseback, his entourage stopped first in Georgetown, then Charleston; they continued south to Savannah and then turned inland to Augusta. Washington jotted in his journal that to reach Columbia from Augusta he spent two days passing through "a pine barren of the worst sort, being hilly as well as poor. This circumstance, added to the distance, length of the stages, want of water and heat of the day, foundered one of my horses very badly." On the evening of May 23, a banquet was held in the first Columbia State House, and the next day he described Columbia, observing that it "had better been placed on the river below the falls. It is now an uncleared wood, with very few houses in it, and those all wooden ones. The State House (which is also of wood) is a large and commodious building, but unfinished."[17]

The simplicity of the State House Washington saw suggests that it was designed by a legislative committee. But by 1789 there were people advertising as architects in Charleston (which was not the case in 1756 when the first State House was built in Charleston), and the design has long been attributed to James Hoban (c. 1762–1831), the most prominent of them. Quoting Governor Charles Pinckney about the creation of the second State House, Edwin L. Green inserted parenthetically that Hoban was the architect.[18] Green's attribution was repeated uncritically

THE FIRST STATE HOUSE IN COLUMBIA, BY JOHN DRAYTON, 1802. COURTESY OF THE CHARLESTON
LIBRARY SOCIETY

by Beatrice St. Julien Ravenel, and other authors have followed suit.[19] More recently, however, historians have expressed doubts, but no proof has been offered either way: "It has been suggested, without evidence, that the Irish architect James Hoban might have designed the first State House at Columbia."[20] Or again: "While there is a mysterious and unfounded legend that the statehouse was the work of James Hoban—the Irish architect of the White House—voluminous documents indicate that it was the product of a collaboration between a committee and a master builder."[21]

The association of Hoban with the State House has persisted because it was both possible and appealing. Hoban arrived in Charleston from Ireland in 1787. He advertised classes in architecture (Robert Mills was probably one of his students) and formed a partnership with Pierce Purcell, a local carpenter. To enter the competition for the new federal buildings, he moved to Washington in 1792 and became well known as designer and builder of the White House and contractor for the construction of the U.S. Capitol. George Washington wrote a letter introduc-

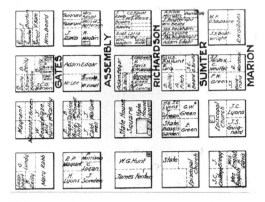

"Map of Columbia, surveyed by Arthur and Moore," drawn by John B. Jackson, circa 1850. Courtesy of the South Caroliniana Library

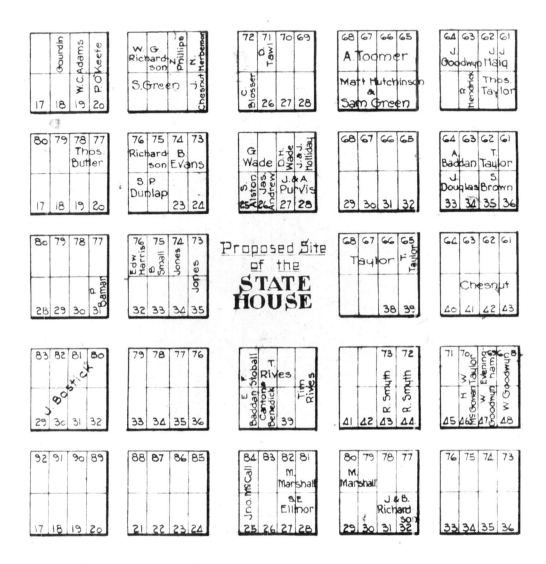

"The First Map of the City of Columbia . . . from the Survey Ordered 1786," redrawn by Tomlinson Engineering, 1931. Courtesy of the South Caroliniana Library

ing Hoban to the commissioners of the Federal District and did not mention the South Carolina State House.[22] If Hoban had designed it, Washington would have mentioned it: only eleven months earlier he had visited Columbia, attended a ball in the unfinished building, and mingled with those responsible for its construction. Washington's silence should stifle any lingering echoes of the mysterious, unfounded legend.

The first State House was begun in 1787, and although still unfinished, was first used on January 4, 1790. Its design was probably the result of a collaboration between James Douglas, a carpenter from Camden who served as general contractor, and the joint Senate and House Commission charged with laying out the new capital city and providing facilities for the government "on the most frugal plan, which, in the opinion of the commissioners, the honor and interest of the state will admit of."[23] The commissioners elected were Thomas Taylor, Richard Winn, Alexander Gillon, Richard Hampton, and Henry Pendleton, all of whom owned land in the Midlands.

Most visitors to Columbia in the early nineteenth century were more enthusiastic about the trees and gardens than they were about the State House. It was not a building that inspired praise. Edward Hooker (1785–1846), a tutor from Connecticut, arrived in Columbia in 1805 and observed that

> The state House is very large on the ground, but yet so low as to be entirely void of anything like just proportion. It has only two stories; and one of these is partly below the natural surface of the ground, and is of brick plastered over. The lower story is appropriated to the Treasurer's, Secretary's, and Surveyor General's offices. There are several other rooms, which, as far as I can learn, are used for little else than lodging rooms for the goats that run loose about the streets, and which, as the doors are never shut, have at all times free access. The court house is a much handsomer building—of brick, two stories high.[24]

Another description of Columbia, written in 1816 to "accompany Mr. Blackburn's map" noted that

> The State-House is a compound of brick and wood, and of the Gothic order, two stories high; the upper part is divided into rooms where the public offices are kept. The Senate Chamber is not so highly finished as that of the Representatives, but is in a higher state of preservation, the other having had its plastering severely cracked by the annual harangues it has been obliged to encounter. They are each ornamented with a blue sattin curtain at the back of the President and Speaker's chairs, which are of mahogany.
>
> The whole building is surrounded by a railing for an acre about, with a gate in front, very curiously fixed to open and shut, upon the principles of gravitation, by means of a cannon ball.[25]

And a final description which touches upon the interior of the upper, or main, floor of the State House:

> The old State House, built of wood, stood near the Southern end of the square, a little West of Main Street, facing East, with a portico in front, reached by a broad flight of steps on each side, beneath which was the entrance to the State executive offices and the Branch Bank on the southwest corner. Above stairs

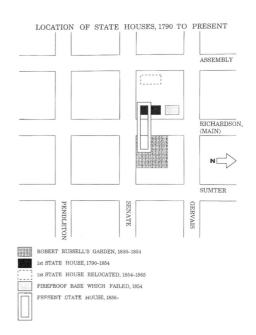

LOCATION OF STATE HOUSES, 1790 TO PRESENT

ASSEMBLY
RICHARDSON, (MAIN)
N
SUMTER
PENDLETON
SENATE
GERVAIS

ROBERT RUSSELL'S GARDEN, 1836–1854
1st STATE HOUSE, 1790–1854
1st STATE HOUSE RELOCATED, 1854–1865
FIREPROOF BASE WHICH FAILED, 1854
PRESENT STATE HOUSE, 1856–

SITE PLAN, LOCATION OF STATE HOUSES. SKETCH BY THE AUTHOR, DRAWN BY WAYNE REDFERN

The first State House in Columbia, one dollar bill, Bank of South Carolina, 1862. Courtesy of the South Carolina Archives and History Center

the House occupied the Northern and the Senate the Southern end, separated by a broad passage or lobby, which was crossed by another leading from front to rear, the spaces between them forming committee rooms.[26]

Hooker says goats lived in lower story of the State House; if so, they were crowded, for office space was in demand. From 1800 to 1840 there were always individuals and agencies requesting or suggesting improvements or additions to the building.

Flammable and poorly built, the State House deteriorated quickly; it was not a safe place to store public records. In 1803 Senator John P. Richardson (the father of Manning's secretary) "observed the decayed and unfinished state of some of the lower apartments of the State House" and the "deranged situation" of court records stored there "in such disorder, that it is almost impossible to obtain any information from the records in the confused situation they are at present."[27] Three decades later the situation had not improved, for a Senate committee reported in 1833

that they have examined the state of the records of the legislature and find them in the most deplorable condition. They have been thrown into closets as though they were mere rubbish. In many instances they are irretrievably destroyed and nearly all of them more or less injured. The floors shelves & chairs are covered with them in utter confusion & disorder. Scarcely a Roll of the House has been preserved. Those that exist are so defiled as to defy the touch of the hand. In short, it is difficult to describe the disgraceful condition which the records of the legislature now present and nothing but prompt attention to them can save them from utter ruin.[28]

Archival Storage and the Need for New State Offices

During the 1786 debate about moving the capital inland, Edward Rutledge maintained that leaving Charleston would be irresponsible, "expensive to the people, inconvenient to the members and extremely dangerous to the public records." He asked rhetorically,

would they agree to carry their records on which the possessions of thousands of individuals depended one hundred and forty miles distance from whence they were now safely deposited, and carry with them what little money might be in the treasury at that time? And for what? Why, only to make a few laws, to remain there six weeks, and then return. The proposal was not only absurd, but also, if agreed to, would prove extremely dangerous. To make the government itinerant exposed its treasure and records to the mercy of a small number of banditti, who might destroy both at their pleasure.[29]

Historically, the issue of archival storage is surprisingly important, for it was the lever used to obtain funding for the second State House in Columbia. As early as 1819 John Wilson proposed a fireproof repository in Columbia. Wilson was State Civil and Military Engineer, 1818–1820, briefly in charge of implementing the Internal Improvements Act of 1817. In his 1819 annual report he pointed out "the expediency of erecting a suitable building for the public offices now kept within the walls of the State House. . . . The critical situation in which the public records are placed in a building constructed of inflammable materials, renders it a subject of serious attention." He "therefore respectfully recommended . . . that a Fire Proof Building be erected."[30]

In 1820 Wilson was replaced by Abram Blanding and Robert Mills, both reporting to the Board of Public Works consisting of Joel R. Poinsett, Robert G. Mills, and Nicholas Herbemont. With some exceptions, Blanding, who was a civil engineer, took charge of the roads, canals, and bridges; Robert Mills was responsible for new buildings. Mills was appointed an acting commissioner on December 20, 1820, and went to work at once. He was hired in part for his reputation as a designer of fireproof buildings. During the period 1821–1829, he designed sixteen courthouses and twelve jails across the state, all as fireproof as funding would permit. He also designed the fully fireproof Charleston County Records Office, a set of fireproof powder magazines on Charleston Neck, and the fireproof core of the South Carolina Asylum. Being responsible for the state's architectural program and having a special interest and expertise in fireproof construction, Mills must have influenced—if he did not in fact write—the recommendation in the Board's 1820 annual report "to convert the present [Columbia] Court House into a jail, which may be easily accomplished; to surrender up the present State House to the use of the courts, and to erect a new building for the use of the legislature, with fire proof offices within it. . . ."[31] This appears to be the earliest, clearly articulated linkage of a new capitol and fireproof offices. Nothing, however, came of this recommendation.

Whether or not Robert Mills participated in the 1820 suggestion, he did propose a new South Carolina State House in 1822, for in an unpublished autobiographical fragment listing his work he wrote, "In anticipation of the erection of a new Capitol Building for legislative purposes—the present structure being of wood—the author projected plans upon an extensive scale commensurate with the rapidly increasing improvements of the state; these plans were hung up [1823] in the Hall of Legislation of the House. No action has ever been taken to commence the work, owing to the extensive pecuniary obligations, to which the state was subject."[32] Mills's plans have been lost, but given the nature of his work at the time he probably proposed a masonry vaulted, fireproof capitol on an extensive scale.

Nicholas Herbemont, President of the Board of Public Works in 1822, must have been describing Mills's proposal when he reported that the Board had considered the need for "fire proof offices . . . so constructed as to form the basement story of a future

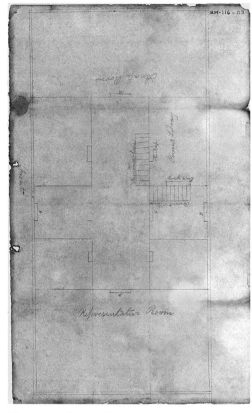

THE FIRST STATE HOUSE IN COLUMBIA, PRINCIPAL FLOOR PLAN, 1839. COURTESY OF THE SOUTH CAROLINA ARCHIVES AND HISTORY CENTER

State House." He said the drawings would produce a building suited to the climate of South Carolina and provide "convenience in the interior arrangement, with simple elegance in its exterior elevation"; the proposed State House also "embrace[d] a design calculated . . . to admit of a gradual progress towards completion." Herbemont recommended that work begin on one wing, which could be occupied, then annual appropriations could be made "until the whole be completed."[33] On other projects Mills had proposed building by stages, and although nothing came of this State House proposal in 1822, the stratagem of getting an appropriation to build a fireproof basement first was used when work finally began in 1851.[34]

In 1821, the year before Herbemont's report and Mills's proposal, the Board of Public Works noted that the legislature had appropriated $50,000 "beyond the specific sums directed to be expended in public buildings [which] was understood by the Board as intended for the erection of fire proof offices, for the State records. But there having been no resolution passed defining the object, the Board did not feel themselves at liberty to act."[35] Perhaps it was this extra $50,000 that prompted Mills to present his plans for a new State House. In the end, however, this money was used to construct the fireproof County Records Office in Charleston, and for the next twenty-five years no major appropriations were devoted to the State Capitol.

The type of repairs and alterations required during the antebellum years indicate that the first State House in Columbia never had been properly finished or furnished. In 1842, for example, the House approved "having the windows repaired, the two committee rooms made private, and the lobby so far protected from the rush of outward air as practicable." They also approved "a contract for heating the House and the Committee rooms . . ." and for "fitting up proper cases to contain the archives of this House, and cause them to be arranged by years, and in such form that they can be easily searched." The basement and the interior of the House itself needed work, for the same report determines "to floor over and properly enclose the basement story of this house, and fit up the Gallery, and curtain the windows of this house, so as to render the same more comfortable; and paint over so much as may be required to give uniformity and finish to the floor."[36]

In 1846 the legislature concluded that perhaps painting and patching would no longer suffice, and a joint committee was appointed to study "the necessity of erecting a fireproof building for the preservation of the Public Records of the Upper Division, and such other matters as may relate thereto. . . ."[37]

Another joint committee in 1848, charged with "providing a suitable room for Senate Records," reported that no room could be found "as all the rooms in the State House are occupied."[38] It is a measure of the need that they suggested removing the west portico and building a small wing on the rear of the State House. This was done and, judging from a nineteenth-century print, the architectural effect resembled a back porch boarded up for a washing machine.[39] During the following year, offices were created for the clerks of the House and Senate by building partitions beneath the galleries in the legislative halls. Although the clerks complained that part of the work was "coarsely and badly done" and "the noise in the offices below from walking in the balcony is annoying," the new quarters were infinitely better than the basement, and on the whole were "well calculated to answer the purpose designed."[40]

By the 1840s, after half a century of use, the first State House in Columbia was showing its age, a bit dilapidated and bulging at the seams. But even when it was new, it was never handsome. It started life as an ugly duckling and never became anything else. According to a Charleston newspaper correspondent, it represented "that very humble order of architecture, which may be designated as *the squat*."[41]

Starting the Present, or Second, State House in Columbia

The earliest hint that something more than minor repairs was being considered is reflected by a payment of $200 in February, 1844, to David Lopez of Charleston for "making trip from Charleston to Columbia. Taking measurements and plans of the Capitol—and furnishing the committee with [a] *report* and *specifications* for *alterations, additions* and *improvements*."[42] Lopez signed his invoice as architect and builder. Today we know little about his proposal for additions. From what we know about him, he usually worked as a builder rather than as an architect. Neither his plan nor his report have survived, but advertisements placed at the end of the year indicate that the committee had a large building in mind:

Contract Wanted . . . plans and specifications for a FIRE PROOF BUILDING, to be erected North of the State House, on the same Lot. The dimensions to correspond as near as may be, in height and size with the State House. Rooms are wanted for the Secretary of State, and his archives; Treasurer and Comptroller, and his archives, Surveyor General, and his archives; Governor's Room; a Deposit for the archives of the House; a Deposit for the archives of the Senate; and it is also desirable to have two Rooms, one for the Court of Appeals at Law, and one for the Equity Court. These Rooms require no arrangements for a Jury. Also a Room for the Court Library. The building to be simple, but in good taste. The basement story to be groined, and all the floors laid in tile; windows and sashes of Iron; all Fire Proof. The upper story to be heated from air furnaces below. All plans and estimates must be hand in by the middle of October, to either of the subscribers.

J. Gregg, Chairman of the Committee of the Senate

Benj. F. Hunt, Chairman of the Committee of the House of Representatives[43]

Lopez's invoice was addressed to Col. Benjamin F. Hunt, whose interest in the building must have been evident to his peers. Two years later he was appointed to a joint committee "with authority to enquire into the necessity of erecting a fireproof building for the preservation of the Public Records of the Upper Division and such other matters as may relate thereto. . . ."[44]

Four more years passed. The State House in Columbia continued to deteriorate, and another joint committee predictably found "the sills, joists and flooring being completely decayed" and the public records in jeopardy: "at present they are kept in the lower rooms of the State House, and their insecurity must be palpable to every one. Their destruction would involve nearly every citizen of the State." Consequently, the committee recommended that "they be authorized to contract for the first story of a fire proof building, to be located on the lot next [to] the State House at present occupied by the Keeper. . . . The erection of this building will remedy a serious inconvenience at present existing. There is, as is well known, no accommodation for a single one of the Senate Committees, and more than half of the Committees of this House are without a place of meeting."[45] Authorized in 1851, this first story of a fireproof building would undergo a metamorphosis and be transformed into a full-fledged State House.[46]

Peter Hjalmar Hammarskold

Public notice of the project appeared on August 26, 1851, when the committee consisting of William Izard Bull, R. H. Bedon, John Wilson, Thomas M. Wagner, Benjamin F. Hunt, and L. M. Keitt advertised for "the immediate construction of FIRE PROOF OFFICES . . . on the State House Square. . . . The exterior to be built with South Carolina granite; the rooms enclosed with groined arches of brick plastered; the doors, window frames &c. of iron, according to specifications and plans in the office of P. H. Hammarskold, Architect, No 122 East Bay, Charleston. . . ."[47]

Peter Hjalmar Hammarskold (c. 1815–1861, active in South Carolina 1849–1856), was the first professional architect to participate in the evolution of the present State House. He was born in Sweden, emigrated to Charleston, and became a United States citizen on November 5, 1849.[48] The joint committee informed the legislature that they had retained him due to his recent work in Charleston. The previous year his entry in the Charleston Custom House competition, although unsuccessful, had received favorable notice; also in 1850 he worked with Edward B. White (1806–1882) on the Charleston High School and at the College of Charleston, and during this period (the date is not precise), he designed a house on Broad Street for William Izard Bull, Chairman of the joint committee.[49]

Three days before the cornerstone was laid on December 18, 1851, the joint committee announced—and the legislature agreed without any recorded discussion—that the fireproof office should be "part of a plan which might be used as a State House."

The fireproof office was designed to become the north wing of a new State House, but as the committee pointed out, it could "be of itself a complete building, should the Legislature determine not to adopt the whole plan." Hammarskold's complete plan was "placed in the Hall for inspection," and exhibited in Charleston:

> . . . left at our office for public inspection. We do not think that any thing more grand in general effect, or more chaste in the details, can be found in any public building in the United States. In the admirable finish of his design, Mr. Hammarskold has shown how completely he is master of his profession, and the plan, as it comes from his hand, is happily touched with the exactness of science, and the mellow and graceful tints of art.[50]

Hammarskold's State House drawings were apparently destroyed when his office at 22 Broad Street, Charleston, burned in 1853.[51] Fortunately, partial specifications for the fireproof office—the first phase of the new capitol—survive, for excerpts from them were given as evidence during an investigation when the foundations failed in the spring of 1854.

The specifications called for a structure more massive and more finely built than anything in the upcountry. The only earlier upcountry building which matched the proposed fireproof office in size and materials was the Graniteville Mill completed in 1849 by William Gregg. It provided a precedent for quarrying stone exposed along a water course (Horse Creek near Aiken). The mill was 350 feet long, 50 feet wide and two stories high, but like the New England mills which Gregg emulated, the Graniteville Mill was made of plain, rough hammered stone without any ornament, and its outer walls supported timbered framed floors, for it was not fireproof.[52]

Hammarskold's plan called for granite walls 4'9" thick, and laid up with carefully cut stone; each stone was to be at least three feet long, one foot thick, and one foot high. The upper and lower surfaces were to be cut or hammered flat so that no mortar joints would be more than 3/16s of an inch thick, and in arches the joints were not to exceed 1/8 inch in thickness. Within the wall there were to be an equal number of headers and stretchers, and the facing stone, the outer layer, was to average fourteen inches in thickness and to be no less than twelve inches thick. Brick arches were to spring from the inside of the granite walls, and these arches were to form the ceilings of the fireproof offices and, ultimately, to support floors above. Plaster would be applied directly to the inner surface of the walls and ceilings.[53] Structurally, Hammarskold's specifications called for the same system of masonry vaulted fireproof construction that Robert Mills had introduced—although Mills's were brick instead of stone—throughout the state thirty years earlier.

On December 5, 1851, Charles McCullock signed a contract to construct the granite outer walls of the fireproof office. The commission had a budget of $50,000, and

McCullock was to be paid for labor and materials as work progressed and was approved by the architect and commissioners. McCullock opened quarries adjacent the Broad River just above Columbia, but "the great freshet" of August, 1852, flooded the site and "swept away all the derricks and other implements."[54] He moved his operations to the banks of the Congaree just below Columbia and trained a labor force composed largely of slaves and set to work again.

For two years everything went well, and just before Christmas, 1853, William Izard Bull, Chairman of the commissioners, lobbying for renewed appropriations and eager to expand the project, published an account of the progress noting,

> In view of the apparent fact, that the present State House has become quite unsuited to the present or prospective wants of the State, and especially as its material is not sufficiently safe or durable for a State Building, intimated, that the object of Fire Proof Offices might be combined with the more enlarged improvement, a new State Capitol, thus saving the double expense; and as the basement story of the new Capitol was the appropriate place of deposit of the public grants, plats, and archives, they caused a plan to be drawn, which would include in one wing of the basement, Fire Proof Offices for the principal class of paper. This has been done, and the Legislature will now perceive that this wing is already erected, and in a short time the public records will be removed to a perfectly secure deposit. Part of a new Capitol is also erected—the foundation.

Bull then briefly described Hammarskold's complete plan, should the legislature decide—literally and figuratively—to build upon what had been done.

> The Capitol will contain every convenience of a State House. The entire basements afford ample rooms for all public offices. The second story will afford a magnificent Hall for the House of Representatives, over the basement story of the north wing; a Senate Chamber on the south; and on the western porch an ample and commodious library; rooms for the Court of Appeals, and numerous committee rooms; Governor's room, and every ample accommodation for all public use required of a State Capitol.[55]

If these benefits were to be realized, Bull pointed out that "means should be placed at the disposal of the Commissioners to enable them to make their contracts in large parcels, so that so extensive a building may progress in some respects simultaneously. The entire basement must be united together—to effect this the old building must be moved off the site; the foundation of the center and wings laid together." He estimated the cost of the north wing basement, or fireproof office, as being $60,000; and the cost to expand the State House grounds, move and restore the existing State House, and build the fireproof basement or first story of the central block and south wing as being $250,000. Informing the public that the commissioners were seeking such an appropriation, he said they proposed "during the next year, to go on with the entire first or basement story."[56] The legislature endorsed the commissioners' proposal, appropriated the $250,000 requested to fund the work outlined by Bull, and further stipulated that this sum was to be deducted from the "one million dollars . . . appropriated for the purpose of completing the new State House. . . ."[57]

The spring of 1854 was a momentous period in the history of the State House. With a budget in place and authorization to build Hammarskold's whole plan—to go beyond the initial one story fireproof office—those involved quickly expanded the work. On January 30, 1854, Hammarskold advertised that "he has taken up Columbia as his permanent residence, and will be found at his office, at the northeast corner of the State House square, where he will be happy to receive any orders in his line of business. . . ."[58] To make room for the new capitol, the commissioners sought proposals for the relocation and restoration of the old capitol on the southwest corner of the block (near what was then the corner of Senate and Assembly Streets), hired additional contractors to finish the initial section, and began to extend the foundations for the recently authorized State House.[59] The old capitol was moved without mishap by mid-April, for a local newspaper noted on April 19, 1854, that "the State House was on yesterday lodged in the position it is to occupy until the New Capitol is finished. This is one of the greatest feats in house-moving we have ever heard of. No chimneys removed, no plastering disturbed, and indeed, the Legislature might have been in session without being at all annoyed by the process of moving. We congratulate the contractors, Messrs. Glaze & Co, and the gentleman who had the job in charge, Mr. Twitchell, on the successful accomplishment of the undertaking."[60]

During this building season, Joseph D. Daly was the major brick contractor. Working with bricks made locally by Halcott Pride Green, men under Daly's direction built wooden centering and constructed the vaulted brick arches of the ceilings which sprang from and were supported by the granite walls of the fireproof office—now designated the north wing of the new State House—prepared by McCullock. As spring advanced and the north wing neared completion, Daly's crews laid its terra cotta floors and assisted in the installation of the eighteen metal window frames and sashes made by Charles (Christopher) Werner of Charleston. Daly worked under pressure, for the plan was to put a temporary roof on the north wing, and use it to store public records and the furniture while the old capitol was restored for the legislature until the new capitol was finished.

Spring turned to summer, and everything appeared to be going well. Daly made boxes for the public records and began moving things out of the old capitol into what

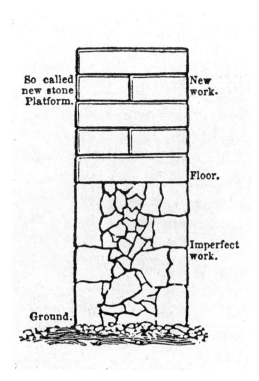

everyone assumed would be temporary quarters in the fireproof north wing. But in late May, like ominous writing on the wall, cracks began to appear. The first signs of disaster were crevices opening in the arched brick ceiling of the northwest corner. The crevices allowed the vault to deform, to settle, and as its weight pushed outward, a network of cracks developed in the north and west walls.

On May 25th Hammarskold reported the problem to the commissioners. Two days later—now thoroughly alarmed—they demanded that he deliver to them "all the notes, working plans, sketches, &c . . . everything connected with the building," and on June 1, 1854, they informed him that "his office was vacated."[61] At the same meeting they decided to request Governor John L. Manning "to communicate with Mr. Niernsee, [architect] of Baltimore, and ascertain whether he can be engaged by the Commissioners to examine the Capitol. . . ."[62]

John Rudolph Niernsee

John R. Niernsee (1823–1885) was described by one of his children as "an immense man, 6-feet tall and at one time weighing nearly two hundred pounds. Fair haired, blue eyed, with a ruddy complexion, erect carriage [and] a very pleasant speaking voice."[63]

Niernsee was born in Vienna, Austria, attended the University of Prague and studied under Schinkel in Berlin. He immigrated to the United States in 1838 and was hired by the Baltimore and Ohio Railroad in 1839. He left the company in 1848 to open an architectural office in Baltimore with Neilson. With his partner James Crawford Neilson, he designed the Baltimore and Ohio Station in Washington (1850–1852) and in 1852 began the Baltimore and Ohio Camden Street Station in Baltimore. Their office was the largest and most successful in Baltimore in 1854.[64] Niernsee had a reputation for dealing with large scale, complex projects. On February 26, 1850, a portion of the interior of the Smithsonian Castle, designed by James Renwick, collapsed; the Regents, the governing board, retained three architects as consultants: Edward Brickell White (1806–1882) of Charleston, William Turnbull of the U.S. Topographical Engineers, and John R. Niernsee.[65] The Smithsonian Regents sought Niernsee's advice because, as an engineer and architect for the Baltimore and Ohio Railroad, he had extensive experience with composite construction—combining cast and wrought iron with wood to exploit the best properties of each material.

Niernsee arrived in Columbia by June 15, 1854, for on that day he met with the commissioners at the Capitol. He reviewed Hammarskold's plans and records, examined the construction, and four days later submitted his analysis in a report co-authored with Kay. They found the construction documents in order—insofar as they went. Hammarskold's plans of the foundations and exterior elevations were complete, but "no details for the construction, finish or decoration of any part of the building above the basement are made out. . . ." They judged the contracts and specifications to be properly drafted, "describing the best kind of work in every branch. . . ." But the work itself was another matter. The exposed foundation of the south wing was "of rubble masonry . . . of quite an inferior kind to the one described in the specification, or what it should be." In the north wing, the brick arches "instead of being cut accurately and of the hardest brick, are frequently cut of the softest kind for the sake of their facility of being so cut. . . ." Niernsee noted numerous other problems, agreed to serve as nonresident consulting architect, outlined his relationship to a resident architect and concluded by noting that more time was needed to determine the precise "causes of the cracks and settlement. . . ."[66] Having submitted the initial report and agreed to serve as consulting architect at a salary of $3,000 per year, Niernsee returned to Baltimore, and, with the commissioners waiting for the response to their advertisement, little work was done throughout the early summer.

Immediately after Niernsee left, the commissioners halted the work and advertised that they planned "to elect, on the 2d of August, a competent ARCHITECT, for the purpose of carrying out and perfecting the plans, &c., of the New State Capitol, now under construction."[67] Now the commissioners were acting with dispatch: the same day McCullock was told to stop work, he was directed to take down the walls to the north wing "to the line of the springing of the window arches," and the next day he was directed to "commence immediately to take up the foundations of the south wing." McCullock refused to comply, for he knew "it would cost more than twice or thrice the amount he was worth and involve him in irretrievable ruin."[68] McCullock dismissed his workmen, left his tools and derricks on the site, and went to see a lawyer.

JOHN RUDOLPH NIERNSEE, CIRCA 1870. COURTESY OF THE SOUTH CAROLINA ARCHIVES AND HISTORY CENTER

George Edward Walker

On August 3, 1854, from the twenty-nine architects who responded to the advertisement, the commissioners selected George Edward Walker (c. 1810–1863) of Charleston as resident architect. Walker had lobbied energetically for the job and believed he would have charge of construction and design of everything left unspecified by Hammarskold's drawings. He was to receive $4,000 per year and $500 for office expenses. Hammarskold's superintendent, John A. Kay, was retained and promoted to assistant architect.

Little is known about Walker's background or training. When he received notification of his appointment as resident architect at the State House, he was working as an assistant to E. B. White, the resident architect, on the construction of the U.S. Custom House in Charleston, which had been designed by Ammi B. Young

(1800–1874). The Custom House was the largest, most substantial and ornate granite building yet attempted in South Carolina. Its grand scale and proposed capitol-like dome (which was never built) have been interpreted as symbols of civic destiny, of assertive ambition, and looming secession.[69] The State House commissioners selected Walker as resident architect, thinking, no doubt, he could assist Niernsee just as he was assisting White. In addition to serving as an assistant, Walker had a reputation for his own work, having designed Charleston Free School No. 6 (1851–1852), remodeled the Georgetown County Court House (1854), and begun plans for the library at the College of Charleston.[70]

U.S. CUSTOM HOUSE, CHARLESTON, CIRCA 1850. COURTESY OF THE LIBRARY OF CONGRESS

ANOTHER VIEW OF THE U.S. CUSTOM HOUSE, CHARLESTON, CIRCA 1850. COURTESY OF THE LIBRARY OF CONGRESS

During his first three months on the job at the State House, Walker recorded activities in terse diary entries.[71] On August 4, the first full entry, he jotted, "the commissioners seem determined to take Mr. Niernsee's advice and only take down the defective N.W. corner." Having examined the foundations before his appointment, Walker was already convinced that they should demolish everything and start over. His brief notation of an initial disagreement was a harbinger of worse to come, for he never established a cordial working relationship with Niernsee or the commissioners. To the contrary, his relationships with almost everyone involved deteriorated. He felt victimized by what he perceived as secret meetings and mendacity, and the more he felt betrayed, the more adamantly he asserted the rights of a resident architect. He bitterly resented Governor Manning's intervention. It was a downward spiral and led inevitably to his dismissal.

But he had a busy first day: on August 5 Walker directed John Kay to supervise the organization of the building site, stacking reusable stone and carting away rubble as the foundations were dismantled. He visited the quarry "a short distance below the old landing on the Congaree, called Granby" and examined the wooden derricks and horse-drawn wagons used to haul stone. Going to and from the quarry, he laid out the course for a planked road leading from the quarry along the river and up the hill to the construction site. Back at the building site, he instructed the stonecutters to recut the shoulders of the granite corbels to provide a footing for the brick groined vaults "at right angles to the tangent of the curve of the arches." At the end of the day he spoke with Niernsee about things they needed to add that did not appear in Hammarskold's plans, including stairs for galleries in the House of Representatives and the library and provisions for the heating, ventilating, and plumbing systems.[72]

The next day was a Sunday, and Walker noted that he left for Charleston "for the purpose of arranging [his] affairs" for a week. The timing of this absence precluded any meaningful consultation with Niernsee, who returned to Baltimore before Walker came back to Columbia. In 1854 the train between Charleston and Columbia took eleven hours: Walker left Charleston at five o'clock Saturday afternoon and arrived in Columbia at four o'clock, before sunrise Sunday morning.[73] Through the night he had ample time to mull over what lay ahead. The commissioners were not scheduled to meet again until the end of September; Niernsee would not be back until then, so Walker had approximately six weeks to get things underway, and many things needed to be done simultaneously.

On the job site he found Daly's men taking down the groined arches of the north wing and carting the bricks away. Walker argued that these bricks belonged to the state, but the commissioners were unwilling to provoke a confrontation. Nonetheless, with their approval, Walker began hiring laborers directly accountable to the state. By September 1 he felt they had "commenced the new system of work" with John Kay, as assistant architect; Peter Suder, foreman of the yard; and Mr. Hewitson, timekeeper.[74]

The derricks and quarries abandoned by the dismissed stone contractor needed attention. From Charleston, Walker obtained coils of tarred rope, two inches in diameter, to be used as guys to support the quarry and construction derricks. These derricks were driven by gears cranked by hand, mechanisms resembling the sprockets of modern bicycles. Walker had broken gears replaced and ordered maintenance for the steam engine which drove the pump at the quarry. There were wagon axles to be repaired and improvements needed on the quarry road. This initial flurry of activity was interrupted by heavy rain on September 8 and 9, which caused the Congaree to rise and flood the quarries the following week.

While getting the work underway, Walker was also studying the plans and trying to look ahead. Both tasks were frustrating: there was nothing in Hammarskold's plans about the depth of the foundations, and the commissioners were not ready "to conclude how much of the work is to be taken down."[75] Walker began a detailed analysis and set of recommendations to present at the next meeting and while working on this report discovered to his chagrin a commission memorandum which—without his knowledge—had doubled Niernsee's salary to a total of $6,000.

Walker was unsettled. The memorandum justified Niernsee's raise "by the increased duties imposed on him, including all plans and specifications." This was a blow, for as resident architect, Walker thought he was to create any plans needed to modify

Hammarskold's design. He had not been informed of Niernsee's salary adjustment or any redefinition of responsibilities. Since the commission had kept the matter from him, he gritted his teeth and said nothing. He grimly put the memorandum aside, "passed by," he wrote, "as if unobserved . . . [but] I knew not how I would be affected. Upon one point, however, my intentions were most unchangeably fixed; that if it was the design of the Commissioners to choke me off and substitute Mr. Niernsee in my stead, that the day could not be far distant when the attempt would be made, and then it would be reasonable and proper, to take a bold and unyielding position in opposition to such a measure."[76] Walker was on his guard, determined to assert himself when the time came.

Burdened now with the knowledge that things were not what they seemed, Walker evaluated everything using Hammarskold's specifications as a gauge and concluded.

> . . . in no single instance are these specifications complied with; the foundations were not constructed in courses; and without any regard to headers and stretchers: all of the stone is of the most irregular form, without level beds or builds, no attempt having ever been made to split or work them out of wind, or to place them in the walls with any regard to bond; they were placed in the work in the same irregular form in which they were blasted from the quarry; the stone could not under such circumstances be brought sufficiently near together to avoid leaving large cavities which did actually endanger the stability of the work; these cavities were often filled with spalls of stone and sometimes brick bats in a loose state without being bedded in mortar; in other cases the cavities were destitute of filling of any kind. Thus it is evident that the foundations instead of being of the best coursed masonry was actually of rubble work of the most inferior character.[77]

He condemned other aspects of the work: flues and downspouts which were supposed to have been built into the walls had been omitted; facing stone was not laid as stipulated. The brickwork, if anything, was worse. Instead of the best hard Columbia brick, "so inferior were many of the bricks used, in not only the walls, but groined arches, that they were most readily reduced to the consistency of clay or totally washed away by rain." Bricks in the arches were not wedged-shaped as specified; instead, wide mortar joints were used, or "many of the joints between the bricks were not filled with either mortar or cement, this was the case to a very great degree in the haunches of the arches, many of the brick of which were piled in dry without mortar." Walker's conclusion was inescapable and uncompromising: "In no case has Mr. Daly approached within the most ordinary requirements of his contract, but has invariably departed from the terms thereof."[78]

The commissioners must have agreed with Walker's report and nodded ruefully at his summation:

It is difficult to understand how any set of contractors could have varied igno-rantly from almost every requirement of specifications so definitely written as those for the New State Capitol; and it is much more difficult to comprehend how the architect who wrote the specifications, and who was vested by the contracts with full power to reject all work which was not in accordance therewith could have passed over unobserved such gross defects in every part of the work.[79]

Walker's recommendation was emphatic: it would be "unsafe and imprudent to attempt to raise the remainder of the building upon such a miserable base."[80] Niernsee, on the other hand, initially tried to devise ways to salvage sections of the walls, but finally he too gave up, and when the meeting convened on September 27, 1854, Niernsee agreed that nothing could be saved.[81]

. From the beginning, Walker had resented Niernsee as an outside expert and gloated when his own diagnosis was confirmed. He wrote that Niernsee's reversal "dispelled all of the sanguine hope which had been entertained by the Commissioners, of speedy and immediate rescue from the snare into which they had fallen. The soothing consolation which had been administered to them by the consulting architect, vanished like a phan-tom, and the stern reality presented itself, that the State House was to be razed to the very foundations." Walker had no sympathy for the plight of the commissioners. He believed their ineptitude was part of the problem, and he wrote that the necessity of total demolition fell "upon the ears of the unfortunate Commissioners, as does the sentence of death upon the culprit arraigned before the bar of justice, leaving them nothing to which to cling but the future hope of Legislative clemency."[82]

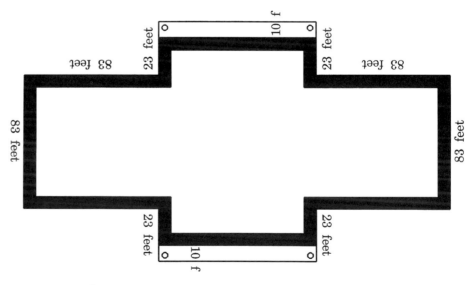

FOOTPRINT OF FIRST STATE HOUSE SHOWING JOHN R. NIERNSEE'S PLAN. DRAWN BY GEORGE E. WALKER, 1854, REDRAWN BY WAYNE REDFERN. COURTESY OF THE SOUTH CAROLINA ARCHIVES AND HISTORY CENTER

Walker vs. Niernsee

Throughout the fall of 1854, tension hung over the project like an approaching storm: the contractors were seeking legal advice; laborers employed directly by the state proceeded with the demolition; a legislative investigation was inevitable; and now the resident architect felt both betrayed by the commissioners and professionally threatened by the consulting architect.

Opening the 1854–1855 legislative session, Governor John L. Manning reviewed the situation and made several recommendations. He observed that $223,213.12 had been spent on the new construction, and without minimizing the loss, observed that "quarrying and working granite is a new business in this state" and "no public edifice of the magnitude of this has ever yet been constructed here." He recommended the appointment of a Special Joint Committee to examine the accounts prepared by Walker and the report prepared by Niernsee. Manning also advocated continuing the project, but suggested relocating the building "at the intersection of Senate and Richardson street [for] with northern and southern exposures it can be seen without obstruction from the four points of the compass and will present an appearance more dignified and imposing." He observed that if the work continued with the state directly employing the labor force (and thereby saving contractors' profits) and if, by starting over, a better site were obtained, then "in the end perhaps it may not be a subject much to be regretted that delay and disaster attended the first efforts to construct a new capitol. . . ."[83]

Governor Manning was identified with the project: he had promoted the expansion of the fireproof office into a full-fledged State House in his 1853 address to the legislature and had recommended Niernsee to the commissioners. Beginning in December, 1854, immediately after he was compelled to report delay and disaster, the governor began attending meetings of the commission as an unofficial, interested onlooker.

On December 22, 1854, with Manning present, a pivotal meeting was held during which the commission directed Walker "to construct the basement of the New State Capitol, of the same plan and dimensions as hitherto adopted, so that it will suit either for a plain substantial superstructure, costing five hundred thousand dollars, or for a handsome ornamental one, costing one million dollars . . . making such slight modifications in the same as may be acceptable to the Commission." They also resolved "that the Consulting Architect, Mr. Niernsee, be requested to make all plans for the future construction of the New State Capitol."[84]

These two resolutions struck Walker as being ill-considered, contradictory, and "an infringement upon my rights" as resident architect. He voiced a "strong and earnest expression of dissatisfaction," arguing that Niernsee was supposed to be a consultant, not a creator. Walker wrote that his "opposition to the will and dictates of so elevated a personage" as Manning "rent asunder all the chords of kindly feeling" and "at this stage of the proceedings of the Commission, the utmost confusion prevailed." Walker was asked to leave the meeting, and he "retired to the State House yard."[85]

Pacing in the yard amidst the debris, Walker was soon joined by Niernsee who had been sent by the commission to find language both architects could agree upon. Niernsee proposed, and Walker agreed, "that Mr. Walker will furnish all of the plans . . . in consultation with the Consulting Architect." But the commission rejected this compromise, and instead passed a resolution calling for "the Resident Architect and the Consulting Architect be each requested to furnish drawings and estimates." A budget of $6,500 per month was approved and a subcommittee of three was empowered to act on the commission's behalf.[86] Walker protested that this resolution made the two architects competitors and thereby removed the potential advantage of having a consultant. Having listened to Walker's objections, the commission agreed to meet again that evening to try to resolve the matter.

If the commissioners reconvened, Walker did not attend; instead, he noted "the Christmas holidays being at hand," he departed for Charleston when the afternoon meeting adjourned. Returning after New Year's Day, he found the commissioners had resolved that he should prepare the plans for the building, but should do so after advising with the consulting architect. Obviously, they could not collaborate: Walker had left before the resolution was approved, and, once again, Niernsee was back in Baltimore when Walker returned to Columbia. Nonetheless, on reading the new resolution carefully, Walker had reason to feel victorious, for it limited Niernsee's role by stipulating that "the Consulting Architect be only requested to prepare plans, drawings and estimates for those parts wherein he may differ with the Resident Architect." Walker interpreted this to mean that he was to be the creator of any plans needed for the new, relocated State House, and he got right to work.[87]

During the month of January, 1855, Walker prepared several alternative plans using Hammarskold's footprint, or outer dimension, of 90' x 227'. Walker was convinced the accommodations needed could not be obtained within a building of this size, so despite the commission's directive that the original dimensions be retained, he drafted "another plan . . . of greater dimensions than those established by the Commission." He carefully drew "front elevations, both plain and ornamental" for each set of plans, and, with the new drawings displayed in his office, must have looked forward to the meeting scheduled to convene there on February 7, 1855.[88]

On the day appointed, Walker was dismayed that only two (out of eight) official commissioners, Professor McCay and Dr. Goodwyn, came to examine his plans. To make matters worse, McCay and Goodwyn were accompanied by Manning, whose term as governor had recently expired, and Niernsee. Walker expected Niernsee, as consulting architect, to critique his new plans, but was shocked when Manning, who had no official standing on the commission, opened the meeting by inviting Niernsee "to place upon the table four sets of plans" which he had created in Baltimore.[89]

Niernsee had no elevations, but explained his plans, all of which were for a larger building than Hammarskold's dimensions approved by the commission. After Niernsee's presentation, the group turned to Walker, now outraged that the consulting architect was being presented as a competitor despite all earlier assurances and resolutions. Describing the scene, Walker wrote that "the utmost exertion and self control" prevented him "from expressing, in strong and unmistakable language" his utter contempt for the commission. He gestured to his own drawings and said, "I desire you to understand, gentlemen, that I do not submit these plans to you in competition with Mr. Niernsee." To which Gov. Manning replied, "We understand you, Mr. Walker."[90]

Nobody spoke as they examined Walker's drawings, and the meeting adjourned without any action having been taken beyond agreeing to meet again the next day. It was now clear that Manning intended for Niernsee to usurp the resident architect's role as creator of the new State House. The lines—literally and figuratively—were drawn, and at this point Walker mounted a determined resistance.

Walker's most vocal advocate among the commissioners, Col. Bedon, delayed any decision and arranged to exclude former governor Manning from future meetings. The commissioners were learning from the repeated clashes between their architects, and on February 10, 1855, they approved a resolution intended simultaneously to shape the building, meet Walker's objections, retain Niernsee's services as a consultant, and move the project forward. After Walker reviewed and approved the language in a draft, they resolved:

> that the resident architect be requested, in consultation with the Consulting Architect, to prepare a plan and elevation for the New State House, embodying the particulars contained in the following. . . .
>
> That the depth of Wing be decreased from about 90 to 80 or 75 feet
>
> That five windows be placed in Wing and in end
>
> That the Senate Room be in the east, and the House in the west end, opposite each other, the former including three windows, and the latter four, both to have a lobby before them, with Clerk's room and Speaker's room at side of lobby
>
> That the projections of center be symmetrical, and have a row of double columns in front
>
> That the Court rooms be under the Senate room.
>
> That a vestibule be placed at the principal entrance
>
> That door be at end of corridor in first story.[91]

Walker was elated; he believed his role as creator had been confirmed. The next day Niernsee wanted to discuss the plans, but Walker rebuffed him saying that the plans would be sent when they were finished and had been reviewed by the commissioners. Once again, Niernsee returned to Baltimore without any consultation taking place.

For the next month, still protesting that the building was too small, Walker worked on plans based on the commissioners' latest criteria. While talking to one of the commissioners in the middle of March, he learned that McCay had asked Niernsee to return to Columbia, and he was expected the next day. Walker recalled "the precipitous manner in which this meeting . . . was gotten up, surprised me as well as aroused my suspicions."[92]

He was right to be suspicious. Niernsee came on or about March 14 with four or five sets of plans, all of which proposed a larger building than the one specified by the commissioners. Walker admitted that his designs appeared cramped by comparison, but only because they conformed to Hammarskold's dimensions adopted by the commission. He had argued for a larger building and had shown its advantages in one of his earlier plans. All of Niernsee's plans, on the other hand, ignored the restraints and therefore naturally depicted more ample, commodious interiors. Niernsee's plans showed a building 260' long with wings 83' wide, that is, 33' longer and 3 to 8' wider than the commissioners' resolution called for. By increasing the size of the building, Niernsee gained 3,879 additional square feet on the interior of each floor, or an additional 11,637 interior square feet on the interior as a whole. It was enough additional space, Walker observed "to form a room 108 feet square, or three times the size of the Representative Hall of the present State House."[93] Predictably, the interior plans of Walker's smaller buildings suffered by comparison, and he quickly made sketches to show he could do as well, "taking the same liberties in exceeding the instruction." Walker suggested to the commissioners present—McCay and Goodwyn—that they ask any board of competent architects to judge the plans, but no decision was reached, and the meeting adjourned.[94]

Walker did not wait for another official meeting. He began seeking out the commissioners; he made presentations to prominent citizens and wrote to the local newspaper. He tried actively to embarrass the commissioners. The bitterness and sarcasm in his prose suggests he foresaw defeat; nonetheless, his resistance is notable, for it prompted descriptions of the proposals which are important, for none of the drawings survive.

Dome vs. Tower: The Origins of the Controversy

Struggling to achieve both dignity and economy, the commissioners pondered how to treat the exterior of the building. They understood the need for a strong vertical feature to balance the long facade and debated the relative merits of a dome versus a tower. After much deliberation, they endorsed the tower proposed by Niernsee instead of the dome suggested by Walker because they believed a tower would be cheaper. The dome versus tower debate erupted again half a century later: it marked the beginning and end of construction like a pair of parentheses.

Before construction began, the commissioners presented their thoughts on this issue to the legislature:

> The original plan had nothing above the roof to crown the structure & to give elevation & grandeur to the work. As the highest line of the roof will not exceed eighty or ninety feet something is still wanting, in the opinion of some persons, to give a lofty & grand appearance to a building whose length is two hundred & sixty feet. Some of our plans contained a rotunda which admitted of a dome. But as the preparations for this had to be begun at the very foundation, we did not feel authorized to introduce so great a variation from our original plan [Hammarskold's] which had already been adopted by the Legislature. A dome large enough for our building ought to be ninety or a hundred feet in diameter, and this would imply great waste of room & great additional expense. To have adopted it would not only have been therefore without authority from the Legislature, but against their implied instructions, since they had directed us to reduce rather than increase the cost of the building.
>
> Our architect has prepared one of his drawings for the capitol with a tower or campanile. This by its great height variety and beauty, & the small outlay required for its erection, presents some advantages over a dome. The view from without would be fine, & the spectator from within, standing at the center of the principal story would be in an open space fifty feet wide & ninety feet long & with an uninterrupted view above him one hundred and fifty feet high. The tower & the style & expense of the building we submit to the Legislature, knowing that they alone can give authoritative decision in these matters, involving as each of them does large expenditures of the public money.[95]

A rotunda was the central feature of the interior of Walker's final plans. He argued that, beyond being beautiful, it was the best means of admitting direct natural light into the interior, for it was to be capped by a dome letting light "perpendicularly through the top of the rotunda."[96] Niernsee's plans solved the problem of lighting the interior with "two shafts of rectangular form, 10 by 25 feet, located near the center of the building, extending from the ground to the roof, at which point they would be covered with glass."[97] None of the commentary describes the exterior he envisioned; however, his skylights, being flush with the roof, were not part of the tower which became the dominating exterior feature of his design.

In Niernsee's plans, windows in the major corridors opened onto the light wells. Walker pointed out that this, at best, would provide only indirect, reflected light, but reserved his most damning criticism for Niernsee's placement of the library which was shown directly behind the main portico so that "it would be necessary to pass through the Library and its alcoves, amongst books and documents" to enter the building. Walker called this feature "an egregious absurdity" committed by "a humbug."[98] He was incensed and did not mince words.

On March 19, 1855, the commission passed a series of resolutions censuring Walker for his repeated failure to consult with Niernsee; they adopted "plan No. 4 of those prepared by Mr. Niernsee, with such modifications . . . as have been orally communicated to him," and they directed him "to draw off as soon as possible, a sketch or plan, so that working plans may be got ready from these for the stone cutters and masons, and that the work of construction shall be speedily commenced."[99]

The commissioners anticipated that Walker would resign, but he did not do so. Niernsee immediately (March 20, 1855) sent Walker a sketch of the footprint of the foundations of the approved Plan No. 4 and pointedly omitted dimensions necessary to do the job. Still Walker hung on. Finally, on April 11, 1855, the commissioners unanimously adopted five resolutions censuring and dismissing Walker.[100] First P. H. Hammarskold and then G. E. Walker had been dismissed. Now John R. Niernsee was to be the sole architect of the new State House.

Chapter Two

Getting Started

The legislative committee investigating the failure of the foundations absolved their peers, the eight commissioners, because they had "been deceived—grossly deceived by employees" and "all bodies of their kind are liable to such incidents, more especially in cases where confidence must be placed in agents or officers."[1] Hammarskold, because he certified the work for payment, was identified as the guilty party, but he had not been required to post a bond, and nothing could be recovered. A committee was considering the claims of McCullock, the stone contractor, and Daly, the brick contractor, who petitioned for payment on the grounds that they had done what the architect told them to do.[2] Throughout these deliberations Walker, the second architect, continued to criticize the commissioners through the press and pamphlets. His strident accusations made him persona non grata, and although he opened an architectural office in Columbia, he never worked for the state again.

The rubble of the dismantled foundations provided a tangible reminder of failure and controversy when the December, 1855, legislative session opened in the relocated old State House. Without commenting on what had gone before, the legislature resolved to replace the commissioners with an agent whom they would elect and pay $5,000 per year. The agent was to have "full power and authority with the assent of the Governor to employ architects and contractors to execute the work."[3]

By a vote of 104 to 3, James Jones (1805–1865) was elected and remained chief administrator of the work until 1861 when he resigned to become a Colonel in the Fourteenth Regiment of South Carolina Volunteers.[4] Between 1855 and 1861, his persistence, political dexterity, and unwavering support of Niernsee provided the administrative climate necessary for the project to flourish. The quality of work achieved during his tenure suggests that his decisive election was justified.

Initially, Jones may have found favor with the legislature because he embodied military virtues valued in antebellum South Carolina. He was the son of Col. Mathias and Clara Jones of the Ridge, Edgefield District. Two of James Jones's brothers, Captain Lewis Jones and Major Edward Jones, had military experience, as did two of his brothers-in-law—General Paul Quattlebaum and Major Tillman Watson. James Jones graduated from South Carolina College in 1824, and soon thereafter was admitted the bar in Edgefield. In 1836 he took leave of his law practice to raise a company of volunteers, the Edgefield Blues, and, as its Captain, participated in the last of the Seminole Wars. He found the military congenial. After the war he became Adjutant and Inspector General of South Carolina and was appointed to a legislative commission processing claims for reimbursement by the Seminole War volunteers. In 1842 he was appointed Chairman of the Board of Visitors of the new, state sponsored, military schools, the Arsenal Academy in Columbia and the Citadel in Charleston. (He remained on the Board until his death.) From 1863 until 1865, he was Quarter Master General of the state. In addition to his military-related service, Jones joined his brother-in-law, William Gregg, in reviving the failed Vaucluse textile mill in 1843 and establishing the Graniteville Mill in 1846–1847 where he participated in the construction of the dam and canal. He was accustomed to the exercise of authority and was a decisive manager. As legislators anticipated, his approach to the construction of the new State House had little in common with the irregular proceedings of the original commission of planters.[5]

Jones immediately reaffirmed Niernsee's appointment "as Architect of the New State House . . . from the first of January 1856" at a salary of $8,000 per year, and requested him to "take up your permanent residence here at as early a day as practicable."[6] John A. Kay was to continue as assistant architect, and Jones noted that Kay would be busy making preparations for renewed work until Niernsee arrived.

John R. Niernsee

But Niernsee did not come at once. It took him six months to wind up affairs in Baltimore and relocate his family. The delay is attributable in part to a deliberate, systematic attention to detail evident in his diaries and accounts. Beyond this, the family must have been in no hurry to move, for their life in Baltimore was comfortable. Niernsee's "Calculation of Expenses for the year 1854" shows that they employed three servants whose wages totaled $18 per month. He kept a horse and carriage ($15 per month), contributed $60 per year to the Catholic Church for pew rent, and budgeted $75 for cigars for the year—carefully figuring 3,000 cigars at twenty-five cents apiece. His wife handled the household accounts which included $160 tuition per year for their older children, Rudolph and Helen, and $80 for the milliner and mantua maker.[7]

Niernsee had been very productive in Baltimore. During his years as chief drafts-man and designer for the Baltimore and Ohio Railroad (1839–1848), he had designed at least five buildings, including the Washington Branch Freight Station which had the first wholly iron roof trusses in the country. In 1848 he left the railroad and formed an architectural partnership with James Crawford Neilson. Before Niernsee left in 1856, they had been responsible for twelve churches, six railroad passenger stations, ten com-mercial and institutional buildings, and numerous town and country houses, including three speculative houses built for Hugh Sisson, who would later be the primary ma-sonry contractor for the new South Carolina State House.[8] Niernsee was successful in Baltimore, and the South Carolina State House promised to add luster to an already satisfying career.

Things had been different for him during his previous extended visit to the deep South. Years earlier, in 1838, just after arriving in America without money or family and with only short-term employment, he traveled on foot and horseback between Mont-gomery, Alabama and Pensacola, Florida as part of a team of six engineers and twenty-four slaves surveying a railroad right-of-way. His diary recounts the heat, bugs, snakes, and discomfort of living in the woods and brushing transit lines in May and June. But he was young, and when the project stalled, with two friends he took rooms by the sea in Pensacola and then in New Orleans. He spent part of his savings on books and used his enforced leisure to study French, English, and mathematics. Finding neither work nor prospects in the South, he went first to New York City and then to Washington, D.C., where he became a draftsman for the government. In August, 1839, Benjamin Henry Latrobe, Jr. offered him a job with the Baltimore and Ohio Railroad, starting as a draftsman at $3 per day with a promise of increasing responsibilities and employment for three years.[9] This induced him to settle in Baltimore where he met and married fifteen-year-old Emily R. Bradenbaugh. Seventeen years after arriving in Baltimore, with a wife and four children and an established professional reputation, Niernsee packed to travel south again.[10]

Niernsee took up his duties on site on June 1, 1856. Columbia, as he knew it before the Civil War, was a bustling community of c. 3,500 which bore little resemblance to the frontier village described half a century earlier by John Drayton and Edward Hooker. Now there was an ice house at the corner of Washington and Richardson Streets which sold ice cut from New England lakes, shipped by sea to Charleston and then by rail to Columbia. Other luxuries, all located along Richardson Street, included six shops sell-ing "confectionery and Fancy Goods," a "dress trimmings shop," three music stores, two book stores, seven fruit dealers, two glass, china, and crockery shops, three milliners, three jewelry stores, four paint stores and three wall paper hangers, four tailors, and—for smokers like Niernsee—four cigar stores. More mundane daily needs were supplied by five bakers, thirty-one groceries, eleven dry goods merchants, and sixteen clothing stores. For rest and recreation there were fifteen boarding houses and hotels and four-

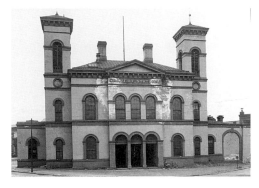

CALVERT STREET STATION, BALTIMORE, JOHN R. NIERNSEE, ARCHITECT. HISTORIC AMERI-CAN BUILDINGS SURVEY, COURTESY OF THE LIBRARY OF CONGRESS

TRAIN SHED ROOF STRUCTURE, BALTIMORE, JOHN R. NIERNSEE, ARCHITECT. HISTORIC AMERICAN ENGINEERING RECORDS, COUR-TESY OF THE LIBRARY OF CONGRESS

teen saloons. Personal, professional services were offered by five dentists, six druggists, thirteen lawyers, and sixteen doctors. A portrait painter, William H. Scarborough, and two photographers recorded the likenesses of antebellum Columbians; there was even a professional gilder, Joseph Brown, at 112 Richardson Street, to frame their products.[11]

A new-comer strolling the unpaved streets would have noted the flour, grist, and saw mills on the canal, the municipal water works and public baths in Sidney (Finlay) Park and the City Hall and Market on the northwest corner of Washington and Richardson (Main) Streets. The City Hall was the hub of commercial activity, and merchants gathered early in its open, arcaded lower story. At nine on weekday mornings they fanned out selling meat and produce from carts. Each night in the tower of the City Hall, watchmen sat and tolled the hours on the town bell; in the event of fire, they rang the alarm.

"Columbia was quite a military town," wrote J. F. Williams, reminiscing of the community he knew as a child in 1856. By law all white males from eighteen to forty-five had to serve in the militia, and "there were the following companies: Governor's Guards, Richland Rifles, Emmet Guards—made up mostly of Irishmen—Carolina Blues, Columbia Artillery, Congaree Cavalry."[12] Other units were formed as the Civil War approached, including the Chicora Rifles, the Columbia Grays, and the Harper Rifles. These militia units represented a long tradition of military preparedness within the state. Intermittent assaults by external enemies—Spanish, English, and Indians—and the on-going fear of slave insurrection served to keep generations of white males armed and ready to defend their inherited prerogatives, property, and way of life.

Niernsee found that James Jones had pressed forward despite significant difficulties with the funding. When Jones took office in December, 1855, the Comptroller General refused to release funds until proceeds from the sale of bonds were deposited in the treasury. As the bonds had not been issued, Jones had no money to work with. To make matters worse, the contractors had not been paid for a month and a half, and the General Assembly directed him to pay Charles McCullock, the dismissed stone contractor, $10,678; and Joseph D. Daly, the fired brick contractor, $1,500. The Comptroller General relented enough to cover existing debts by advancing $25,000 against the anticipated sale of bonds, but the bonds sold slowly, and in an effort to keep the labor force together Jones borrowed from the Bank of South Carolina in both Charleston and Columbia to meet payrolls though October, 1856. Having carried the project for ten months, both banks refused to extend any more credit.

In his first annual report (November, 1856) Jones requested an appropriation of $300,000 "to relieve me, both from my present unpleasant position towards the operatives and other creditors, and my liabilities to the Bank."[13] He had reason to be anxious: from November 1, 1855 through September 30, 1856, he had disbursed $173,162.42 most of which—$150,701.03—was borrowed and represented unsettled liabilities at the end of his first year as agent for the new State House.[14] Among his other tasks, James Jones had to convince the legislators that the work had to be put on a business-like footing if it were to succeed.

When Niernsee arrived, he immediately set about making the quarries more efficient and improving the labor force. Writing the legislature to bolster Jones's request for an appropriation, Niernsee emphasized the complexity and expense of building with stone. Eight times in the previous eleven months the Congaree had risen and flooded the main Granby quarry, and each time this had happened, pumping out water and cleaning out mud had cost time and money.[15] Niernsee found they had been hauling the quarried stone in wagons and, as the unpaved road near the quarry ran along the river, wet weather made it difficult to haul the large blocks required for the foundations. Once the stone reached the site, Niernsee insisted on carefully cutting it to specified shapes. In each aspect of the work, his standards were different from Hammarskold's or Walker's, and he reorganized things accordingly.

Niernsee's technical training and experience are evident in his initial reports. To increase the supply of stone he argued successfully for the construction of a three-mile tram line or mule-drawn railroad. He meticulously presented the differences in initial cost, maintenance, and operation of a common unpaved road, a plank road, and a railroad. Taking into account the weight a mule could pull on each type of surface, he demonstrated that a railroad would be five times more efficient than the existing common unpaved road.

Within six months of arriving, Niernsee had completely reorganized work at the site. His office consisted of himself, John Kay as assistant architect, a draftsman, a timekeeper, and a general clerk. Working on site were 100 stonecutters directed by a foreman and his assistant; there were also three masons, twenty carpenters, four blacksmiths, thirteen tool sharpeners, three machinists (working on the fireproof metal window frames), two painters, twelve general laborers, and a day and a night watchman.

Most of the stonecutters were foreign born: there were thirty-nine Irishmen, eleven Scotsmen, eleven Englishmen, five Germans, and two Welshmen. The remainder, with one or two exceptions, came from the northern states—New York, Massachusetts, Maine, and Connecticut. The presence of imported labor underscores the fact that physically as well as conceptually, from its very foundations, the new State House, unlike the old State House, was a cosmopolitan undertaking.[16]

The local labor force was dominated by slaves. In 1856, for example, the 216 stonecutters at the quarries were all slaves; 65 more slaves worked as general laborers at the building site; 10 worked as carpenters; 4 worked as blacksmiths, and one as a rigger. The wages paid to owners for slave labor ranged from 38 cents per day for general laborers to $1.15 per day for the carpenters and blacksmiths. By contrast, the white general laborers received $1.25 per day and the white carpenters $2.25 to $2.50. The white stonecutters, masons, and blacksmiths all earned $3.00 per day.[17]

During his first summer and fall on the job, Niernsee stockpiled cut granite and imported marble. John F. Williams recalled that "it was an interesting sight to see the large blocks of marble being sawed into slabs at the State House. The blocks would be put under the saws and as many saws as you wanted slabs could be put in the gangs. The saws were long steel blades without teeth, the block was covered with sharp sand and the saws started a water sprinkler system which would keep the sand washed down in the grooves and that would do the cutting."[18] (Nothing in the records suggests that Niernsee's predecessors used mechanical stonecutting tools.)

While stockpiling stone, Niernsee also finished the foundation piers of the north and south porticos and began the base course of the foundation walls. He directed work at three quarries and planned "to commence laying bricks on or about the 1st December." Niernsee had received some 400,000 bricks from H. P. Green. Based upon his calculations, he anticipated completing one story each year and assumed "it will take about a year to put on the roof and put in the iron ceilings and arches and another year for the general interior finish. . . ."[19] He thought the job could be done in five years, and he was almost on schedule when war halted the work.

Niernsee's Plan in Its National Context

Professional training and experience enabled Niernsee and Jones to get underway efficiently. They were also intangibly—but substantially—assisted by the recent history of State Houses in America, for State Houses had evolved as a new building type, and Niernsee's plan was firmly rooted in that evolution. Niernsee, Jones, and those sponsoring their work were able to proceed with the assurance that they were operating within an honored tradition, for during the second quarter of the nineteenth century American state capitols had become recognizable as a specific, special building type.

Not until the states began to acquire self-identity through experience, after the Louisiana Purchase, the War of 1812, and the Missouri Compromise of 1820, did the State House as a building type began to emerge. Fifteen of the seventeen State Houses built between 1783 and 1820 still resembled Georgian or colonial governmental buildings. The two exceptions were the Massachusetts State House in Boston (built 1787–1798) designed by Charles Bulfinch and the Capitol of Virginia (1798) designed by Thomas Jefferson. The Massachusetts State House was based on English prototypes and introduced the large scale dome, later to become a key component of the typical American capitol. The Capitol of Virginia, an adaptation of a Roman temple, promoted the use of classical forms as the insignia of governmental architecture in the new republic.

Westward expansion, prosperity, fire, and the relocation of capital cities caused eighteen state capitols to be built between 1820 and 1862. These buildings shared features meant to promote a sense of grandeur, dignity, and power reflecting the role of the states in the republic. Excepting the Gothic revival Louisiana Capitol in Baton Rouge (1847–1849), the state capitols that spanned the Jacksonian era invariably used large scale, multistory, classical columns, and other Greek and Roman motifs and forms. The classical image proved so attractive that historians have said "the Jacksonians made the Greek Revival their emblem."[20]

Since prestigious classical buildings had been built of stone, ten of the antebellum capitols were built wholly or partially of stone, and two others, the remodeled North Carolina Capitol in Raleigh and the Arkansas Capitol in Little Rock, were built of brick then stuccoed to imitate stone.[21] Psychologically and structurally, stone promised permanence. The commissioners of the Ohio State Capitol, embarking on a new stone capitol, expressed the appeal of building for posterity:

> We have commenced a work, not for ourselves only, but for future generations; posterity will view it as the work of a former age, the enlightened views and intelligence of which will be clearly indicated in the structure—it is thus that the architectural monuments of a country cherish national pride and patriotic sentiments, and contribute, in a great degree, to identify the citizen with his country. A state destitute of great public works . . . is not likely to have its institutions cherished and sustained, and its soil defended, with that zeal and tenacity which has always distinguished those regions adorned with monuments of art and architectural magnificence, to which the citizen can, at all times refer, as lasting evidence of the glory of his ancestors.[22]

Rearing above a classical stone base, the dome, or lantern, became a principal feature of state capitols after 1820. Bulfinch's dome for the Massachusetts Capitol and William Thornton's proposed dome for the national Capitol (finally completed, though wholly modified, in 1865) provided the most widely used conceptual models. All except four of the Jacksonian or antebellum state capitols had domes or lanterns. Of those four, Louisiana was Gothic revival, and a dome would have been stylistically inappropriate; the other three exceptions—Connecticut (1827–1833), Arkansas (1833–1840) and Florida (1840–1845)—were all adaptations of the classical temple on the Jeffersonian model.

The typical state capitol, c.1820–1860, consisted of a stone building with classical details having two wings (expressing a bicameral legislature) and a grand formal entry (expressing seriousness of purpose and public access), all capped by a central dome or lantern (symbolizing unity). Twelve of the eighteen capitols designed during the second quarter of the nineteenth century fit this mold and Niernsee's South Carolina State Capitol was one of them.

Judging from nineteenth century prints—for none of Niernsee's drawings survive—he proposed to place the State House on a raised terrace surrounded by a balustrade.

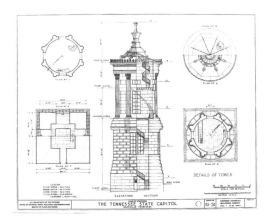

TENNESSEE STATE CAPITOL CUPOLA. HISTORIC AMERICAN BUILDINGS SURVEY, COURTESY OF THE LIBRARY OF CONGRESS

MODEL OF TOWER OF TENNESSEE STATE CAPITOL. HISTORIC AMERICAN BUILDINGS SURVEY, COURTESY OF THE LIBRARY OF CONGRESS

The main facade would face north, but entries on the south, east, and west sides aligned the building with all points of the compass as envisioned by Manning. Niernsee wanted the porticos to project dramatically from the facade; both were supposed to be two columns deep. The exterior walls were to resemble the national Capitol with a heavily rusticated ground floor serving visually as a base for the elaborate framing of the windows on the principal floor. A balustrade, echoing the terrace below, was to be the crowning feature of the exterior walls.

The most unusual feature of Niernsee's plan was a 180' high tower, 30 feet square at the base, capped by a lantern based upon the Choragic Monument of Lysicratus.[23] The tower was to rise above the main entrance over the central lobby like a vertical exclamation mark. Niernsee's proposed tower is based upon a design by William Strickland (1788–1854) for the Tennessee State Capitol (1845–1859).

Niernsee knew Strickland as one of the first generation of American born, professional architects. Strickland dominated architectural practice in Philadelphia during Niernsee's early years in Baltimore. He had trained under Benjamin Henry Latrobe (whose son hired Niernsee to work for the Baltimore and Ohio Railroad). Strickland gained prominence in 1818 by beating Latrobe to win the commission for the Second Bank of the United States. The bank, built in Philadelphia (1818–1824), was based on the Parthenon and established Strickland as a leading figure in the Greek revival.

But Strickland was not content to work in one style. He produced Gothic and Egyptian Revival designs in addition to his classically based work. The abruptly vertical tower crowning the Tennessee Capitol was a departure from the dome which by 1845 had become more or less standard as the crowning element of antebellum capitols. Juxtaposed to the classical horizontal balance of the body of the capitol, the tower reflects Strickland's interest in Victorian Picturesque Eclecticism. Although he had used a similar lantern two decades earlier on the Philadelphia Merchants' Exchange (1832–1834), the Tennessee tower was unique and avant garde on a state capitol. Niernsee, recognizing it as an innovation, was drawn to it.[24]

National attention had focused on Nashville in 1850, for the slave states convened there (June 3–12, 1850) to consider unified opposition to abolition and the exclusion of slavery from the western territories. The Nashville Convention disbanded without ratifying unified action, and the South Carolina delegates advocating secession were dismayed. But they brought home with them an impressive symbol of statehood, for by 1850 the gray marble walls of the Tennessee capitol had reached the eaves, and Strickland was getting ready to take bids for the iron roof.

Strickland's Tennessee Capitol was sited at the summit of Campbell's Hill, the highest point in the Nashville. Like the Temple of Jupiter, the Capitolium on the Capitoline Hill in Rome, and the U.S. Capitol on Jenkins Hill in the District of Columbia, the Tennessee capitol was meant to dominate the skyline. John L. Manning had the same effect in mind in 1854 when he recommended building the new State House facing north at the intersection of Richardson and Senate streets. He envisioned, he wrote, a State House which could be "seen without obstruction from the four points of the compass."[25]

To realize Manning's suggestion, the state consolidated the old State House block bounded by Gervais, Assembly, Senate, and Richardson (Main) streets with the block immediately to the east bounded by Richardson, Gervais, Sumter, and Senate streets. Richardson was then closed between Gervais and Senate, and the new foundations spanned the two blocks and were centered on Richardson Street. The rear portico was laid out parallel and close to Senate Street. The effect was dramatic. The old State House had simply occupied an ordinary block near the center of the town, but the new site broke the street pattern and created a specific, prominent focal point.

Unfortunately, the reconfiguration necessitated the destruction of Russell's Garden, the first commercial and recreational landscaped, parklike setting in Columbia. Niernsee saw the remnants of Russell's work amid the debris as work began. In 1836 Robert E. Russell (1785–1854) had leased from the state a one-acre lot at the southwest corner of Richardson and Senate streets.[26] The lot was directly opposite the front of the old State House and had been reserved for public use in the 1786 city plan.[27] Here he developed a nursery business and attracted customers by selling ice cream and ginger pop and offering walks through a "mystic maze" made of clipped hedges. By midcentury Russell's Garden had become one of the places visitors to the city were taken.[28]

Beyond his garden, Russell promoted city beautification through horticulture. In 1846 he sold to the state and planted on the old State House grounds thirty-nine large live oaks, eight orange trees (boxed, presumably so they could spend winters in his greenhouse), fourteen cedars, each seven feet high, ninety-nine small cedars, fifty-two mock oranges, fifty-five small live oaks, one balsam fir, and two magnolias. For selling and planting these trees and shrubs and undertaking some minor brickwork and fencing, he charged $243.75. In 1846 Russell requested $100 for "my services superintending the grounds." At his death his wife petitioned for his 1853 salary as "gardener for the grounds"; she noted that his salary was $300 per year.[29] Robert E. Russell was the first person to promote ornamental planting on the State House grounds.

Russell's business blossomed. In December, 1853 he advertised 50,000 plants for sale, but it was a going-out-of-business sale, for immediately below Russell's advertisement was a notice from Hammarskold seeking bids to move the old State House. Russell died that spring (March 3, 1854).[30] He was buried in Trinity Churchyard, across the street from the site of his garden and near the grave of one of his children, Camellia Japonica Russell.

As Russell's garden disappeared beneath piles of brick and stone, the only ornamental feature remaining was the cast iron and copper palmetto tree made by Christopher Werner of Charleston. Werner was one of three Germans who dominated the production of cast and wrought iron in Charleston in the mid nineteenth century. He had supplied iron sashes, doors and pillars for Hammarskold's ill-fated fireproof building.[31]

TENNESSEE STATE CAPITOL, CIRCA 1850.
COURTESY OF THE LIBRARY OF CONGRESS

Just before Niernsee arrived, Werner brought his palmetto tree to Columbia (c. 1852) and erected it on the grounds as a speculation. It had not been commissioned by the state, but Werner had good reason to assume the state would ultimately purchase it to honor the Palmetto Regiment or as a symbol of the state itself. Werner knew the palmetto was a powerful symbol and, like a fisherman casting and letting the bait settle, he put it in front of the relocated old State House without any labels or markers.

In 1776 William Henry Drayton and Arthur Middleton had designed the state seal with a palmetto as a central motif. They used it because the tree was indigenous and because the walls of Fort Moultrie, made of palmetto logs and sand, had recently sheltered Col. Moultrie and his men in their victory against the British fleet. In the following decades, the palmetto was also used on banners in various forms; it was adopted as the principal symbol on the state flag proposed by Robert Barnwell Rhett, Jr., on January 28, 1861.[32]

Having become a symbol during the Revolution, the palmetto tree was adopted as the regimental emblem of the volunteers who left Charleston on December 23, 1846 to participate in the Mexican War. The war was enthusiastically supported by the slave states (they sent 43,232 soldiers versus the 22,136 from the more populous North), for southerners anticipated territorial gains that would allow the expansion of slavery and the cotton economy. The Palmetto Regiment was young and aggressive (the average age was twenty-three) and lost 501 of its original 974 to wounds and disease. Its leader, former governor Pierce M. Butler, was among those who died. At the battles of Churubusco, Chapultepec, and Mexico City the Palmetto Regiment suffered greater losses than any other American unit.

In 1851 Governor John H. Means noted that the Palmetto Regiment survivors had "taken steps to erect a monument at their own expense." He urged the state to intervene and "pay the last tribute" to those who died.[33] Werner, whose iron tree was already in place on the State House grounds, must have been optimistic, but not until 1856 did the legislature resolve to purchase "the cast Iron Palmetto Tree now in front of the State House" for a sum not to exceed $5,000.[34] James Jones, as agent, directed Werner to "have the foliage of the Palmetto tree completed upon the top" instead of a perching bronze winged eagle which had been discussed by the legislature.[35] Jones also asked Werner to prepare plaques bearing the names of the dead. When the plaques were installed, twenty-seven misspelled names raised howls of complaint, and Jones, having paid Werner $4,000, refused to advance any more money until the plaques were corrected.

Werner was disgruntled. Although he admitting having undertaken the monument of his own volition, he claimed to have spent $11,000 producing it. In response to Werner's petition for reimbursement, the legislature authorized only an additional $1,000 to be paid when the monument was complete, and he saw that they had no intention of paying what he maintained the work was worth.

Palmetto Monument, circa 1902. Courtesy of the South Carolina Archives and History Center

PALMETTO MONUMENT. PHOTOGRAPH BY JET LOWE, 1995

Werner installed revised plaques, but more mistakes were found, and Jones felt the plaques themselves were improperly made. (The letters were welded on instead of engraved and tended to fall off.) Werner "declined to do anything more towards its completion."[36] Jones finally authorized another payment in February, 1859, bringing Werner's total up to $5,000, when the errors were corrected.[37] The supplemental appropriation of $1,000 was never paid.

Visitors were drawn to the large, bustling construction site. On July 15, 1857, Micajah Adolphus Clark, passing through Columbia, wrote in his diary that he "went up to the capitol, the State House, now being erecting—it is a very costly, and magnificent building . . . and is designed to be the finest State house in the

New State House north elevation on Confederate ten dollar bill, 1863. Courtesy of Harry McDowell

New State House north elevation. Print from the collection of Henry K. Brown, circa 1860, courtesy of the Library of Congress

South. There appears to be enough Rock on the Yard, dressed to complete the building."[38] Clark was impressed by the millions being spent and the size of the building, for even a casual observer sensed the scale of the work. Unlike Clark, who was born and lived in the South, Niernsee thought of the whole operation in national terms. In explaining the quarrying and stone cutting to the legislature, he

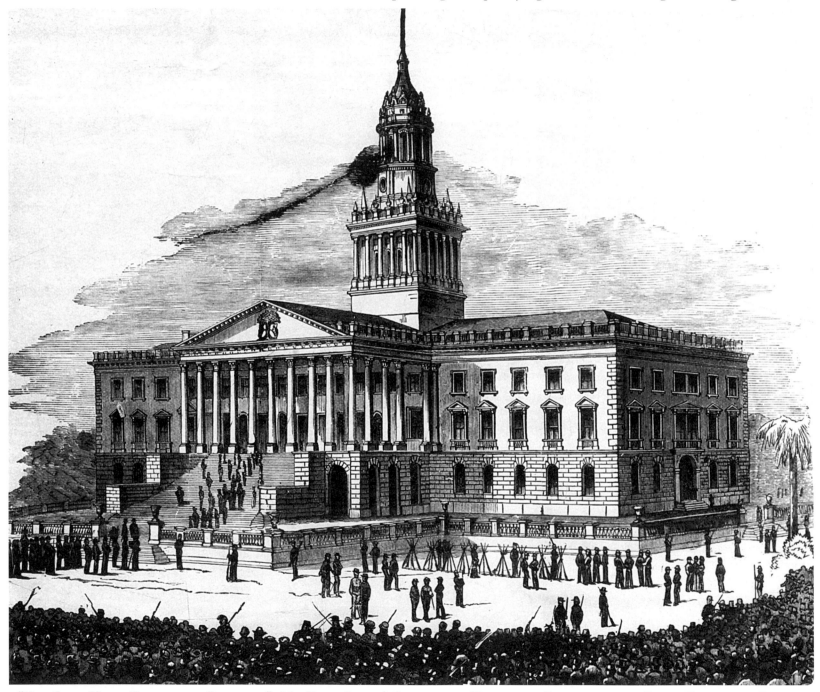

"NEW STATE HOUSE DEPICTED AT COLUMBIA," 1861, *FRANK LESLIE'S ILLUSTRATED NEWSPAPER*. COURTESY OF THE SOUTH CAROLINIANA LIBRARY

compared it to work in Massachusetts, Maryland, and the extension of the U.S. Capitol which was then underway.[39]

Niernsee had spent the summer and fall of 1856 improving the quarry, gathering a labor force, setting up his office, starting footings for the new walls, and stockpiling brick and cut granite. The preparatory work began to pay off in 1857, and during the next three years the building rose steadily like a well-watered tree. The walls had reached a height of twenty-six feet above the footings in 1857 when Micajah Clark visited the site; two years later they were fifty-two and one-half feet high. By 1860 the walls were sixty-five feet, nine inches high; and by 1861 the cornice line, at seventy feet, three inches above the footings, had been reached.[40]

Above the foundations, more finely finished stone was required; consequently, from 1857 through 1860 the labor force increased each year. In 1857 a total of 307 men were working on the job; there were 546 the next year, 573 the next, and 607 at the peak of activity in 1860. In 1861, with most of the stone work done and war approaching, the labor force fell to 277 men; by 1863 it had dropped to 103. The labor force always fluctuated seasonally, declining during the hottest months and peaking in October and November.

Problems to Overcome

Niernsee had to make three major improvements in the operations in order to insure an economical, steady supply of large blocks of stone. First, a dam was needed to keep the Congaree from flooding the Granby quarry; second, a railroad was essential to transport the stone to the site, and finally, steam engines were required both to keep the quarry pumped free of water and to power the derricks lifting the stone from the ever-deeper quarry and onto the ever-higher walls.

Ten times during 1856 the river flooded the quarry making work there "not only expensive but unreliable."[41] Niernsee solved this by building a dam along the river side of the quarry. The dam required moving 101,484 cubic yards of earth with men and mules; it was 1,100 feet long, 12 feet wide on top, and 35 feet wide at its bottom. Half of the inner face of the dam was reinforced with a rubble stone wall containing 3,000 perches of stone. With the exception of one record-breaking flood in 1861, the dam was an unmitigated success, and flooding was no longer a problem.

But the river was not the only source of water in the quarry. As the excavation grew larger, both surface and ground water became increasingly troublesome. On a typical rainy day as much as 200,000 gallons of run-off drained into the quarry. And even in dry weather springs within the quarry were a constant nuisance. Hammarskold and Walker had used Archimedian screw pumps operated by an average of forty men to lift the water thirty-five feet and pump it into the river.

Justifying the expense of setting up a steam-driven pump, Niernsee observed dryly that the hand-driven pumping had proved precarious. He dug a well in the lowest part of the quarry, or seventy-eight feet below the top of the dam. The well acted like a sump, and over it he set a steam powered pump which lifted 40,000 gallons an hour. The steam pump kept the quarry free of water and freed forty men to quarry stone. As if that were not enough, Niernsee also coupled the steam engine to the seven quarry derricks. Using mechanical power to lift stone at the quarry freed another thirty men who had previously been needed to crank the derricks.

In 1856, as they began laying the finished part of the superstructure, stones "from 15 to 20 tons weight" were required, and it quickly became apparent that the old method of hauling stone in wagons on a "common road" would no longer suffice. In 1856 and 1857 Niernsee built the railroad track for mule-drawn trams. The track was 3 miles 208 feet long and ran "down Richardson street [South Main], turning Westward at Narey's brewery, and from there extended straight to Granby. . . . Large, strong flat cars, built especially for the purpose, and each drawn by a team of thirty-six mules, were employed in transporting the granite."[42] Using iron rails supplied by the state, James W. Gibbes built the line for $12,500, including culverts, bridges and the ties, and longitudinal timber supports for the rails. Both financially and functionally the tram line was successful. Before it was finished, the cost of hauling stone during 1856 and 1857 had been $36,000, but with the tram line in operation expenses for mules and teamsters fell in 1858 and 1859 to only $14,000. As Niernsee pointed out, the tram line paid for itself in the first two years of operation.

More importantly, Niernsee noted that using the tram line "we have been enabled to haul weights on the railroad which we should have been unable to transport on the common road, having hauled the large columns, weighting upwards of thirty-four tons apiece, (in the rough) in little more than an hour for each column, drawn by sixteen mules."[43]

The tram line was indispensable. Forty of the monolithic columns weighed twenty-six tons or more apiece. One Architrave—a single stone—weighed fifty-two tons, and Niernsee proudly wrote that insofar as he knew, it was the "largest rock moved (or at least recorded as moved) in this country."[44] He also claimed it was impossible, at any price, to obtain such massive stones from the New England quarries and ship it to the site, for no vessels were equipped to handle it.

Cutting the granite and moving it to the building site was less than half the battle. The stones arrived rough cut and larger than needed; finishing the ashlar blocks and columns was done by specialized carvers in wooden sheds on the State House grounds. Whereas all the quarry men were black slaves hired by the state, all the finish carvers were white employees of the stone contractors. The major contract was signed in 1858 by Hugh Sisson of Baltimore. For $335,000 Sisson agreed to supply almost all of the carved granite and marble. Most of the decorative carving was done in 1859–1860 when the corps of carvers increased from 59 to 121. By the fall of 1861 there were only 36 stonecarvers remaining on the job, for most of the work was completed, and the outbreak of war made many of the stonecarvers eager to depart.

Quarrying and shaping the stone were the labor intensive parts of the work.[45] After each block was finished, it was lifted into place by steam powered derricks and set by a handful of stone masons. In 1860, for example, all of the stone was set by "Mr. Macomber and his assistant, with five black laborers." At a time when only 7 men were required to position the finished stone in the walls, there were 138 men in the quarry and 121 stonecutters laboring in the yard.[46]

As the stone walls rose to each floor level, the floors were constructed by setting iron beams into the stone walls and then building shallow brick arches between the beams. Sections of the exterior walls revealed by the current renovation suggest that every other course of the granite facing of the exterior walls is keyed into a brick wall approximately twenty inches thick. Many bricks were required; for example, 1,017,466 bricks were laid in the walls and arches during 1860 by a team of twelve bricklayers who were kept constantly supplied with bricks and mortar by the general laborers.[47]

Henry Kirke Brown, Principal Sculptor

The most intricate, figural stone carving was directed by Henry Kirke Brown (1814–1886). Forgotten by the public today, he was one of the most famous sculptors in mid nineteenth century America. His reputation was such that while he was in Columbia working on the new State House, he was also serving as head of the Art Commission for the National Capitol, and in recommending him to Congress, President James Buchanan said, "Brown is in the prime of life, full of knowledge and experience as well as inspiration, and no man in America is so well fitted to head this commission and lead this national enterprise."[48] Like Niernsee, Brown had studied abroad and had a substantial professional record and reputation when he came to work on the new State House.

Brown was born in Leyden, Massachusetts. As a young man he trained for four years in Boston under Chester Harding, a successful portrait painter; he then moved to Cincinnati and supported himself for four years as a surveyor while studying anatomy under Dr. William Parker. With this foundation Brown went abroad and spent two years in Florence and then two more years in Rome. Returning to America in 1846, he established a studio in New York and became a leading advocate of a recognizably American style of sculpture. His subsequent reputation as a realist was based upon an understanding of anatomy and the analytical eye of a portraitist.

HENRY KIRKE BROWN, CIRCA 1860. COURTESY OF THE LIBRARY OF CONGRESS

He achieved success quickly. In 1846 his first major figure, a technically complex bronze of a young Indian stalking, entitled the Aboriginal Hunter, received favorable reviews. People found the American subject and realistic presentation a refreshing change from idealized, mythological figures. Brown's Aboriginal Hunter was followed by a statue (1850–1852) of DeWitt Clinton in Greenwood Cemetery, Brooklyn, and an equestrian statue (1853–1856) of George Washington in Union Square in New York City. The Washington is considered his masterpiece; Charles Sumner, speaking on the floor of the U.S. Senate, hailed it as the best of its type in the country.[49]

In 1855 Brown was invited to submit a design for the pediment of the House of Representatives wing of the U.S. Capitol. He wrote his wife that the building inspired thoughts "more eternal than buildings . . . strange notions . . . about groping in darkness . . . about good men and about bad men, men in power, and men without certain kinds of power."[50] Visiting the Capitol and waiting for Montgomery Meigs, who was in charge of the work, Brown spent the morning perched on a scaffold beside an Italian fresco painter. When Meigs arrived he took the sculptor on a tour of "every nook and turn of that growing pile." Meigs invited him to submit plans of a bronze door and "a pediment to match Crawford's."[51]

As a realist interested in establishing a distinctly American art, Brown prepared a model in which laborers symbolized regions of the country. The only classical, allegorical figure in the design is a woman in the center representing America. Her raised arms shelter a kneeling immigrant. The other nine figures are recognizably contemporary. To the viewer's right are a farmer, a fisherman, and a hunter; to the left are an explorer, a young mariner, "a stalwart Negro sitting upon a bale of cotton" and a trapper.[52] The proposal was rejected, for Meigs "refused to have a Negro represented in the pediment; and when Mr. Brown asked what substitute he had to propose by which the industry of the South could be more appropriately represented than by a Negro and a bale of cotton, Mr. Meigs was dumb, but declared, nevertheless, that he would not allow the figure to remain. 'Well,' said Mr. Brown, 'I will make that Negro yet; and I will make him in the South, too!'"[53] This anecdote—recounted in Brown's obituary—succinctly links his penchant for realism and his association with the national and the South Carolina Capitols.

MODEL FOR HOUSE PEDIMENT OF U.S. CAPITOL, HENRY KIRKE BROWN, 1855. COURTESY OF THE LIBRARY OF CONGRESS

The rejection of the proposal is not surprising, for before the Civil War no public monuments in America included blacks or depicted slavery.[54] Public monuments are rooted in broadly agreed-upon values, and the intensifying debate about the social and political status of blacks insured that Brown's proposal would be controversial. The contrast between the body language of the active, free laborers and the pensive, seated slave suggests that Brown meant to draw attention to the evils of slavery.[55] As a sculptor, however, he was drawn to the U.S. Capitol, so he modified the design in an attempt get the commission. He wrote a friend "about my Washington affairs I do in no way get discouraged. I felt at the time that Capt M[eigs] was acting under restraint & that he had a good and true heart and had a strong desire for my success. . . . see what restraint rests upon all who desire success in our governmental affairs. They have to skulk and dodge in many ways which must be repulsive to them. . . ."[56] Describing the revised design, he said he ". . . left out the soldiers and put the Ballot Box in their stead which if regarded aright will attain our brethren of the South more than my poor sleeping slave. . . ."[57]

The modified design was rejected, but his time in Washington was not fruitless, for there he apparently made contact with Carolinians seeking sculpture. Several months after losing the U.S. Capitol pediment, he wrote his friend again: "I . . . expect to go to Washington in the course of a few weeks to see about making a statue of Calhoun for the Chivalrous of S.C."[58] Four years later, when Brown went to South Carolina, it was to produce sculpture for the State House and its pediment.

A contemporary described Brown as being "tall, slender, and very pale, with dark hair and whiskers, and eyes very black and expressive. His manner is child-like, yet calm and dignified."[59] He arrived with his wife in Columbia in early April, 1859, and wrote to a friend:

Columbia, April 22, 1859

Dear Maynard,

We reached this place on Thursday morning. . . . We are delighted by the appearance of . . . lovely views in all directions from the Capitol or State House, and the City itself is a city of gardens full of fine shrubbery, fruits and flowers. . . . I found Niernsee in point of flesh all that he had said of himself and a good warm-hearted German, well Americanized. He is having a studio prepared for me and everything else I want, and seems to have formed full as favorable opinion of me as I deserve. . . . The Capitol has been already three years in progress, and the walls are not yet up. It is being constructed of granite which they find not far off, and seems equal to any I have ever seen. The whole work is being executed more thoroughly and in better taste than the U.S. Capitol. . . . This is the first letter I have attempted to write from here so please excuse all eccess of enthusiasm.[60]

COLUMBIA STUDIO, HENRY KIRKE BROWN, 1861. COURTESY OF THE LIBRARY OF CONGRESS

The sculpture studio was in one of the wooden sheds on the State House grounds near the relocated old State House. In these sheds Brown made plaster models to guide the stonecarvers. Brown's assistant, Johnson Munday, writing to his sister in Baltimore, described the growing tension in Columbia. Munday also described the statues which were meant to be the most prominent and telling ornament of the new State House.

Columbia, S.C. Feb. 20th 1861.

My Dear Sister,

I have become so settled in my new home that life has assumed the monotony inseparable from familiarity with objects and facts. The city has become common-place, and the din of workmen about the State-house falls upon my ear as an old story. I vibrate between the studio and my home quarters, seeing nothing but the opening buds, and hearing nothing but rumors of Wars, which last, by the way, is the least of novelties in this chivalrous Republic.

When I last wrote to you, there was some uncertainty in regard to my staying in S. Carolina. We are still kept in suspense upon this point, not knowing what day we may find it advisable to seek for more peaceable quarters. In the event of War, it will hardly be possible for the state to continue the work upon the Capitol, and even if it were not suspended, to remain in the midst of the excitement and confusion would not be at all agreeable. . . .

But however much I may be isolated by these prejudices, I find kind and sympathizing friends in Mr. and Mrs. Brown. They seem to be tender of me sometimes, so that I feel guilty almost in being subject to their kindness, for I am sure that all that I can do, can never make it appear that they have found a worthy subject. We are stopping in the same house and a few steps take me to their room which is often sought. There the evenings pass pleasantly with reading, drawing, card-playing, and occasionally, a hot whiskey toddy to get up some degree of patriotism. We get on nicely at the Studio through the day. It is a large and very complete, and Mr. Brown is modeling some fine statues. I find enough to do, and the experience is of great value to me. The sculptures are indicated in the wood cut of the State-house, in the pediment over the main entrance. They form a group of twelve figures. The three central figures represent the Hope, Justice and Liberty with their usual emblems and the statures on either side are of Negroes, represented in the cotton and rice fields. The three principal figures are each eleven feet in height; those on either side, each about nine feet. They are to be executed in Italian Marble, which will require yet nearly three years. The State house is constructed of granite, iron, and marble. The floors and inside walls will be of polished marble. The furniture will be of iron. As no wood is to be used in its construction, the building will be fireproof. Mr. Brown considers it the finest building in the country, not excepting the new Capitol at Washington. It has been in process of erection the last seven years, and will be completed in about three more years. The cost will be between three and four millions. It is a satisfaction to have a finger in so fine a pie as this, and I really hope that the "dogs of war" will not force us to leave the work unfinished.

Your Aff. Brother
Johnson M. Mundy.
Miss Mary E. Mundy[61]

Architecture, Ornament, and Symbolic Meaning

Brown wrote a friend that he was modeling the pediment for the north front on a metal armature and using the unraveled ends of old manila rope to support figures made of sand and plaster. He applied a smooth, finish coat of plaster mixed with marble dust and added "a little lemon juice to prevent its setting too quickly. . . ."[62] Photographs of the completed model, along with several descriptions, allow us to visualize and interpret the design.

According to Brown's son, the central figure represents South Carolina "bear-

MODEL FOR NORTH PEDIMENT OF SOUTH CAROLINA STATE HOUSE, HENRY KIRKE BROWN, 1860–1861. COURTESY OF THE LIBRARY OF CONGRESS

MODEL OF CENTRAL FIGURE FOR NORTH PEDIMENT OF SOUTH CAROLINA STATE HOUSE, HENRY KIRKE BROWN, 1860–1861. COURTESY OF THE LIBRARY OF CONGRESS

MODEL OF LEFT WING OF NORTH PEDIMENT OF SOUTH CAROLINA STATE HOUSE, HENRY KIRKE BROWN, 1860–1861. COURTESY OF THE LIBRARY OF CONGRESS

GEORGE MCDUFFIE, BY HENRY KIRKE BROWN, CIRCA 1860. PHOTOGRAPH BY HUNTER CLARKSON, 1998

MODEL OF RIGHT WING OF NORTH PEDIMENT OF SOUTH CAROLINA STATE HOUSE, HENRY KIRKE BROWN, 1860–1861. COURTESY OF THE LIBRARY OF CONGRESS

ROBERT Y. HAYNE, BY HENRY KIRKE BROWN, CIRCA 1860. PHOTOGRAPH BY HUNTER CLARKSON, 1998

ing the star of empire on her forehead and the laurel branch of victory in her right hand." (Johnson Munday said she symbolized Hope.) She is flanked by Liberty, carrying the Phrygian cap of the French Revolution, and Justice who holds her scales. On either side of the allegorical figures are the "Eagle of soaring dominion," "the Lion of majestic power," the "anchor of Hope," the "protecting shield" and the "broad rays of the rising sun which give promise of future glory and enlightenment." Adjacent the eagle is a horseman who "represents the controlling mind of a dominant race, giving direction to the brute energies of the laboring masses." To the left are slaves harvesting rice; to the right are "herculean forms of the slaves handling the cotton bales." Slaves stretched out in the outermost angles represent "the peace of mind and content of the enslaved laborer with his lot."[63]

When Brown presented the model, his friend William Morris Davis said "silence fell upon the assembled judges as they looked upon the bold conception. . . . General Jones, superintendent of construction, suggested that the artist should favor the committee with the conceptions he sought to embody." Brown told them monumental sculpture was "prized as faithful records of the times in which they were made. In . . . monuments we read the customs, manners and institutions of past ages." He said the design

> endeavored to record in enduring form the institutions and productions of your native state, and a testimonial to present and future generations of your conviction that the institutions thus portrayed are the most favorable to an advanced civilization, as well as a more perfect human government. This you believe, and are prepared to defend, I simply give art expression to your convictions.[64]

A New York newspaper credited Brown with the design, but he obviously worked closely with Niernsee, for the pediment was not yet built, and its planned dimensions determined the size—and to some extent the postures—of the figures.[65] Combining allegorical and realistic figures, the design resembled Brown's proposal for the national Capitol, but the South Carolina sculpture was meant to present the planters' argument that slavery, Justice, South Carolina (or Hope), and Liberty were compatible—sentiments which presented a bold contrast to the federalism implied by the bronze statue of Washington purchased only two years earlier by the state.[66]

Ornament above the entries of monumental buildings traditionally makes institutional values concrete and visible. Viewed by themselves the allegorical figures would have referred only vaguely to ideals, but when juxtaposed to laboring slaves, Hope—if Munday was correct—or the appearance of the anchor of hope, probably alluded to an assertion often repeated from antebellum southern pulpits and press that Christianity condoned slavery. Hope figured prominently in this argument: it was claimed that Africans were fortunate to have been brought into a Christian culture and thereby exposed to the hope of a Christian salvation; furthermore, it was said that since all Christians must have faith in God's inscrutable beneficence, they live in the hope that all things—even slavery—work toward a good end.[67] The star of empire, the laurel of victory, the rising sun, and the lion and eagle all alluded to the power and glory of the state. The statue of Justice was probably meant to evoke respect for a government of laws, and like the adjacent figure of Liberty, Justice would have reminded the viewer that South Carolina's politicians believed that just or constitutional laws guaranteed states' rights as a foundation of liberty. This interpretation of the statues is substantiated by the use of John C. Calhoun's last speech at two successive cornerstone dedication ceremonies.

When work began on the new State House, states' rights was a major—perhaps the major—political topic in South Carolina, and John C. Calhoun's last major speech in the U.S. Senate (March 4, 1850) was widely viewed as one of the most forceful presentations of the southern states' rights position. Calhoun's death (March 31, 1850) transformed his address into a legacy. South Carolina politicians identified strongly with the speech: it was the only document placed beneath the cornerstone on December 15, 1851 when Hammarskold began the initial fireproof building.[68]

George E. Walker had removed Hammarskold's cornerstone during the demolition of the failed foundations and "found its contents totally destroyed, it being impossible to handle the papers. . . ."[69] The copy of the speech had crumbled, but the ideals expressed by Calhoun still commanded allegiance. A second cornerstone ceremony was held on June 9, 1856, as Niernsee got underway, and once again Calhoun's last address was the only document deposited beneath the cornerstone. At this second ceremony Niernsee made comments which were not reported. The principal address was delivered by Professor J. L. Reynolds of the South Carolina College, and he said a State House should represent "the dignity and majesty of the commonwealth," that "such buildings . . . are among the most efficient educators of the people. . . ." Architecture, he said, "is the external representation of their inner-life and embodies their views, feelings and hopes."[70]

Professor Reynolds concluded by "turning from the glorious recollections of the past to survey the future. . . . Clouds loom up in the distant horizon, muttering thunders break upon the ear, and the convulsed and agitated elements seem to portend an approaching storm." Like Munday who foresaw "the dogs of war," Reynolds feared, "the erection of a new State House—commenced in times of national tranquility, might be completed amid the clash of arms." He closed by echoing Calhoun: "we have not invited the contest. We stand upon the broad platform of the Constitution and the law, and however few in number, [we] constitute the country. All others are rebels and traitors."[71]

Brown's pedimental sculpture and the doctrine it personified was shattered by the Civil War.[72] Nonetheless, the symbolism embodied in the lost figures is perpetuated on the north facade by his medallions portraying George McDuffie (1790–1851) and Robert Y. Hayne (1791–1839). Both served in the U.S. Senate and as governors of South Carolina. Both were allies of Calhoun and were famous advocates of nullification, the 1830s prelude to secession.[73] Beneath each medallion is an eagle surrounded by fifteen stars which are "symbols of the prospective fifteen Confederate States." These portraits flanking the main entry were installed before the war halted the work. They are the most forceful antebellum symbols surviving on the State House.[74]

Construction of the New State House during the Civil War

Johnson Munday's description of the pedimental sculpture was written during the tension-filled interlude between the passage of South Carolina's Ordinance of Secession (December 20, 1860) and the firing upon Fort Sumter (April 12, 1861). As the new year dawned, H. K. Brown wrote a similar letter home. Without taking sides, he noted that war was inevitable, and "every son of South Carolina" was ready. Having been awaken "by the tread of soldiers" on their way to Charleston, he was saddened by the trauma he foresaw. With his wife and Johnson Munday, Brown left Columbia on or shortly after May 13, 1861, and by January, 1862, he was residing in Washington, D.C.[75] Before the war was over, and in failing health, he returned home to Newburgh, New York. For the next decade he sought commissions in New York City and at the U.S. Capitol, but he never returned to South Carolina.[76]

As Munday anticipated, war first impeded and finally halted the State House work. But construction did not stop suddenly, for Jones and Niernsee struggled to keep everything going in order to protect the state's investment in the quarry, the railroad, and the partially completed structure.

Anticipating war and the suspension of funding, James Jones ordered all paid contract work halted, effective March 15, 1861, but he arranged for the owners of the quarry men and Sisson and Dougherty and Company, the stonecutters, to accept, in lieu of cash, stock paying six per cent issued by the state.[77] For the next two years a smaller labor force continued the work under these new terms. Having made these arrangements, Jones resigned to become the colonel of a South Carolina regiment preparing defenses along the coast.

With Jones gone, Niernsee agreed, c. December, 1861, to serve as architect and superintendent of the new State House at a reduced salary of $2,000 per year. He had three principal goals for 1862. First, he wanted to quarry enough stone to complete the building before the quarries were allowed to flood and their equipment deteriorated through disuse; secondly, he wanted to finish all stone carving before the skilled stonecutters dispersed, for gathering and training a new set of carvers would be difficult and expensive; and, finally, the materials and the structure itself had to be made secure for an indefinite period until circumstances allowed them to finish the building.

Niernsee described the status of the building at the outbreak of the Civil War in his October 1, 1861, annual report. The exterior walls were virtually complete, and he wrote, "we have now finished the building, necessary to sustain and build the permanent iron roof upon, to within an estimated value of $19,440 worth of granite cutting and setting, and $8,250 worth of brick-work." Although the exterior walls were almost complete, there was no roof and nothing had been done to make the interior habitable. The porticos had not been begun, but "all the engaged columns and capitals connected with the building proper [were] being set now. . . ." None of the marble detailing or veneer intended for the interior had been installed, but Sisson and Dougherty, "contractors for the execution of the external Corinthian granite capitals, have completed that part of their contract to within the value of about $8,000. Their contract calls for its completion on the 1st of January, 1862." Most of the marble was cut, polished, and stored in sheds on site ready for installation, and Sisson and Dougherty had a foreman, two toolsharpeners, thirty-four marblecutters, twelve polishers, an engine man, and thirteen black laborers finishing the stone cutting. The state labor force, on the other hand, had been reduced to one white carpenter and one black carpenter's assistant working on site, and two whites and 128 blacks working at the quarry.[78]

Major John R. Niernsee and the War Effort

Throughout 1862, finished stone, both granite and marble, accumulated on the yard, but as the war intensified, others began to requisition materials from Niernsee. During the year he supplied 71,000 bricks for a powder magazine and arsenal in Columbia, 54,000 bricks for the confederate powder works in Charleston, 430 barrels of cement to General Trapier in Charleston, 957 pounds of rope to Major J. J. Pope, Chief of the Ordinance Department, and 1,300 feet of heavy chain to General Ripley in Charleston.[79]

Niernsee's two oldest sons, Frank and Rudolph, had joined Hampton's Legion as volunteers as soon as the war broke out.[80] Niernsee himself became engaged in the war effort as a military engineer on April 1, 1862, when he left Columbia to examine potential invasion routes and defensive positions in the largely unmapped mountains of South Carolina, North Carolina, and Tennessee. This initial reconnaissance expedition lasted a month. It was not leisurely. Bad roads, few bridges, inclement weather, and the press of time made this a strenuous undertaking.[81]

With John McRae, four slaves, six mules, a wagon, and a carriage, and equipped with camping gear and surveying instruments, Niernsee took the train from Columbia to Walhalla. From there the party set out in the wagon and carriage and climbed to Cashier's Valley. They examined routes along the Chatuga and Little Tennessee rivers and crossed Rabun Gap. They went to Franklin, Asheville, Caesar's Head, and Jones Gap; everywhere Niernsee noted distances between landmarks, the nature of fords and places suitable for fortifications. He concluded there were four routes from Knoxville across the Smoky Mountains "thro which the western part of NC & consequently SC could be invaded." These routes lay along the Little Tennessee River through Franklin and Walhalla, or along Little Pigeon Creek and through Oconee Luftin [?] Gap, or along Big Pigeon Creek from Newport, Tennessee to Waynesville, North Carolina, or finally along the French Broad through Asheville and Flat Rock. (Two years later when Union forces invaded from the west, they avoided the North Carolina mountains altogether by swinging south to Atlanta.)

Niernsee's first expedition returned to Columbia on April 30, 1862. In the fall he left again to undertake a series of reconnaissance missions (November 13 through December 21, 1962) along navigable rivers throughout South Carolina. The first of these was an excursion by boat from Granby down the Congaree seeking battery

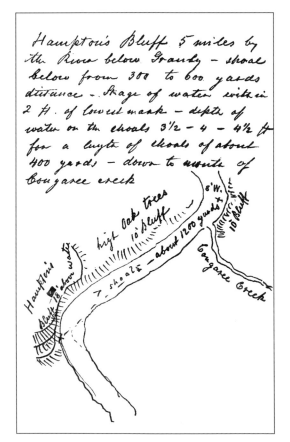

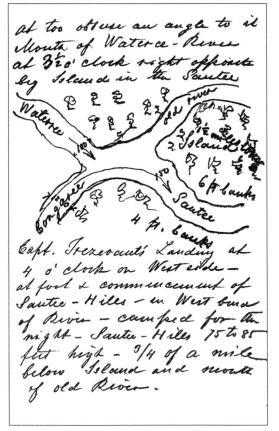

RECONNAISSANCE MAP OF CONGAREE RIVER, BY JOHN R. NIERNSEE, 1862. COURTESY OF THE MARYLAND HISTORICAL SOCIETY

RECONNAISSANCE MAP OF SANTEE RIVER, BY JOHN R. NIERNSEE, 1862. COURTESY OF THE MARYLAND HISTORICAL SOCIETY

sites on the High Hills of the Santee. As a result of this scouting foray, on December 12th he embarked with twenty men and four boats to obstruct navigation on the Santee River. Having taken a series of soundings to determine shoal water, they sunk boats and built log cribs filled with stone in the channel and returned to Columbia on December 21, 1862.

During the five months that followed, much of Niernsee's time was spent with approximately 100 men from the State House quarry reinforcing the Santee obstruction and building earthworks for a battery on Dr. Taber's Point overlooking the river. Having fortified the Santee and thus defended the approach by water from the coast to the capital, Niernsee conducted a reconnaissance (June 19–22, 1863) on the Waccamaw, Black, and Great Pee Dee Rivers and Lynches Creek. As summer waned, he poled and paddled along the forks of the Edisto (August 13–September 9, 1863). Attempting to coordinate the confederate and state defensive plans, having first obtained Governor Bonham's permission, Niernsee submitted a full report of his surveys and recommendations to General Beauregard. In the end, none of this work bore fruit, for General Sherman elected to march overland from Savannah to Columbia.[82]

In his annual report for 1863, Niernsee noted that defense work had reduced the quarry force to an average of only thirty-three laborers during the last nine months of the year. Nonetheless, these men had been able to quarry the foundation blocks for the north portico. Meanwhile, Sisson and Dougherty had completed the Corinthian capitals for the porticos and believed them to be the first ever executed in granite.[83] The supply of marble, however, was running out, and although forty-six stonecutters were still productive, Niernsee reported that their work must soon "virtually cease for want of material." From October, 1862, through September, 1863, the state only employed an average of ten whites and forty-seven blacks (including the quarry men) per month on the project.[84]

By the fall of 1863, the progress slowed due to reductions in the work force; nonetheless, whenever Niernsee visited the site between reconnaissance excursions, he could take satisfaction in the steadily growing supply of finished marble and granite, all carved, polished, stacked, and ready for installation.

The War Draws Near

The Civil War initially drew men and materials away from the new State House, but as the war effort intensified, the tide turned and the unfinished building and its environs became the scene of bustling, military-related production and activity. James Jones, for example, returned to Columbia in 1864. As Quartermaster General of the state, he established a factory on the State House grounds to make cotton cards which were needed for the production of uniforms, bandages, and bedding. He doubtless made use of the idled builders' sheds and equipment. The card factory "consisted of three buildings, one of which contained nine machines and another of which housed a steam engine that powered the entire establishment. Nearly one hundred cards were produced each day by a crew consisting primarily of women and young white and black lads."[85]

As an inland rail center located on navigable water, the capital was well situated as a point of manufacturing and distribution. John F. Williams, a teenager in Columbia during the war, wrote, "there were three railroads into Columbia at that time, the Charlotte, the Greenville, and the South Carolina." In addition to the railroads, Williams recalled, "there was a boat line running to Columbia which played a good part in the business of the city. The boats ran to Granby and the goods were hauled by drays to town, and cotton was shipped in return. There was also a line of river boats that ran to the up-country, bringing cotton and carrying back goods. The river boats ran to the foot of Elmwood avenue, then known as Boundary street. . . . It was an easy job coming down, but a pretty hard one going back, as it was all done with poles and ropes. In places men would get out on the banks and haul with ropes, and others pushed with poles."[86]

The transportation network encouraged the establishment of a variety of wartime industries. At the State Fairgrounds, then located at the northwest corner of the city, Joseph Leconte, a professor of chemistry and geology, directed the production of medicine, alcohol, chloroform, and nitrate of silver. He was also responsible for the development of a large government distillery which produced between two hundred and five hundred gallons of whiskey and alcohol per day. The confederate government operated a gunpowder mill on the canal embankment just north of the Congaree Bridge and maintained an armory and military warehouse near the corner of Huger and Hampton streets and another arsenal on the bluff above Finlay Park. At the corner of Lincoln and Laurel Streets, the Palmetto Iron Works produced ammunition and cannons. Kraft, Goldsmith, Kraft and Company, at the corner of Richardson and Upper Boundary Streets, produced swords, sabers, and bayonets. Munds and Henning on Washington Street employed "a large force of hands" making shoes for the army. The Saluda Factory, a mile above the city on the west bank of the Saluda River, was the largest industrial facility. It employed 1,000 spinners and weavers making cloth for the confederate government. Saltpeter for the gunpowder factory was made on the State Hospital grounds, and there were other factories devoted to the production of wool hats, buttons, buckles, uniforms, and socks for military use.[87]

In addition to supplying materials for the confederate forces, Columbia was also the site of two prisoner of war camps, several military hospitals, and a military academy. Beginning in 1861, governmental records from Charleston were moved to Columbia and stored in the old and new State Houses for safekeeping. The City of Charleston also sent a statue of Calhoun commissioned by its citizens. The statue, by Hiram Powers, presented Calhoun in a Roman toga, leaning on a palmetto trunk and holding a scroll on which had been inscribed: "Truth, Justice and the Constitution." It was placed out of harm's way in the entry hall of the old State House.[88] In 1862 the confederate printing presses were also shipped to Columbia from Richmond, and the city became the center for the production of confederate notes and bonds.[89]

John F. Williams recalled that "Columbia was quite a military town."[90] And the modern historian, Marion Brunson Lucas agrees: "Its military installations, its railroads, and the fact that it was to a great extent the last breadbasket of the Confederacy made the city far more important than Charleston. From a military standpoint the South Carolina capital was Sherman's next logical objective once Savannah had been taken and his army resupplied."[91]

Vivid images of Sherman's campaign through Atlanta, Savannah, and Columbia were taken by George N. Barnard (1819–1902), photographer for the Topographical Branch of the Department of Engineers of the Army of the Cumberland. The Union Army used photography as an administrative tool. The West Point curriculum included engineering, mapmaking, and drafting; consequently, Federal officers valued photography as an efficient means of reproducing materials needed in the field. In 1862–1863 Barnard worked in Washington on the photo duplication of maps, and in the spring of 1864, he was assigned to Nashville where he participated in the reproduction of maps, plans, diagrams, and topographical photographs being assembled by General William T. Sherman for the assault on Atlanta. Using a 12 x 15" and a 18 x 22" camera, Barnard was able to reduce, enlarge, and duplicate images of all types.[92] Compared with Niernsee's topographical sketches, the technology available to and used by Barnard and the union engineers presents a stark, sobering contrast.

Atlanta fell on September 2, 1864. Two days later Barnard was ordered to bring his equipment there to document the condition of the city, photograph the confederate defenses, and ultimately to reproduce maps needed for the remainder of the campaign. Mary Boykin Chesnut, who fled Columbia just before it fell, could have been composing captions for Barnard's pictures of its ruins when she wrote: "They say no living thing is found in Sherman's track; only chimneys, like telegraph poles, to carry the news that Sherman's army passed that way."[93]

Despite the speed of Sherman's march from Atlanta to Savannah, and notwithstanding the military importance of Columbia, neither state nor confederate authorities undertook timely measures to avert disaster. Mary Chesnut observed that after the fall of Atlanta both officials and ordinary citizens in Columbia seemed paralyzed by despair, denial, and disbelief:

December 1st [1864]

Through the deep waters we wade! . . . The girls went with the Martins to the State House. The Senate was deliberating how much cotton they would allow a man to plant next year, while the House put off until noon tomorrow a bill to raise men for home defense. While the enemy is thundering at their gates, they can still fool themselves with words; and yet the men who would not join Noah in his Ark-building must have left no descendants. They do not count Sherman among the devastating forces of nature. I do believe they forget his existence.[94]

Three weeks later she wrote again in the same vein:

December 19th [1864]

The deep waters are closing over us; and we in this house are like the outsiders at the time of the Flood. We eat, drink, laugh, dance, in lightness of heart! . . . Neither the Governor of Georgia nor the Governor of South Carolina is moving hand or foot. They have given up. . . . Our Legislature is debating State's Rights and the encroachments of the Confederate Government, with an occasional fling backwards at the Governor and Council; the much abused Council who wanted to train the militia, and fortify Columbia, and who did put Negroes to work on fortifications.[95]

While the Union forces rested in Savannah and prepared to continue the campaign, the biggest public undertaking in Columbia was a spectacular three-day bazaar mounted by ladies of the city in the old State House; it was the last public event staged there.

The bazaar opened on January 17, 1865 (exactly one month before Union troops crossed the Congaree), and was designed to raise money for confederate hospitals. One of its organizers, Grace Elmore, alluded to the ironic contrast between the social gaiety and the gravity of the military situation, observing in her diary:

How strangely is the serious and the gay intermingled in our life. . . . I can now, in some measure, understand the spirit that pervaded the Aristocracy of France during their sojourn in the Bastille, that philosophical rather than reckless spirit that accepted and used everything cheerful and bright in their prison life; a spirit which enabled them to laugh and chat with gaiety though they knew in the next few hours they would be headless. We romp with the children, receive our friends, and eat our dinner, just as tho' Sherman were a thousand miles away instead of only 200, and our hearts not filled with anxiety and gloomy anticipations.[96]

The bazaar was considered a dazzling success: 3,800 tickets (at $1 apiece) were sold on the first night; $24,936.50 was donated to the Wayside Hospital in Columbia. The interior of the old State House was transformed by banners and booths representing each of the confederate states (including those which for months had

been occupied by union forces). The food, games, trinkets, dancing, and decorations created an illusory fairyland, and "to give a just description of this royal festival," wrote a reporter, "would require a pen dipped in the hues of a thousand rainbows, or the power to catch the fantastic shapes that live in the changing pictures of a kaleidoscope." Attendance suggests the bazaar was welcomed as a bright spot against the gloom.[97]

John R. Niernsee and the Defense of the City

As Sherman left Savannah, patterns of life in Columbia seemed fragile—as the reporter said of the bazaar—like images in a kaleidoscope. Governor Andrew Gordon Magrath sought reinforcements from the government in Richmond, but Lee was hard pressed and sent only 2,000 cavalry and a handful of officers, including Major General Wade Hampton who came with no troops to command. Magrath also appealed to Joseph E. Brown, Governor of Georgia, who refused to send the Georgia militia, perhaps because South Carolinians had not rallied to the defense of Atlanta. Confederate General P. T. G. Beauregard, the ranking officer in the state, chose not to consolidate his 33,000 troops in Columbia. Instead, believing Sherman would attack either Charleston, Augusta, or Branchville, Beauregard divided his forces in an attempt to defend three points. Sherman swept around them much as he had bypassed the mountain passes surveyed by Niernsee.

Even before capturing Savannah, Sherman planned to attack either Branchville or Columbia and let Charleston, with its hinterland roots severed, fall on its own. From Savannah he had written to U. S. Grant:

> I feel no doubt whatever as to our future plans. . . . I left Augusta untouched on purpose, because now the enemy will be in doubt as to my objective . . . whether it be Augusta or Charleston, and will naturally divide his forces. I will then move either on Branchville or on Columbia, on any curved line that gives me the best supplies, breaking up in my course as much railroad as possible; then, ignoring Charleston and Augusta both, occupy Columbia.[98]

By Christmas Magrath had lost hope of effective assistance from Lee, Beauregard, or Governor Brown of Georgia; Sherman was ready to move north and west into South Carolina, and on December 20, 1864, Magrath ordered Niernsee to determine what had been—or could be—done to fortify Columbia.

Niernsee had recently returned "from the vicinity of the Savannah River, on a mission" (presumably similar to his reconnaissances on the Edisto, Pee Dee, and Waccamaw rivers).[99] He told Magrath he had never received orders from anyone concerning "commencing with the defenses of the city" despite the fact that he and other citizens had frequently alluded to the need to prepare for the worst. Insofar as Niernsee knew, the only thing being done was a survey "reconnaissance & location of the lines with a view to the general military operations" being conducted by Captain I. A. Haydon (or Hayden), a confederate engineer.[100]

Governor Magrath expressed dissatisfaction with "uncertain[ty] and delay . . . on the part of the Confederacy" and directed Niernsee, as a State Engineer, to cooperate with Haydon and General Gene M. Lovell in creating fortifications. For several weeks Captain Haydon had been surveying a potential line of defense on the east side of the Congaree River, but no ground had been broken. Niernsee arranged to go with him "to view the various positions prepared & selected by him for the location of the works." At this point Haydon was ordered to Charleston, and without waiting for his return, Niernsee decided to examine the western shore of the Congaree in Lexington and "concluded to commence the work under my personal direction on the part of the state."[101]

Governor Magrath confirmed Niernsee's decision to press ahead, and gave him "the final order 'of commencing work at once on the part of the State independently of waiting any further proceedings of the Confederate Officers and to avail myself simply of the able military services of Gene Mansfield Lovell. . . .'" Niernsee submitted to Magrath a list of "tools, teams & other implements & material and 2000 Negro laborers & the necessary subsistence shares" needed. But the state no longer commanded the resources to do the work, and the governor joined the mayor of Columbia, Thomas Jefferson Goodwyn, in an appeal to the public, seeking volunteers to build the defensive entrenchments and gun emplacements. The initial response was disappointing.[102]

Mayor Goodwyn said that the appeal produced "few hands and fewer tools."[103] Niernsee reported to Magrath that he began work in January "with but twelve (12) Negro hands, under the local superintendence of Capt T. L. Webb who was assigned by your Excellency to me as Assistant Engineer. . . ." By February 12th the work force reached a peak of 750 hands, and with this "comparatively small force" on the west side of the Congaree Niernsee completed two lines on the western side of the Congaree: "the inner line of Caseys Creek about two miles from town from its junction with the Congaree River following the farms up by Col Taylors pond, toward Monkey Spring, some four miles of Strong Entrenchments with three heavy Batteries for five Guns each with a view of extending said Entrenchments beyond that spring over the Ridge toward Saluda Mills on double Branch and across the fork between the Broad & Saluda Rivers. . . ." The outer defensive perimeter consisted of "four miles of Entrenchments about five miles from town near the mouth of the Congaree Creek on the River . . . following up the former creek thence along Six Miles Creek contemplating a junction on the Ridge near the sources of double Branch & thence to the Saluda near the Factory. On this outer line there were five Strong Batteries completed and in course of construction besides the clearance of extensive & heavy masses of timber, in front of both lines above mentioned. . . ."[104]

In addition to eight miles of trenches, gun emplacements, and clearings on the western side of the river, Niernsee "also commenced work at the same time, on the Eastern or Richland side of the River—commencing and completing a line of heavy Entrenchments from the River nearly opposite the Garer Creek between the Bruhls Gill's Creek following up a connecting line of heavy timbered gum-ponds between Harwell's & Trenholm's plantations and extending up those ponds for nearly two miles to the Bluff Road at Hampton's Mill pond near the bridge with a light Battery for three guns at a Sandy Ridge between those ponds and commanding the large and open field of Trenholm's Plantation on the River . . . thence across the country in the commanding eminences around the Eastern section of the town."[105]

"SHERMAN'S ARMY ENTERING COLUMBIA," *HARPER'S HISTORY OF THE GREAT REBELLION*, FEBRUARY 1865. COURTESY OF THE SOUTH CAROLINIANA LIBRARY

After the city fell, Niernsee reported that only "another two weeks labor . . . would have completed the whole of the works on the Lexington or western side of the River." He told Magrath that "several of the Enemies officers" said "that even with the incomplete works on those lines if properly manned by an adequate numerical force of men & guns . . . would have offered sufficient resistance to abandon their design of a direct or persistent attack on Columbia . . . as they were not prepared with heavy guns nor instructed to run the risk of a heavy fight for the possession of the place—their object seeming [to be] an extensive raid of destruction and rapine through the State with a view of an early & as much as possible an unimpaired junction with their forces from the coast in South Carolina or Grant's in Virginia."[106] But in mid-February, 1865, Columbia could not muster "an adequate numerical force of men & guns," nor did Niernsee have two weeks to finish the job. He was still in the field directing the work when union forces arrived.

John F. Williams was fifteen years old in 1865 and his account of the attack is vivid:

When Sherman was on his way here, everything was excitement and turmoil. . . . Every day increased the excitement, and on the 14th of February, they had approached so near that you could hear the booming of the cannons. On the fifteenth it became more distinct, and the home guards, which consisted of men in the various shops here, and the Arsenal Cadets, were called out. On the morning of the sixteenth the Confederate troops retired across the Congaree River and burned the bridge behind them. The Yankees planted a battery on the Mayrant Hill, just opposite the penitentiary and began to shell the city. They kept it up all day, and I watched them. You could see the cannons every time they would fire, and hear the shells whistle through the air. Some of them would explode in the air and others would not. Several of them hit the State House, but they did very little damage, as they were all small shells. . . . The Yankees put the pontoon bridge across and on the morning of the seventeenth they came across and marched into the city. Then the work of plunder started. . . . plunder kept up all day, and when night came on the work of burning began. Rockets were sent up from the State House grounds, and immediately the fiends started their hellish work. In a few minutes' time the whole of Main street, from Bouknight's Shop on upper Main, to the State House, was in flames. There was only one house left on Main street in that distance. It was the home of Alex. Riley, on the nineteen hundred block of Main street, on the east side. It was occupied by the French Consul, who had come here from Charleston and put up the French flag, thus saving it.[107]

Although Niernsee was in the field when the shelling began, his wife, two small daughters (Emma Josephine, seven years old and baby Lill, about two) and a son (Charlie, ten), were at home with several slaves in the center of the city. Emma Josephine, writing memoirs for her grandchildren, recalled:

I think I had better tell you now of the shelling of Columbia. . . . Our house was opposite the Presbyterian church which had a very beautiful tall spire, that was used by the Yankees as their target, so our house was well in range of the shells. Mother had some of the cellar rooms cleaned out & beds were put up & rugs laid down, & the women & children slept & lived for many days in the cellar. The servants occupying the wood cellar, under the opposite side of the house. In the "milk cellar," so called because of the large milk cupboards built safes standing out in the middle of the room, there were bags of horse feed all along the wall, & my chief delight was to run along the tops of them all along the side of the cellar. We younger children enjoyed those days in the cellar immensely. The governess, Miss Clark if she had to go up to the upper part of the house (which could only be reached by going up the outside cellar steps then on to the back porch) always amused the family by taking & opening a umbrella. My brother would tease her, & she would say "she did not want to see the shell coming even if she could hear it." Once a shell took the corner off the house & burst in the kitchen garden behind the house. Another smashed the high brick wall on the lower side of the garden [& demolished] all the windows in the servants quarters.

I remember my Mother, Miss Clark & the maids all falling down on their knees & crying. I don't remember being afraid, when they whistled overhead, I wanted to go out & look for them. I suppose I was too young to realize the danger we were in at the time. . . . The night the town was burned, [February 17, 1865] all the population of white people went out on the railroad tracks beyond the town to pass the night. Mother, the children & the nurses & some few of the house servants, carrying as many blankets & quilts as they could. Eliz & Emeline [slaves] carried the old mahogany cradle with my sister sitting in it with two hams & two bags of some packages of books, & a milk can of milk. Bro. Charlie, with his maimed arm still bandaged [Charlie, in a hunting accident, lost his right hand before the war.] All night those helpless women, children & old men lay out there on the grass & watched the town burn. Near daylight one of the soldiers came & told Mother her house was standing, Father in the meantime had reached the city & the Yankees wanted to hang him.[108]

Chapter Three

The Hiatus

South Carolina, Columbia, and the State House evoked the wrath of union troops as symbols of secession. "The state house on the highest ground stood boldly," wrote a soldier in the Seventh Illinois Regiment, "but the soldiers all were cursing that spot as the cause of our being here—Our gun was planted & occasionally fired a shot at the state house."[1] Another union infantryman recalled "the imposing walls of the new capitol, yet unfinished, rose in massive beauty; the white marble of column and cornice—each stone was said to have cost a round thousand dollars—glittering in the sunlight like immense gems. Near this magnificent edifice stood its less conspicuous neighbor, the old capitol, dingy and forbidding."[2] And yet another soldier remembered seeing General Logan with "a rifled cannon in a road that led to one of the burned bridges. When the gunners had the cannon loaded, Logan would sight it, then climb on the high bank beside the road, adjust his field-glass, give the order to fire, and watch to see where the ball would strike. If I remember rightly he was aiming at the State House, and aiming well, for he would wave his hat and call for three cheers for South Carolina after each discharge."[3]

George M. Wise, a lieutenant with the Forty-third Ohio Volunteers, wrote his brother that while a pontoon bridge was being assembled, "a brigade from the 17th crossed in old flat boats and raised the stars & stripes on the State House, while the cheers of the grand Army on the opposite bank almost rent the heavens. We had captured the proud Capital of the first & meanest rebel State & planted the National flag on the building in which treason had it birthplace, and grown up into this terrible rebellion."[4]

When the union troops crossed the river

> . . . later in the day, a jolly party met in the old senate chamber, where, thirty-three years before, the legislature of South Carolina proclaimed its hostility to the federal union. A mock senate was organized, and a vote of censure was passed against John C. Calhoun, the great nullificationist, whose states' rights doctrines had found their logical sequence in the existing wicked and unhappy rebellion. His marble bust, a conspicuous ornament of the hall, was made the target for ink stands and spittoons. The secession ordinance was repealed, "John Brown" was then sung with great enthusiasm, and the "senate" adjourned to reassemble at Raleigh, North Carolina.[5]

That afternoon rioting erupted throughout the city, and Mrs. Niernsee hurried her little group away along the railroad tracks. As darkness fell, arson, alcohol, burning cotton, and a stiff northwest wind combined and soon "a quivering molten ocean seemed to fill the air and sky" as a thirty-six block area, some 458 buildings comprising approximately a third of the city, burned.[6]

John R. Niernsee was not hanged, and when the union troops moved north, he assessed damage and reported that the new State House "sustained but slight injury by the shelling—none indeed which cannot be easily repaired." Six shells struck the west facade, "none of them doing any material damage, except the one which shattered the moulded window-sill and balusters at one of the windows on the principal floor." Four shots passed through the vacant windows into the interior of the building, but there was nothing inside to hurt.[7] Although the artillery had caused little damage, the effects of the rioting and fire were disastrous. Nothing remained of the old State House "but the blackened ruins of the brick walls of the basement." The stonecutter's sheds, "Sisson & Dougherty's steam-works for cutting, rubbing and polishing marble," the sculptor's "atelier, model and work-shops, containing all the small original, as well as colossal models, and some of the unfinished statues, designed to decorate the main gable field, or tympanum, of the Northern portico." The blacksmith and carpenter's shops and the cotton card factory established during the war by James Jones "were all burnt, and their respective contents utterly destroyed."[8]

Niernsee lamented:

> The consuming flames devoured not only my own library of valuable architectural and other scientific books, pictures, engravings, instruments, and several thousand drawings, the result of a practice of twenty-five years, but all the valuable documents relating to the new State House, specifications, memoranda, books and papers, which had accumulated in those offices during the past ten years, all have been utterly swept away during that terrible night.[9]

"Raising the Stars and Stripes over the [Old] Capitol," *Harper's Weekly*, April 8, 1865. Courtesy of the South Caroliniana Library

"13TH IOWA REGIMENT . . . RAISING THE STARS AND STRIPES ABOVE THE [NEW] STATE HOUSE," *FRANK LESLIE'S ILLUSTRATED NEWSPAPER*, APRIL 8, 1865. COURTESY OF THE SOUTH CAROLINIANA LIBRARY

"Columbia after the Fire," by William Waud, 1865. Courtesy of the Library of Congress

"Columbia . . . Portion of the Burnt District," *Frank Leslie's Illustrated Newspaper,* April 8, 1865. Courtesy of the South Caroliniana Library

Main Street looking north from State House, by George Barnard, 1865. Courtesy of the Library of Congress

Building materials ". . . accumulating in the yard and work-shops during the past four years" were substantially damaged. Forty granite capitals were destroyed; "out of some sixty-five of the Corinthian capitals, wrought in Italian marble, intended for the great marble hall and staircases on the principal floor, only five are saved," and all of the Tennessee marble shafts for them were demolished, as was the polished marble wainscot and stone balus-trade intended "to crown the building and the terrace, designed to surround the lower part." The quarry was flooded—a portion of its dam had been destroyed—the quarry railroad dismantled, and all the buildings at the quarry had been burned.[10]

Immediately after the fire, and until laborers stopped accepting confederate money, Niernsee directed a crew sorting through the rubble. Six hundred (out of 1,400) of the granite balusters were salvageable, and these were carried from one of the burned sheds and stored in the new State House along with some tools and hardware. Niernsee boarded up the roofless shell of the new State House and hired a watchman to discourage pilfer-ing. He calculated losses to the state as being $700,000 and prepared estimates and options which he addressed—as if everything were normal—to the legislative Chairman of the Committee on the New State House.[11]

Niernsee outlined four ways to secure the unfinished building until construction could be resumed. He also presented four additional ways the building could be made at least partially usable. Cost estimates accompanied each of his eight alternatives. The cheapest estimate for simply securing the building was $63,070. This entailed leveling the walls enough to put on a temporary, timber-framed, tin-sheathed roof, boarding up doors and windows, and erecting a stout fence around the site. The most expensive estimate, $359,780, allowed a portion of the interior to be put into use. It included finishing the exterior walls, completing the granite cornice, putting on an iron-framed, copper-sheathed roof, installing the fireproof, iron window frames and sashes, finishing the interior of the House of Representatives and installing courtrooms, offices, and the Senate Chamber in the basement. The report gently reminded the legislature of "the importance of the adoption of early measures" to preserve the building and noted that before anything could be done an architect with an able assistant would need "to remeasure the whole of the building for the purpose of drawing anew all of the requisite plans, sections, details and working drawings, so as to prepare all the necessary specifi-cations." He estimated this preliminary work made necessary by the loss his office, "will take the best part of the year to accomplish."[12]

When they received Niernsee's report, the legislature was meeting on the South Carolina College campus.[13] The 1865 and 1866 sessions necessarily focused upon the reorganization of state government and the re-establishment of civic and economic order. In this context, resuming work on the State House was not a priority, and Niernsee's report languished. At the end of the 1866 session, the assembly authorized the governor "to call for plans and estimates for covering the New State House building with a light tin roof, and to close the windows and door openings with rough shutters to protect it from injury" and to "appoint the Architect whose plan shall be adopted superintendent of the work . . . at the earliest day practicable."[14] By issuing a call for new plans and estimates and asking only for a light tin roof and rough shutters, the legislature made it clear they were by-passing Niernsee and looking for a cheap, simple solution.

Niernsee Returns to Baltimore

While waiting for a response to his proposals, Niernsee had sought work elsewhere, for he needed money. His salary had been cut in half (to $2,000 per year) in 1861, and even this had not been paid in 1865. As a volunteer, he had received nothing for his work as a military engineer. In 1866, he applied for an appointment as architect of the unfinished U.S. Custom House in Charleston, but this was awarded to A. B. Mullet, architect for the U.S. Treasury Department. Mullett delegated the job to Thomas Oakshott, a stonecutter and contractor from Massachusetts.[15] (Predictably, no federal work in South Carolina was awarded to architects associated with the Confederacy.) Seeking employment, Niernsee wrote Governor James L. Orr requesting an appointment as agent to direct the sale of surplus building materials at the State House and various fortifications. Niernsee noted he could be paid from the proceeds of sales, but nothing came of this.[16] There was little hope of obtaining private work, and when the 1866 legislature only called for rough repairs and made no appropriation for an architect of the new State House, Niernsee decided to return to Baltimore.

Baltimore had not been devastated by the war, and he was able to reestablish himself professionally without difficulty. He moved his family into one of several rental houses he owned on Courtland Street and rejoined J. Crawford Neilson who had carried on the work of the firm in Niernsee's absence. During the next decade Niernsee and Neilson, architects, were responsible for twelve commercial buildings, seven houses, a concert hall, and four institutional buildings. Niernsee began to take work outside Niernsee and Neilson in 1876, for his son Frank, who had studied engineering at the University of Virginia, joined him, and for the following decade Niernsee and Son was one of the major architectural firms in Baltimore. Niernsee and Son designed several commercial buildings, including the Chamber of Commerce Building, the Spiller Building, the Merchants' Club, a residence for George W. Gail, an Orphans' Asylum, and a Hospital for John's Hopkins—all in Baltimore—and an Opera House in Lynchburg, Virginia. Emma Niernsee (then a teenager living at home) recalled, "Father [was] during these years at the top of his profession, & was financially very well off. We lived in a large house, with plenty of servants, & money seemed to flow easily. I heard my father say to my older brother one afternoon . . . that his profession was now bringing him in twenty & sometimes thirty thousand a year."[17]

Having ignored Niernsee's eight alternatives for the State House, the General Assembly, in December, 1866, appropriated $12,000 for a tin roof to protect the walls and arches from the weather. Governor Orr advertised for proposals and reported that "although various designs were presented looking to the construction of a roof imposing in appearance, the limited appropriation made compelled me to adopt the plan submitted by Messrs. Kay & Heweston, Architects, of Columbia."[18]

John A. Kay (1830–?) had worked on the building as Hammarskold and Walker's assistant and had been retained by Niernsee. He was born in England and became a Master Mason in Richland's Masonic Lodge #39 on May 2, 1855. In 1859 and 1860 he was listed in city directories as an architect living at the northeast corner of Lady and Bull streets with his wife Mary E. (Hewitson) Kay, who had been born in Ireland c. 1836. When the war broke out, Kay joined the Richland Rifles, served as a Confederate Engineer, and was 6th Sergeant at Morris Island during the campaign to capture Fort Sumter. He apparently left South Carolina shortly after working on the State House roof, for in August, 1869, he notified the Masonic Lodge that he had moved to St. Charles, Missouri.[19]

The Heweston mentioned in the *House Journal* as Kay's partner was probably Ralph E. B. Hewitson (1830–1881) who had worked as a timekeeper for Niernsee at the State House. Hewitson became a Master Mason in the Richland Lodge on October 16, 1855 and served as the Master of the Lodge from December 1859 through December 1860. At that time he was living with Kay (and may have been Kay's brother-in-law) and was listed in city directories as an engineer. During the war Hewitson became a major and served in Virginia as a Quartermaster in Company C, Regiment No. 1, the Maxcy Regiment. After the war he advertised as an architect with offices at the corner of Main and Taylor Streets and a residence at 80 North Main Street.[20] The temporary State House roof is the only project known by Kay and Heweston, architects.

Niernsee's departure and his replacement by obscure practitioners was part of the pattern of professional life in South Carolina after the war. Charleston, for example, lost notable architects when Edward C. Jones moved to Memphis (1867); Francis D. Lee moved to St. Louis (1868); and Edward Brickell White left for New York City (c. 1879).[21] Architecturally, the only silver lining in the situation was that the poverty which drove trained architects away also prevented major work by those—like Kay and Heweston—who eagerly filled the void. Because funding was unavailable, only minor work took place at the State House during Reconstruction; nonetheless, the building quickly became entangled in turmoil and fraud; consequently, it became for a time symbolic in ways never envisioned by its creators.

New State House, south facade, photograph by George Barnard, 1865. Courtesy of the Library of Congress

New State House with temporary roof, circa 1870. Courtesy of the South Caroliniana Library

New State House with roof by Frank Niernsee, circa 1890. Courtesy of the South Caroliniana Library

Reconstruction

Governor John L. Manning and his peers had planned a building that would portray their own political, social, and economic preeminence. Events, however, temporarily transformed their architectural portrait into a fun-house mirror reflecting the economic dislocation and social and political tension of the postwar era. For two decades following the war little work was done on the State House; Governor James Orr reasonably observed in 1868 that "there is no probability that the completion of the building, according to the original design, will take place for years."[22]

Despite the "impolicy of taking any steps whatever towards a resumption of the permanent work upon the building," the legislature decided to fund temporary accommodations in the unfinished shell.[23] On March 13, 1869, an appropriation not to exceed $25,000 was approved "for Fitting up of certain portions of the State House."[24] With this budget, James M. Allen, a contractor from Greenville, prepared "the inside parts of the Capitol Building for the use of the next General Assembly of both Senate and House, and also for the use of the different offices of the State."[25] The west wing was made usable first. Allen installed wooden floors, doors, and moldings in the House of Representatives and in eight rooms below it as offices for the Governor, the Secretary of State, Attorney General, Comptroller, and Auditor, "and nine large rooms in upper part of [the] building used as Committee rooms."[26]

Making even temporary use of the building promoted a number of things which many people in the late twentieth century would consider indelible attributes of state government. As the postwar legislature settled into its work, for example, employees were added; competition arose for desirable space; questions were raised about the personal use of state property; and there were charges of fraud, extravagance, and theft. The Republicans, being in power, began to use the State House and its furnishings as their own, and the Democrats quickly initiated audits and investigations. Before the first year (1869) was out, the building was considered too small; consequently, space was rented throughout Columbia at what some claimed were exorbitant prices.

Knowledge of the interior work and furnishings during this period is based largely on testimony taken during an investigation by the Democrats after they returned to power in 1876. Their inquiry painted a sordid picture of their Republican predecessors. Modern historians have amended this image by relating misrule in South Carolina to contemporaneous corruption in other states and by pointing out the racially based intimidation, violence, and electoral fraud that marked the resurgence of the Democratic Party.[27] Records from this era must be used with their bias in mind; nonetheless, the records are important, for they recount the first use of the State House.

"Rogues on the Ragged Edge: Liquor and Cigars at the Public Expense" was the headline in *The News and Courier* as the investigation began in 1877.[28] The Democrats were determined to prove Republican corruption and misrule, and their Joint Investigating Committee published 1,700 pages of sworn testimony and documents demonstrating "a carnival of fraud and extravagance."[29] The evidence was damning. In addition to six restaurants which had operated in the lobby of the State House, the Senate had maintained a barroom adjacent its chamber. Lewis Grant, porter, or bartender to the Senate, testified that he stayed open from eight in the morning until the wee hours—two to four A.M.— "Sunday was no exception." He served free whiskey, wine, beer, ale, porter, and champagne to members and their friends. "When some of them would leave they would put a bottle of champagne in their pockets. . . . I found it hard to keep a sufficient amount of cigars on hand [because] on leaving [they] would generally fill one or two of their pockets."[30]

Although members of the House had no bar within the State House, they were not abstemious. They received whiskey by the bottle from John Williams or A. O. Jones. A Columbia supplier, Hardy Solomon, testified that Williams and Jones purchased, with state vouchers, $9,560 worth of whiskey between February 12, 1872 and March 28, 1872.[31] This must have been a dry spell: the Investigating Committee reported that in one session, under the heading of "supplies, sundries and incidental expenses," $125,000 was spent on "the finest wines, liquors and cigars."[32]

Buying furnishings for the State House and for thirteen committee rooms outside the State House (in the Hardy Solomon Bank Building, the Greenfield Building, and the Callahan Building) provided a wonderful opportunity for graft. Influential legislators found the experience so profitable that committee rooms—and many rooms in the State House itself—were completely refurnished annually between 1870 and 1876. Whole rooms of furniture, including carpets and cast iron stoves, simply disappeared at the end of each session. Testifying under oath in 1877, John Williams, Sergeant-at-Arms for the House of Representatives, said the furniture "was stolen by those who had charge of it."[33]

The initial furniture was purchased in the summer of 1870 from Stewart, Sutphen, and Company and Nicol, Davidson, and Company of New York by General John B. Dennis, a Representative from Charleston, who signed himself "Superintendent of State House Repairs." Dennis fits the popular image of a carpetbagger. (The "General" appears to have been a pretension.) A tinker in civilian life before the war, he became an artillery captain in the Connecticut Seventh Regiment Infantry and served along the South Carolina coast—at Port Royal, Hilton Head, Tybee, Daufuskie, and Folly Islands—during 1862 and 1863. He was captured near Petersburg, Virginia, in 1864, and soon after the war moved to Charleston. He was a Representative from Charleston 1868–1872 and Superintendent of the State Penitentiary 1873–1875, and "was known as a ring leader among the plunderers."[34]

During the investigation of 1877–1878, Dennis claimed he had gone to New York in 1870 with Mr. M. H. Berry, a Columbia merchant, at the request of F. J. Moses, Speaker of the House of Representatives, "authorized and instructed to purchase the necessary furniture." Dennis admitted they had no specific contract or budget.[35] They ordered opulent walnut chairs and desks, satin and silk upholstery, chandeliers, and cuspidors and arranged for a team of decorators from New York to install everything.

Shortly after the furniture-buying trip, in November, 1870, Dennis was reelected to the House and became Chairman of the Committee on Contingent Accounts—the committee charged with reviewing the bills for the furnishings. Predictably, Dennis's committee approved payment, but the adjusted bill for $90,506.31 raised protests, and the resulting inventories and investigations simmered until the Democrats came to power in 1877. When the political tables turned, Dennis and other Republican chairmen were exposed.

Abuses became more ambitious as legislators settled into power. Moving into the State House, for example, during the session of 1869–1870, they modestly ordered $5 clocks, $4 benches, $1 chairs, $4 mirrors, and $2 curtains, but the following year they ordered $600 clocks, $200 crimson plush sofas, $60 crimson plush Gothic chairs, $600 mirrors, and $600 brocaded curtains. The range of purchases also expanded as prices escalated. By 1872 the state was paying for pocket knives, jewelry, carriages, and—according to the sworn testimony of M. H. Berry—the furnishing of at least forty bedrooms: "but [he] does not know who occupied them all or what became of the furniture. He was paid for it in legislative pay certificates."[36]

Fraudulent certificates for payment by the state were a common technique. Many were issued in the name of John Williams, Sergeant-at-Arms, but he testified, "I know nothing of most of these accounts. I allowed my name to be used to assist the members from time to time. . . . I did not know my name was used so often, nor for such large amounts, until now [1877]. I am sure that it was arranged by introducing a legislative claim in my name and adding the words 'and others' to it, thereby getting it passed without creating any suspicion that it was a fraud." But Williams was not innocent. He concluded his statement saying: "I remember the $3,500 account; that was for the Committee on Contingent Accounts. I think they took $500 apiece; they promised me $500, but never gave it to me."[37]

Another technique was to obtain authorization for payment to wholly fictitious persons or businesses, then "pay certificates were drawn for them and delivered to different members." Bills submitted for payment also often bore "unmistakable evidence of alteration." For example, "In the item of 'fitting closets,' the figure 3 is inserted, making $340 instead of $40 as originally. In the two items of 'partition in cloak room,' the figure 6 is inserted, making $650 instead of $50 as originally. Sometimes, without resorting to a ruse of any kind, money was simply divided up.

Lawrence Cain, a farmer from Edgefield who served in the legislature from 1868 until 1876, testified that when he was a member of the Senate Committee of Contingent Accounts at the end of the 1875 session, "after all the contingent accounts were settled, there remained . . . a balance of enough to give each member of the Committee who was present (seven in number) something over two hundred dollars apiece."[38] And they took it, Cain included.

Bad as it was, the use of fictitious accounts and fraudulent vouchers by legislators was mere shoplifting compared to the grand larceny indulged in by state executives. One of their most outrageous schemes tangentially relates to the unfinished State House. After Niernsee's departure, his proposal to sell surplus State House building materials was used to mask a major fraud. On March 1, 1870 a bill was passed to establish a sinking fund commission empowered to sell "all such real or personal property, assets and effects belonging to the State as is not in actual public use." It was anticipated that the commission, composed of the Governor, Attorney General, Comptroller General, Chairman of the House Ways and Means Committee, and the Chairman of the Senate Finance Committee, would sell unused granite, bricks, marble "and other material lying around the State House grounds."[39] This, however, was not what the commissioners, who had drafted the law, had in mind.

The day after their enabling legislation was passed the commissioners sold themselves, as private individuals, a block of stock in the Greenville and Columbia Railroad. The state had acquired the stock for $20 per share to encourage the construction and subsidize the operation of the railroad. The commissioners acquired the state's investment of $433,960 for $59,969, or $2.75 per share. Worse yet, they paid the state with its own money which they obtained from H. H. Kimpton, who was in charge of the sale of South Carolina bonds in New York. Kimpton simply underreported the amount realized from the sale of bonds and used the balance to pay for the railroad stock.[40]

The *Columbia Register,* a Democratic organ, like a child picking a sore, continually called attention to the disheveled condition of the State House and its grounds. Its editors delighted in pointing out dilapidated fencing, construction rubble, weeds, or a fouled well. Poor maintenance was taken as prima facie evidence of slovenly stewardship by the Republicans. At the same time the newspapers approvingly reported the progress of the South Carolina Monument Association which formed in 1869 to create a monument to the state's confederate dead. The monument was to serve as "a constant testimony to the costly sacrifices which true men must be ever ready to make in asserting and defending their principles."[41] Appealing to white sentiment, this monument, together with the later Wade Hampton statue and the monument to the Women of the Confederacy, established the grounds as a focal point of Lost Cause remembrance.

The Confederate Monument was an early example of its type.[42] Because it was begun during Reconstruction, nobody imagined that it would be placed on the State House grounds. On March 4, 1869, a group of Columbia ladies gathered in a chapel on Washington Street to form the Monument Association; Wade Hampton and the Rev. William Martin addressed the initial meeting. The Association set the minimum contribution at $1 and began raising money primarily from the women of South Carolina. In August, 1872, the Association paid the city $600 for a lot on Arsenal Hill overlooking Sidney (Finlay) Park, and the following July they retained Muldoon and Walton, architects, from Louisville, Kentucky, to design and deliver the monument for $10,000.

Michael McDonald Muldoon (1836–1911), who was responsible for the Confederate Monument on the State House grounds, was an Irishman who began his career as a stonecutter. He worked in Steubenville, Ohio briefly before settling in Louisville, Kentucky circa 1860. The Civil War created a stunning boom in tombstones and memorial sculpture. Monuments sprouted across the South like mushrooms after a sum-

NEW STATE HOUSE, NORTH FACADE, 1896. COURTESY OF THE SOUTH CAROLINIANA LIBRARY

MULDOON MONUMENT CO. ADVERTISEMENT, *CONFEDERATE VETERAN*, APRIL 1900. COURTESY OF THE SOUTH CAROLINIANA LIBRARY

mer rain, and by 1871 Muldoon had several hundred employees in marble cutting yards in St. Louis, Memphis, and New Orleans as well as Louisville. One of his partners, the aptly named Charles Bullett, operated the firm's marble quarries in Carrara, Italy.[43]

While the monument was being carved in Carrara by one Nicolini, the Association began laying foundations on Arsenal Hill using granite donated by Judge John S. Green. Unfortunately, the soil on their lot proved unstable, and at a cost of $585 the granite base was moved to a lot donated by Elmwood Cemetery. With the base completed, the Association made an initial payment of $5,000 to the architects. However, when the crated monument arrived in Columbia in September, 1875, the Monument Association was unable to pay the balance due Muldoon and Walton or hire anyone to erect the monument; consequently, it lay in its crate like a butterfly in a cocoon for three years awaiting the end of Reconstruction.

In addition to keeping up with the difficulties encountered by the Monument Association, the newspapers often commented upon the condition of the cast iron palmetto tree. It had been toppled by a storm in 1875 and lay prostrate in the capitol grounds. The *Register* compared its restoration to the possible resurrection of the state in the upcoming elections of November, 1876: "The iron palmetto tree, the emblem of the State, which was blown down by the big cyclone still lies prostrate in the capitol grounds. Big hopes are entertained however, by thinking people, that it and the State of which it is so truly emblematic will be lifted from the mud and mire in which they have both fallen ere the ides of November pass."[44] The prediction was correct on both counts, for when Hampton was elected, the Confederate and Palmetto Monuments were both erected (as discussed below), flanking the main entrance to the State House like a pair of exclamation points celebrating the end of Reconstruction.

The elections of 1876 were the most hotly contested—and most fraudulent—in the history of the state. Symbols used during the campaign by the Democrats forecast how they would use allegorical ornament at the State House. Although Hampton presented himself in a Jeffersonian plain style without personal finery, his campaign used emblems in a manner typical of nineteenth-century public life. At Democratic rallies before speeches began, the crowds were entertained by bands, parades and transparencies, or painted banners, and dramatic tableaux—groups of young women dressed and posed to personify allegories. At Sumter, for example, the state was represented by a young woman draped in black and bowed beneath chains. As Hampton approached the platform, she rose and shed the shroud and chains and stood "pure white . . . tall and stately, head uplifted and eyes shining like stars." At Winnsboro "the prostrate figure of South Carolina was raised by Liberty, with cap and pole, while Justice held on high the evenly balanced scales and the sword of State, and Fame with her trumpet stood ready to proclaim the glad tidings. The thirty-seven sister States, all appropriately draped, stood on either side."[45] These tableaux, with their messages modified to fit the times, were, in effect, animated versions of the destroyed pedimental sculpture.

Another symbol, the red shirt often worn by Hampton's supporters, was a stern contrast to the tableaux. Armed horsemen wearing red shirts attended Democratic rallies as an honor guard; at Republican gatherings they menacingly surrounded the crowd and platform. Their red shirt was first used to symbolize the violence of the Hamburg riot of 1876. (One white and seven blacks died when an organized group of whites attacked a black militia company.) Unlike the tableaux, the red shirt was an assertive symbol of defiance. Benjamin R. Tillman, a participant in the Hamburg riot and present when the first red shirts were produced and worn, recalled that when he and his peers, all members of the Sweetwater Saber Club, were escorted to Aiken for arraignment after the riot, they wore the shirts during a defiant gallop through all the principal streets around the court house. Tillman said the idea came from Senator J. Z. George of Mississippi, who suggested that to intimidate black voters they should "parade long processions of armed white men through the country" wearing "splendid uniforms" to "impress the Negroes both as to our strength and . . . purpose. . . ."[46]

The feminine version of the red shirt was the red ribbon, which became popular enough to be noted by a local bard:

Red ribbons round their waists,
Red ribbons in their hair,
Red ribbons to their tastes,
Pinned to them everywhere.[47]

The streaming ribbons were like stigmata. It is tempting to link the ribbons and Bloody Shirt, as it was called, with the confederate dead, but Tillman was more inclusive—he associated the Hamburg Riot with the martial spirit of the Revolutionary War:

The spirit of 1776 which made Moultrie . . . man his palmetto log fort . . . pulsated in the bosom of every brave Carolinian, when they learned that a body of 75 poorly armed whites had dared to attack a legally organized militia company, capture its armory, and then put to death some of its members. If there had been no Hamburg riot, it is extremely doubtful whether there would have been any straight out campaign in 1876.[48]

The Dual Government and the End of Reconstruction

The tense campaign resulted in a contested vote which, in turn, led to a confrontation in the State House when the legislature convened, for both parties claimed victory. Attempting to prevent the Democrats from seizing control, Governor Daniel H. Chamberlain had a company of U.S. troops secretly occupy the State House during the night of November 27, 1876. The next morning, Hampton Democrats found "soldiers on each side of the doorway, with guns carrying bright and glistening bayonets crossed over the doorway."[49] John B. Dennis, flanked by soldiers, was checking credentials, and only people with passes from Chamberlain or the Board of Canvassers, a commission responsible for certifying election results, were permitted to enter.[50] The Democrats adjourned to the Choral Union Hall on Richardson Street; they determined that they had a quorum, declared themselves to be the duly elected House of Representatives and elected General William W. Wallace Speaker of the House.

Back at the State House the Republicans also organized and elected E. W. M. Mackey of Charleston as Speaker. At ten o'clock the following morning the Democrats, led by former governor James L. Orr, marched in a body down Richardson Street to the State House, and this time they were permitted to pass unmolested into the building. The Republicans had not begun business for the day and were caught offguard. The Democrats filed into the chamber and General Wallace, the Democratic Speaker, took possession of the Speaker's Chair. Mackey and his Clerk, A. O. Jones, hurried into the chamber. Mackey mounted the Speaker's stand, and he and Wallace argued over possession of the chair. Tension mounted:

Several Democrats and Radicals ascended the stand and stood behind their respective leaders. Neither Mackey nor General Wallace moved, and there was a general crowding towards the Speaker's stand, as if all parties anticipated a row—but no row occurred, both parties holding firm, and the two Sergeants-at-Arms stood on either side looking at each other like two chicken cocks when pitted for a fight.[51]

For four days and nights neither party abandoned the chamber. Both sides went through the motions of conducting business. Both Speakers were recognizing legislators; speeches were being given simultaneously, and as "the long watch and fitful sleep [began] telling upon many of the members" many expected "a bloody end." Governor Chamberlain finally broke the impasse by informing the Democrats that they would be evicted by military force; consequently, on December 4, 1876, they "withdrew in a body" and reconvened in Carolina Hall (now Longstreet Theater). Two days later the South Carolina Supreme Court ruled that the Democrats were the official House of Representatives, and they immediately certified the election of Wade Hampton as Governor. Meanwhile, the Republicans had certified the reelection of Governor Chamberlain, so throughout the spring of 1877 the state had two governors and two Houses of Representatives.

Troops and the Republicans occupied the State House from the end of November, 1876 through early April, 1877. This period of dual government came to an end when President Rutherford B. Hayes invited both Chamberlain and Hampton to Washington at the end of March, 1877. As a result of these conferences, Chamberlain agreed to withdraw. Hampton became the uncontested governor, and at noon on April 10, 1877, "the south door of the capitol building opened wide and a captain of the United States Army commanding about thirty men, filed out of the building. . . . Thus end[ed] the carpet-bag reign in South Carolina."[52]

For the State House, the post-Reconstruction era began on April 13, 1877. That morning a large squad of convicts marched from the penitentiary by the river up Gervais Street to clean the building from top to bottom. Before noon, while they were still at work, Democrats began moving in records and setting up their offices, and by afternoon Wade Hampton was receiving visitors in the governor's office.[53] The next eight years were a period of active maintenance, minor improvements, and finally the beginning of efforts to complete the building. R. M. Sims, Secretary of State under Hampton, took an active interest in the State House; consequently, for the first time since the departure of James Jones in 1861, planning and construction had an effective, influential advocate. At first much of the work was devoted to landscaping, which was relatively inexpensive and very visible. However, the roof also required urgent attention, and Niernsee was soon brought in from Baltimore as a consultant. His report marked the beginning of serious discussions about when the building would be finished and what form it would take.

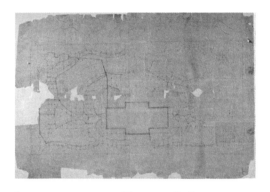

LANDSCAPE PLAN, BY EDWARD O. SCHWAGERL, 1878. COURTESY OF THE SOUTH CAROLINA ARCHIVES AND HISTORY CENTER

Since the destruction of Robert Russell's garden in 1854, the grounds had been a construction site: sheds, building materials, and machinery were scattered everywhere. When the Democrats met for their first full session in the winter of 1877–1878, the most notable features of the grounds were an outhouse which "smelled loud," a well, and the toppled Palmetto Monument. There were no walks or ornamental plants. Weeds sprouted amidst stacks of brick and stone; the debris from the destroyed first State House was strewn across the west end of the lot.

On March 4, 1878, the secretary of state was authorized to spend $500 and use penitentiary labor to improve the grounds.[54] Plans must have been in motion when the appropriation was approved, for the following week the local newspaper began

"BIRD'S EYE VIEW OF THE CITY OF COLUMBIA," DETAIL BY C. DRIE, 1872. COURTESY OF THE SOUTH CAROLINIANA LIBRARY

reporting what was to be done. A landscape architect from Philadelphia, Edward Otto Schwagerl (1842–1910), was already in town and had "made three plans—one for working, another for planting, and the third to show the grounds as they will be when the other plans are carried out."[55] Schwagerl was paid $100.[56] His presence indicated that the Democrats intended to maintain the high standards set by Niernsee. Schwagerl's plan, which was implemented by Secretary of State Sims, may have been the earliest project by a professional landscape architect in South Carolina.

A number of architects had previously designed parks in South Carolina. Robert Mills, for example had unsuccessfully proposed (1822) a formal park at the center of Charleston to serve as a fire break and provide a campuslike setting for governmental offices and a projected academy of the arts. Had it been developed, this would have been Charleston's first formal city park.[57] Fifteen years later, the architect Charles F. Reichardt designed White Point Garden on Charleston's Battery (1837–1838). Half a century earlier, the commissioners who laid out Columbia as the new capital city had set aside eight squares for public use, but these remained as blank on the ground as they were on the plat. Robert Russell, whose garden had been on the old State House grounds, did not design landscapes as a profession; he was a horticulturist, and perhaps a landscape gardener in the eighteenth century tradition which focused upon plants rather than plans serving a multiplicity of uses.

Landscape architecture, as a profession, was new in America when Schwagerl designed the State House grounds. Landscape architect as a title was first used by Frederick Law Olmsted and Calvert Vaux in 1858 in connection with their work on Central Park in New York City. Officials there first used the term in 1863, and Olmsted's subsequent success as a designer of open spaces—parks, cemeteries, campuses, boulevards, and estates—established landscape architecture as a distinct profession. The landscape architect aimed—and still aims—to shape outdoor spaces to serve human uses including health, active and passive recreation, vehicular and pedestrian transportation, and sometimes education and inspiration.[58] Schwagerl's plan addresses these needs and by doing so links the State House site to national trends.

Schwagerl was born in Wurzburg, Bavaria, lived in Paris as a child and emigrated alone to America when only twelve. After working as a clerk in New York and attending Tilton Seminary in Tilton, New Hampshire, he returned to Paris at the age of 23 and worked for an architect, Mons Mulat, who was then designing the grounds of the 1867 Exposition Universelle. In 1868 he returned to America and spent almost two years with Jacob Weidenmann, a landscape architect based in Hartford, Connecticut. During the 1870s Schwagerl moved often; he worked in Omaha, St. Louis, Cleveland, and appears in the Philadelphia City Directories of 1877 and 1878 as Edward O. and Hermann J. Schwagerl, Schwagerl and Company, Landscape Architects. While based in Philadelphia, he visited Columbia and designed the State House grounds in the spring of 1878.[59] Like J. R. Niernsee, H. K. Brown, and F. W. Ruckstull—the sculptor discussed in the following chapter—Schwagerl was a recognized professional. His 1878 plan for the South Carolina State House grounds is his only known work in the South.

Along with one tattered drawing which survives, the best record of the Schwagerl plan is a detail on a 1895 city map. The plan was in the French Beaux Arts tradition: balanced and symmetrical, with axes focusing upon each side of the building. On the north and south sides there were four points of access from the street—pedestrian pathways on the corners and carriageways in the center of the block. The pathways and carriageways were graded and surfaced with crushed granite. They divided the block into curvilinear lobes. On paper the plan resembled the pattern of flower petals. Sites for the Confederate and Palmetto Monuments are shown as small squares on the north

"Map of Columbia . . . and Its Suburbs," detail by Niernsee and LaMotte, 1895. Courtesy of the South Caroliniana Library

side of the State House. The major landscape feature, a butterfly-shaped lake, appears near the northwest corner of the block, and the solitary grave of Swanson Lundsford is indicated by a small square near the southwest corner.[60]

Secretary of State Sims—or rather the convicts working at his direction—set to work at once. By early May, 1878, fifteen tons of gravel had been crushed and laid in the main carriage way. Cow peas were planted, and those that survived foraging cows during the summer were turned into the soil the following fall. By midsummer the pond had been excavated to a depth of five feet. Four fountains were installed, and the pond was filled with water. A bridge—too massive to be graceful—was built over the lake; local wits called it the bridge of size. Goldfish, carp, turtles, and two alligators were put in the lake, and along with them came a boat: "two expert marines who are engaged at the capitol attempted to navigate the skiff 'Mamie' on the lake yesterday afternoon and got capsized and handsomely ducked." Despite, or perhaps because of, the wildlife, the lake became a popular place for shenanigans: "the police came upon a party of lively bathers in the lake Sunday night." Sims supervised the planting of trees and shrubs, and by early 1879 the grounds were "becoming quite a popular promenade," and evening walks were especially recommended; "if you want a frog serenade, walk about the State House lake at night. The notes are distinct and protracted. 'Knee deep,' 'Better go round,' 'time to go home, etc.'"[61]

While work on the grounds was underway, the Confederate and Palmetto Monuments were installed as the principal ornaments. The Confederate Monument was centered on the east wing, and the Palmetto Monument, on the west wing. The legislature allowed the Association to select a site for the Confederate Monument and appropriated $650 to pay for its granite base to be moved from Elmwood Cemetery. Anticipating the installation of the Confederate Monument, a local journalist wrote that "the fact that the monument is to be placed in the State House yard indicates the final recovery of South Carolina from the domination of her enemies."[62]

On May 13, 1879, after a parade of bands and somber, limping corps of veterans, the principal orator, General Preston, spoke to a hushed crowd of 10,000 who had come from all corners of the state. He began by pointing out how rare it was to raise a monument to a defeated cause: "In every attribute this monument is an anomaly. It is without precedent, without example, almost without analogy in human history." Carolinians were not "in view of the promised land"; instead they were standing "on the dust of desolation, met with silent tears of defeat." Confederate soldiers were viewed by the world as "defeated and degraded . . . traitors to truth and liberty." But despite what others might think, the monument was not "an altar to treason and infamy." Far from it, Preston asserted, it was a "sanctuary to which in pious pilgrimage you may lead your sons in all the days to come. . . . to worship the valor which demanded this monument and the virtue which has builded it."[63]

In the excitement surrounding the erection of the Confederate Monument, the restoration of the Palmetto Monument attracted little attention. Working with an appropriation of $2,000, Mr. Hoefler, a local iron worker, raised the repaired trunk by April 12, 1878, and during the months that followed, he made new fronds and repaired those that could be salvaged. The following spring he installed an iron railing around the monument.

The Mexican War had been overshadowed by the Civil War; nonetheless, the Palmetto Monument is historically significant as a rare example of civic sculpture made of cast iron. Cast iron was in vogue as an architectural material when Christopher Werner fabricated the Palmetto Monument, but it was never accepted as being suitable for sculpture. This fact, and Werner's verisimilitude, make the palmetto tree more historically notable as a work of art than the nearby Confederate Monument.

The South Carolina Confederate Monument is notable primarily as an early example of its type. Outside of cemeteries, only six other public Confederate Monuments were dedicated between 1865 and 1885. As the South recovered, the movement to erect monuments gained momentum, and thirty-four were erected between 1886 and 1899; the movement peaked between 1900 an 1912 when 192 were completed. By 1912, most cities and towns throughout the South had monuments, and since then only sixteen have been dedicated. The Muldoon Company claimed to have "erected nine-tenths of the Confederate Monuments in the United States." In Kentucky they were responsible for monuments in Cynthiana, Lexington, and Louisville; their work in Georgia included monuments in Macon, Columbus, Thomasville, Sparta, Dalton, and Chickamauga; in Tennessee they placed monuments in Nashville, Columbia, Shelbyville, and Franklin. Their largest monument in Kentucky, the Louisville Confederate Monument (1895), resembles the Columbia, South Carolina monument: an infantryman at rest, leaning upon his rifle atop a tapering pillar.[64] The soldier atop the South Carolina column is generic, but it is noteworthy that Isabella D. Martin, the Recording Secretary of the Association, supplied the architects with a photograph of General Stephen Elliott, the hero of Fort Sumter.

During Wade Hampton's term, while work was underway on the grounds and monuments, leaks made the roof the first priority in the State House. The low-pitched tin roof designed by John A. Kay and Ralph E. B. Hewitson in 1866 had never been satisfactory. It needed extensive repairs almost every year. In 1875, before it was ten years old, a proposal—which was not adopted—was made to the legislature to contact the Baltimore firm thought to have in storage the trusses designed by Niernsee.[65] Two years later Secretary of State Sims reported that "no amount of patchwork will ever be entirely satisfactory in making it secure" due to the "bad character of the material and construction."[66] The 1877–1878 legislature concluded that "it is poor economy, if not extravagance, to allow such valuable property to injure from the want of an adequate cover," and they invited Niernsee to come to Columbia and advise them what to do.[67]

Niernsee arrived on February 20, 1878, and informed the Committee on the State House and Grounds that contracts had never been let for the roof; consequently, no quick solution was in storage in Baltimore. He must have advocated finishing the building, for after his visit the issue was raised with increasing frequency during the next five years. But the legislature continued to vacillate, and despite repeated repairs, "In one office . . . a stream of water as large as a man's arm comes flowing in every time there is a hard rain and almost every part of it suffers and becomes more or less damaged every Winter. . . ." Or again: "the State House roof leaks like a sieve, and the interior walls are greatly damaged. This damage, let it be remembered, gets worse with each succeeding storm."[68]

Finally, on September 24, 1883, Governor Hugh S. Thompson requested Niernsee to return and develop "estimates of the cost of completing the State House in detail according to the original design" and to determine how much of the labor could be done by convicts.[69] Niernsee spent October and early November in Columbia and submitted a detailed report for which he was paid $600. He estimated that without the central tower the State House could be completed for $738,475; however, a savings of $163,454 could be realized by reducing the projection of the porticos and not building the "great flight of steps" leading up to the porticos.[70]

Niernsee was now sixty years old. He had been injured in a railroad accident in 1883, suffered from rheumatism, and was nearing the end of his career. His report was garrulous and acerbic, chiding the legislature for requesting estimates based on the original plans when they knew those plans no longer existed. He reminded them he had repeatedly pointed out that the "first requisite is to have a thorough set of working plans." He urged them to retain him to make drawings "while my scraps of notes, sketches and a retentive memory of my original ideas of the plan yet serve me for that purpose." He reminded them that a full set of plans would take six months to a year to produce and warned that his estimates were necessarily based upon the rough general plans produced in only six weeks while simultaneously making a survey of labor and material costs in Columbia. He concluded that unskilled convict labor was potentially a liability rather than an asset and urged them to act promptly for two reasons. First, the repaired roof was currently keeping rain out of the interior of the building, but it was not protecting the tops of the exterior walls. Water was seeping in and leaching out the mortar. Secondly, because his terrace and drainage system had never been developed, water was percolating into and softening the clay subsoil all around the base of the building. He warned ominously that it would be "very injudicious to accumulate all the falling waters around this foundation [for] another period of twenty years."[71] Nature soon emphasized the urgency of Niernsee's recommendations, for that spring and summer, storms blew off sections of the roof and severely damaged the interior.

Finally, on January 2, 1885, Niernsee was reappointed architect, but now his health was precarious, and he relied increasingly upon assistants. Twenty years to the day after the city burned—on February 17, 1885—Gustavus Theodore Berg (1823–1905), as Niernsee's assistant, opened Niernsee's new office in Columbia. Berg had been educated at a European polytechnic school. He was born in Koenigsberg, Germany, emigrated to Baltimore in 1850, and first came to Columbia as a draughtsman with Niernsee in 1856. Unlike Niernsee, however, Berg never left. He married Caroline Muller, and the census of 1870 shows they had seven children living at home on Gates Street. They were pillars of the Ebenezer Lutheran Church. Berg, like Kay and Hewitson, began to practice as an architect after the war. He joined Richland Masonic Lodge #39 in 1867, became Master pro tem in 1869, and was elected Master of the Lodge in 1870, 1872, and 1886–1889. Prior to Niernsee's return, Berg designed the Masonic Temple and Fire House at the corner of Main and Washington streets (1867), the Ebenezer Lutheran Chapel (1870–1874), the Robertson- Hutchinson House, 419 North Main Street (c. 1880), and the North Wing of the South Carolina Lunatic Asylum (1880–1882). During Nicrnsee's return to Baltimore, Berg had grown as a professional. He was ready to be more than a draftsman.[72]

With an appropriation of $75,000 Nicrnsee and Berg prepared plans and specifications needed to advertise for cut granite to finish the entablature and cornice. By May 15, 1885, they had placed notices in newspapers in Columbia, Charleston, Richmond, Washington, Baltimore, and Boston. The bids were to scheduled to be opened on June 10, 1885, but Niernsee, who had not been well all spring, took a turn for the worse and died three days before the deadline.[73]

Chapter Four

Substantial Completion

J. Crawford Neilson

The death of John R. Niernsee left the State House commissioners in a difficult position, for no drawings or plans existed. They concluded sadly that "if Major Niernsee ever had any fixed designs for the completion of the work, they died with him. Certainly he left nothing whatever beyond the work that was actually completed." Niernsee, they said, came to Columbia in declining health and in less than four months after his arrival he died leaving only stonecutting specifications for the exterior walls.[1]

A week after Niernsee's death the commissioners invited his partner in Baltimore, James Crawford Neilson, "to visit Columbia to confer . . . with regard to the work on the State House. . . ."[2] And the following week they hired him effective July 1, 1885. Neilson's salary was to be only $2,500 per year (Niernsee had initially been paid $3,000 per year), but he was not required to live in Columbia and could thus retain his practice in Baltimore. The commissioners also agreed that Neilson could select an on-site assistant whom the state would pay $1,800 per year. They assumed Neilson was qualified to bring Niernsee's vision to fruition. Unfortunately, by allowing Neilson to reside out of state, and by selecting him quickly without advertising the job, the commissioners antagonized in-state interests and triggered conflicts which ultimately resulted in Neilson's dismissal.

With Neilson hired, the first order of business was to examine bids submitted for the stone work needed to complete the main exterior walls (minus the porticos, which were considered nonessential and consequently were deferred). This was done on June 23, 1885. Five firms submitted bids (White and Viett of Charleston, $75,234.43; Omar and Stewart of Nashville, $62,704.44; Westham Granite of Richmond, $57,005, Lane and Malnati of Washington, $62,600; M. A. McG[?] of Washington, $65,656). The low bid from Westham Granite of Richmond was accepted.

Before the war, Niernsee had taken pride in the fact that the state was supplying the stone from Columbia. But after the war, due to a lack of capital and skilled labor, few bids were submitted by local contractors. Postwar conditions prevented the State House commissioners from reopening and operating the Granby quarries, and from this point forward much of the work would be done by out-of-state contractors.[3]

In July, 1885, Neilson recommended T. J. Schmidt and the commissioners hired him as the on-site assistant architect for $125 per month. During his initial examination of the building, Schmidt found a pile of finished granite balusters in the basement, hidden by Niernsee after the fire, beneath the Secretary of State's office. Schmidt had convicts pass the balusters up through a trap door in the floor which had been concealed beneath a bookcase and a rug. Four hundred and thirty-two usable ones were recovered; consequently, the Westham Granite contract was reduced by $6,500.[4]

Neilson reported that Schmidt had been exploring the basement in order to plan a system of drains and sewers, for the existing downspouts "delivered their water into the foundation of the building."[5] A brick drainpipe was built (eighteen inches in diameter) leading from the building to the lake in the northwest corner of the square, and plans were made for a sewer leading from closets to be located in the basement. Only temporary repairs were made on the roof, for everyone anticipated that a permanent, fireproof roof would be installed in a year or two when the exterior granite walls were finished.

Having reviewed Schmidt's work, Neilson concluded his first annual report as State House architect by offering two alternatives to what everyone understood as Niernsee's plan. Thirty years had passed since the foundation had been laid, and Neilson pointed out the building was being completed "under conditions very different from those under which it was commenced."[6] Niernsee's plan had provided only two committee rooms for the House, no interior bathrooms, and few executive offices; now Neilson became the first architect to propose enlarging the original plan. Neilson's first alternative was to develop the basement—wholly unoccupied in the original plan—into nineteen rooms, seventeen of which would have one or more exterior windows. Using the basement would require cutting doors and windows through granite foundation walls which were eight feet thick in places. At best, it would be difficult, and he admitted being "unable to estimate the risk of shaking the building in opening windows near the corners." Assuming windows could be cut through the exterior foundation walls, he proposed to trench around the perimeter of the building to allow light into the below-grade windows. He admitted this would create a drainage problem as it would "obliterate the present continuous stone sewer now encompassing the entire building."[7] Given its obvious flaws and uncertainties, this first alternative may have been designed solely to make his second proposal acceptable.

Neilson's second alternative was the first time anyone publicly attempted to change the exterior adopted in 1854. Neilson proposed to finish the wings as originally planned but to delete the $200,000 square iron tower and to add two full stories to the central block. He claimed this would create "twenty-two new excellent rooms, besides the water closets, coat rooms and a quantity of storage." Moreover, all this could be accomplished within Niernsee's 1884 estimate of $738,475 to finish the building.

The press reacted critically to the drawings which were exhibited in Neilson's office. They warned legislators to guard against being seduced by "technical sophistry" or "beautiful, colored drawings or plausible suggestions."[8] The commissioners did not endorse the proposals; they merely forwarded them as Neilson's portion of their annual report and observed that their role was to implement whatever plans were approved by the legislature. The legislature never debated either of Neilson's proposals; instead, they appropriated $75,000 to build the exterior stone and the interior brick walls to their full height, remove the temporary roof, and install the permanent roof and to make preparations to finish the interior based upon Niernsee's plan as it was understood.

Neilson never again offered new designs. During the remaining two years of his tenure as architect of the State House, he lived and worked in Baltimore; there he prepared specifications, reviewed bids, consulted with Schmidt, and periodically came to Columbia to meet with the commissioners. Predictably perhaps, his status as an outside expert provoked caustic comments in the local press: "Architect Neilson left yesterday, having given an entire day to the business of the State House."[9] As a distant administrator, he was responsible for the installation of Niernsee's iron framed roof and the completion of the masonry walls, but as a designer he did little to shape the building.

The administration of the project under Neilson and Schmidt was quite different from the antebellum Niernsee-Jones era. Unable to contract for slave labor as Niernsee had done at the quarry, Neilson used convicts whenever possible. In 1884 a law had been passed requiring the superintendent of the state penitentiary to supply convicts and guards on demand at no cost for work on the State House and grounds. Niernsee had argued against this; he considered it false economy, for convicts rarely possessed the skills required. J. Q. Marshall, who, as Secretary of State and State House Keeper, directed the work of convicts on the grounds, complained in 1889 that "the convicts that have been furnished me during the year have been of a convalescent class, weak and feeble, utterly unable to do any but the lightest work."[10] Despite problems, fifty convicts worked almost full time throughout 1885, and prisoners supplied 850 days of labor in 1888 and 1,842 days in 1889. Convict labor was even more significant off-site, for prisoners made most of the bricks needed to build the interior walls. In 1886, the commissioners agreed to furnish forty convicts and guard to John G. Guignard, who in turn contracted "to make brick on shares, the agreement being that the Commission should have one-half of the bricks burned, with the privilege of buying as many as they needed of Mr. Guignard at $7.50 per thousand."[11]

Contracts made with out-of-state vendors attracted more publicity and controversy than any other aspect of the work during the Neilson-Schmidt era. The primary materials—granite and brick—needed before the war were produced locally. But much of what Neilson needed simply was not manufactured in South Carolina. Neilson needed a steel frame, slate, and copper for the permanent roof; to finish the interior he needed prefabricated ceilings of galvanized iron, cast iron stairs, brackets and railings, plumbing fixtures, and steam heating apparatus. Before the war, importing out-of-state marble and stonecutters had been welcomed as signs of well-being and sophistication; now the practice was decried as an unfair economic threat.

Charges of favoritism and corruption prompted the commissioners in 1887 to publish a history of contracts made during Neilson's tenure. To rebut the charge that "Carolina bidders . . . are unjustly and invariably discriminated against" and refute "systematic opposition which has been so industriously created against the Architect," they documented that "in every single case, with one exception, the Commission have awarded the contract to the lowest bidder." The commissioners also pointed out that Neilson merely drew up the specifications on which the advertisements of work bid were based; normally he was not present when bids were opened. The exception concerned the roof. Metal work for the roof was won by Bartlett, Hayward, and Company, a Baltimore firm which offered a heavier gauge metal which Neilson and the commissioners decided would be more substantial than the material proposed by two less expensive bidders.[12]

Stung by repeated charges of "injustice to home enterprise," the commissioners pointed out that "in only six cases have South Carolina and Baltimore competed for the same work . . . the result was three contracts awarded to Columbia, two to Baltimore and one to North Carolina." Carolina businessmen bid on a total of fifteen contracts and won eight of them. Nonetheless, public opinion unjustly blamed Neilson and the commissioners for the fact that businesses based in Richmond, Nashville, Baltimore, Cincinnati, and Greensboro were able to underbid local interests fifty percent of the time. The commissioners explicitly rejected the notion "that it is the duty of the State to give all the work upon the State House to local contractors, even though they be not the lowest bidders" and concluded, "this . . . has really been the cause of the violent and groundless attacks which have been made upon their management of the work with such persistence."[13]

During Neilson's first year as architect, the major contracts were advertised and Schmidt focused on drainage and the repair of the temporary roof. By the summer of 1886 everything seemed ready for work to begin again in earnest: the Westham Granite Company was delivering stone from Winnsboro; Guignard's bricks were being stockpiled on the grounds; and on August 7 the local newspaper reported that "the ponderous steam hoisting machine" had arrived by rail, and "a short temporary track has to be constructed in front of the machine, which is a steam derrick mounted on a platform truck . . . the engine furnishes the motive power to the truck. The track is laid about four lengths in front of the machine, and as the machine moves forward the track which has been passed over is taken up and replaced in front. It is a slow process. . . ." It took a week to move the derrick from the depot on lower Gervais to the State House and another week to set it in position near the western end of the building and adjust the various guys, stays, blocks, and tackle. The process was watched with interest by "knights of leisure assembled in the State House yard."[14]

A week after the derrick was in place, without warning on August 31, 1886,

> A terrific earthquake of full three minutes' duration struck this city at 9:45 o'clock. . . . The whole city swayed and shook like a leaf. Men, women, and children rushed from hotels and houses into the streets in wild alarm . . . walls of buildings were cracked, crockery rattled, and strong men found it difficult to stand. Nothing so alarming has ever before occurred here.[15]

This was the earthquake which devastated Charleston. In Columbia there were a total of twelve shocks over a period of twenty-one hours. On the campus of the South Carolina College, just two blocks south of the State House, DeSaussure College lost its chimneys and gables and its north wall was badly "sprung." North of the State House, chimneys were toppled throughout the town. T. J. Schmidt was asked to examine the Court House (now City Hall) and the Governor's Mansion, and found both had suffered minor damage. Neilson arrived to examine State House on the September 11 morning train and "stated that while the capitol exhibited evidence of the shake-up, no material damage was done." Then without lingering, he took the afternoon train for Charleston.

Neilson's assessment proved correct, but his judgment was challenged by Ashbury Gamewell LaMotte (1868–1929), an eighteen-year-old aspiring engineer. Acting on his own, Lamotte examined the State House and wrote the governor that "the injuries were so serious as to make it a matter of question whether the work of raising the walls should be continued." The commissioners asked Neilson to return and review Lamotte's assessment. He did so in early October and again assured them there was no significant damage. One of the pilasters on the north wall had been skewed from its base, and there was now criticism in the press about gaps in the new stonework on the west wall. (The contractor setting the granite, Omar and Stewart and Company, said blocks were being cut too short by the Westham Granite Company, and mortar joints had to be widened to make up the distance required in each course.) Neilson must have viewed these as minor problems, for his comments, if any, were not recorded; instead, he told the commission that work on the exterior should continue and would soon be complete. Moreover, construction would soon begin on the interior, and the 1886–1887 legislature would have to convene in the Agricultural Hall at the state fairgrounds (then located in Elmwood Park). There is no evidence he did anything to curry favor or avoid criticism.

PILASTER, WEST SIDE OF NORTH PORTICO. PHOTOGRAPH BY HUNTER CLARKSON, 1997

As the exterior walls were completed in the fall of 1886, the work entered a more complex phase. For the remainder of the job, several contractors were typically on site simultaneously. What one did often affected the others; consequently, coordination became increasingly essential, and Neilson's absence became a larger and larger liability. Omar and Stewart, for example, fell behind schedule with the brick and stonework footings for the metal roof trusses, so Bartlett and Hayward, who had the roof contract, billed the commissioners for a month's wages, claiming their supervisor in Columbia had been unable to begin. Omar and Stewart promptly claimed that the delay was caused by extra work due to problems created by prior construction or altered instructions given by Schmidt. (The commission negotiated settlements with both contractors' attorneys.)

Neilson, in Baltimore, was unable to keep things running smoothly, and the commissioners were directly exposed to an ongoing litany of problems. The most acrimonious dispute centered around the heating contract. As a fire precaution, Neilson originally specified a freestanding, brick boilerhouse to be built on the State House grounds; the boiler was to supply steam to radiators throughout the State House. Bids for this system were received, but rejected, for after advertising, Neilson and the commission had decided to place the boilers in the basement. The same bidders responded to revised specifications, and the relative expense, or rank order, of their bids did not change (Thomas C. Basshor and Company, Baltimore, $14,550; H. M. Crane, Cincinnati, $14,620; and Walworth Manufacturing Company, Boston, $14,720). Walworth Manufacturing was represented locally by McMaster and Gibbes, and after the contract was awarded to Basshor and Company, McMaster and Gibbes bitterly protested the change in the specifications and claimed that their system, although slightly more expensive, was vastly superior. Neilson's analysis of both systems confirmed the commissioners in their decision to award the contract to the out-of-state low bidder.

Although the heating system was not completed, Neilson wisely pressed forward on the legislative halls. The House and Senate opened the 1887–1888 session in ornate chambers boldly painted in the Pompeian style. Unfortunately for Neilson, reaction was lukewarm, for South Carolinians never wholly embraced the exuberant forms and colors of the Victorian styles. Instead, they continued to prefer the clarity of the Greek revival or the pale harmonies of the federal style, settings reminiscent of another day.

As the scaffolding was being dismantled in the House, a reporter visited the halls and wrote, "the general effect is at first startling, at least to those who . . . in their ignorance of 'high art' have not cultivated an admiration for red, green and blue in comparatively immediate conjunction. It is, however, executed according to the ideas of the architect, and is said to be correct, according to all the cannons [*sic*] of the Pompeian school; therefore it is presumable that little guns should not be heard from on the subject."[16]

The House of Representatives had a checkered floor made of white Italian and dark Tennessee marble framed by a black marble baseboard. The wainscot above the baseboard was made of a cream-colored ceramic tile with bands of chocolate brown tiles at its upper and lower edges. Above the wainscot was a heavy, wooden chair rail painted Tuscan red with gold-gilt trim where it intersected windows and doors. The wall above the wainscot was painted "a delicate shade of terra cotta with panels in sienna shades to harmonize with the wood work." The galleries matched the chair rail and had a brass rail with ornamental fittings. The uppermost walls above the galleries were "a slightly deeper shade of terra cotta than those below, and like them are paneled in sienna shades . . . wooden rosettes at the corners of all the casings of windows and doors and in other parts of the wood work are picked out in gold leaf, which wonderfully brightens up the dark tone of the body of the work."[17]

The reporter found the cerulean ceiling the most unique feature in the House of Representatives. Ultramarine blue dominated the ceiling and its intensity was heightened by accents of contrasting colors. Judging from the reporter's description, it must have been the boldest, most colorful ceiling in the state:

Beginning where the ceiling springs from the wall the cove of the cornice is outlined with a narrow stripe of Tuscan red ornamented with gold, then comes a wider band in ultramarine, then a bronze molding beneath the graceful brackets, which are themselves painted a dark bronze, with ornamental work in silver on the front, and the wide ground behind them is blue. Above the brackets is a bronze rail with golden edge, then a wider band of dark vermilion, then a wide strip of lighter blue with a panel in a darker shade of the same and adorned with scroll work in sienna tints. Next is seen the raised leaf-like ornaments all in gold upon a ground of blue, next to the graceful brackets the prettiest part of the ceiling. Beyond this row of ornaments comes the flat portion of the ceiling, the surrounding frame of which is outlined in light blue, paneled in old gold lined with Chinese vermilion.

The ceiling proper is divided into eight recessed panels and a center one, where a skylight is placed. Each of these panels is outlined by a bronze molding, next [to] which is a stripe of ultramarine green, then a stripe of white 'to harmonize' then another bronze band and [then] the favorite blue. These large panels are divided into smaller panels . . . finished in ultramarine blue, picked out with gold and outlined with Chinese vermilion. The center of each is a raised square of blue, in which depends [hangs] a knob of gold from a smaller square of light green.[18]

The Senate had a different, but equally exuberant, color scheme. Here the ceiling and wood work were painted in various shades of olive green relieved by the liberal use of gold. The Senate walls were paneled in shades of pink. Within both the walls and ceiling were bands painted sienna, vermilion, and chocolate brown.

The House and Senate color schemes were visible evidence that Neilson did not understand the taste of Carolinians. Moreover, he had other liabilities, for unlike Niernsee, who had moved to Columbia, Neilson remained an outsider. He was not on hand to deal with day-to-day problems, and it is not surprising that the 1887 Act to Make Appropriations, which provided $35,000 "for the completion of the repairs of the State House," also stipulated, "this amount is [to be] expended under the personal superintendence of a competent architect, who shall reside in the city of Columbia, in this State, during the progress of the work."

Someone had inserted a residency requirement sure to result in Neilson's dismissal. The commissioners notified Neilson and Schmidt at once "that their services would be stopped on and after this date [January 4, 1888] . . . and that Mr. Schmidt . . . turn over to the Secty the keys of the Architects offices."[19]

Francis (Frank) McHenry Niernsee

This time the commissioners advertised the position, but only in the *Columbia Daily Register* and the *Charleston News and Courier*. They probably assumed the residency requirement, low salary, and political climate all meant they must search for a South Carolinian. Despite its limited circulation, their notice produced "a volumous batch of papers" from at least thirteen applicants.[20] Nine applications came from South Carolinians (four from Columbia, three from Charleston, and two from Greenville); the others came from North Carolina, Alabama, Arkansas, and Washington, D.C. Today the applicants are obscure: "F. Niernsee, Columbia, H. Gabler, Greenville, Tilman Watson, Columbia, Geo. W. Waring, Columbia, E. B. Rutledge, Greenville, T. J. Schmidt, Columbia, Mess, Abrams & Seyle, Charleston, L. R. Gibbes, Charleston, E. R. [J.] White, Charleston, A. J. Armstrong, Birmingham, Ala., B. J. Barlett, Little Rock, Arkansas, Byron A. Purgin, Greensboro, N.C. and J. F. Denson, Washington, D.C."[21] Established architects from major cities were not attracted by a project with declining appropriations in the still-impoverished South.

Although they submitted their applications separately, E. J. White of Charleston and Francis (Frank) McHenry Niernsee, joined forces and were hired as White and Niernsee, architects, at a salary of $1,800 each per year. White played no role as an architect at the State House, for White and Niernsee was dissolved on October 1, 1888, and Niernsee was then appointed "sole Architect at a salary of $2,100 per annum."[22]

Frank Niernsee was energetic and gregarious, and like his father, John R. Niernsee, he felt at home in South Carolina. He kept a twisted artillery fragment on his desk, and when visitors picked it up he would recount the morning of February 17, 1865, when the shell struck the State House while he was crossing the grounds as a confederate cavalry courier.[23] He identified with the building and with Columbia, these were the scenes of his youth.

He was born in Baltimore in 1849 and was five years old when the family first moved south. Throughout his childhood and adolescence, his father was working on the State House. When the war broke out, Frank and his older brother volunteered. Both survived unscathed, and after the family returned north, Frank studied engineering at the University of Virginia, then joined his father in Baltimore in 1878. We do not know exactly when Frank Niernsee returned to South Carolina. As early as 1875 he presented material on the construction of roads to the Reconstruction legislature. (Nothing came of this.) He may have accompanied his father on a visit in 1882 and decided to stay, for Frank Niernsee's obituary says he moved back in 1882. John R. Niernsee moved back to Columbia in 1885, but none of the records indicate that Frank came with him. In 1887 the local newspaper noted that drawings and specifications for the restoration of the Colleton County courthouse and jail in Walterboro could be seen in Frank Niernsee's office; this is the earliest evidence that he was in business in Columbia. In 1888 he was listed as an architect for the first time in the city directories as "White & Niernsee, State House."[24]

Unlike his father, Frank Niernsee did not focus exclusively on the State House, for the job was no longer considered full-time and did not pay a living wage. In addition to working at the State House, he designed St. Paul's Lutheran Church and Chapel in Columbia (1888); prepared plans for St. Peter's Catholic Church, Columbia (1889); was hired to construct a cotton seed oil mill in Winnsboro (1889); and designed municipal water works (1891–1894) for Columbia. In nearby Sumter he designed a school and jail and sheriff's residence (1891–1892). In 1893 he formed a partnership with A. G. LaMotte, the young engineer who examined the State House after the earthquake, and as Niernsee and LaMotte, they were responsible for at least fifteen architectural and engineering projects in the midlands before their association ended in 1896. Together they designed individual residential and institutional buildings, but they also published an updated map of Columbia (1895) and designed the mill village of New Brookland for the Columbia Mills Company (1896). The attributes which enabled Frank Niernsee to work with public and private clients stood him in good stead at the State House, and he experienced none of Neilson's troubles with contractors or the commissioners.

Frank Niernsee appears to be the earliest architect based in Columbia with a recognizably modern office. Others—Walker, Kay, Heweston, and Berg—had advertised as architects prior to 1882, but none of them retained draftsmen or simultaneously served a variety of clients in various locations. Frank Niernsee, on the other hand, maintained two offices, one in the State House and a private office at 1528 Main Street, and both offices were busy enough to justify salaried assistants. At the State House, Edwin J. White was the assistant until White and Niernsee was dissolved on October 1, 1888, and White was replaced by Charles Schramm. That spring George Waring joined the State House office as supervising architect "under the direction of the architect," for the commissioners concluded that Frank Niernsee's private business had grown and was taking him away from the State House. Gadsden E. Shand, having just graduated from the South Carolina College, replaced Charles Schramm as draftsman in the State House office in June, 1889, and Shand moved to Niernsee's private office the following month and worked there until September, 1890. Shand then left to study engineering at the School of Mines at Columbia University in New York. A. G. LaMotte took Shand's place in the private office and worked with Niernsee until 1896. Niernsee needed assistants, for reconstruction in a positive and literal sense had begun in the South.

Niernsee's staff reflected a growing class of urban professionals whose livelihoods did not depend upon antebellum agrarian skills. In this regard, the career of Gadsden E. Shand is especially telling. After studying in New York, Shand returned to Columbia and became chief engineer of W. B. Smith Whaley and Company. His early career is important in the evolution of the State House, for at the turn of the century he would be among the first to propose a dome (discussed below) in lieu of John R. Niernsee's tower.

The Whaley Company specialized in the design of textile mills and designed or expanded twenty mills—fifteen in South Carolina and others in Alabama, Georgia, North Carolina, and Massachusetts. In Columbia Whaley designed and had an interest in the Richland Cotton Mill (now called the Whaley Mill) (1895), Granby Cotton Mills (1897), Olympia Cotton Mills (1899), and the Capital City Mills (1900). Although technologically advanced, Whaley's own mills were undercapitalized, and at the turn of the century a combination of labor problems, fluctuating prices, and accumulated debt forced him into bankruptcy.[25]

Whaley left South Carolina in 1903, but Shand stayed, and for twenty years focused upon the practice of architecture. Initially, he practiced alone, and the major surviving work from his early practice is the Richardsonian Romanesque Canal Dime Savings Bank (1893) on Main Street in Columbia. From 1903 through 1912 he worked in partnership with George E. Lafaye as Shand and Lafaye, Architects and Engineers. Together they designed the five story, reinforced concrete Ottaray Hotel (1907–1908) in Greenville and numerous banks, schools, and commercial buildings throughout South Carolina, North Carolina, and Georgia. Their major surviving buildings in Columbia include the Shandon Baptist Church (1908), the Waverly School (1910), the YMCA Building (1911), the Elmwood Baptist Church (1911), and the Columbia City Jail (1912).

Shand left architecture in 1912 to form Shand Engineering Company and for two more decades specialized in "industrial power, water power projects, and municipal works."[26]

The original justification for a new State House had been to provide secure storage for public records. When Frank Niernsee was hired to direct the work, he found his father's fireproof exterior subdivided by wooden floors and covered with a timber-framed roof. John R. Niernsee had planned a fireproof building with a marble interior—marble stairs, walls, multicolored patterned polished marble floors—but the fire that burned his plans also destroyed most of the stock-piled marble.[27] Remnants of marble were salvaged and adapted for decorative details in the library, but for the most part Frank Niernsee had to design a fireproof interior using metal and ceramic tile, for South Carolina could not afford polished marble in the 1880s.

The interior detail is Frank Niernsee's most visible contribution to the State House. Excepting the legislative halls, he designed galvanized metal ceilings (of which only the cornices survive) in all the major rooms except the House and Senate, the cast iron staircases, the galleries and balconies, the spiral stairs, and stained-glass window in the library. He also designed the tile baseboards and patterned marble floors. Beneath these details are his fireproof floors and walls: every aspect of his interior design fulfilled the fireproof mission begun forty years earlier by his father.

The fireproof interior began to take shape in 1888–1889, for during his first full year as architect, Frank Niernsee began removing wooden floors and ceilings and re-placing them with nonflammable materials. The new floors, which he would install throughout the building, were composed of molded, hollow ceramic tile or brick form-ing shallow arches between I beams. The soffit, or underside, of the beams, was pro-tected by tile slabs and the upper surface received two courses of bricks set in cement and covered by a marble tile floor. Frank Niernsee calculated that these floors would support five hundred pounds per square foot without deflection.

The State House floors appear to be the earliest use of this fireproof technique in upcountry South Carolina. Although the technique had been used in France and En-gland for decades, suitable iron beams were not produced in America until Edward Cooper and Abram S. Hewitt were able to do so at the Trenton Iron Works in 1847. They intended to make rails for the Camden and Amboy Railroad, but the iron proved too brittle, and the material was salvaged and reused for fireproof buildings. Subse-quently railroad rail was purposefully used as fireproof joist-footings for brick arches at the Cooper Hewitt Foundation Building, New York City (1854), at the U.S. Assay Office (1853–1854) on Wall Street, and at Nassau Hall at Princeton (1855); by the outbreak of the Civil War, this technique was widely accepted. As the production of suitable rail increased, this method of fireproofing spread in commercial, institutional, and governmental architecture. Much of the iron needed for the State House came from Carnegie and Company in Pittsburgh.[28]

While installing the new fireproof floors, Frank Niernsee also began hanging pressed metal ceilings. In 1888 he finished eleven committee rooms, the office of the Secretary of State, and the Supreme Court Library. Neilson had selected the metal ceilings for the legislative chambers from catalogues, but for the library and the central lobby, Frank Niernsee designed his own. These ceilings consisted of sections of 24- to 29-gauge iron sheets, varying in size from 2' x 2' to 2' x 8'; each section had a design stamped in it at the factory; on site the sections were assembled like a puzzle and hung by wires from a grid of iron bars. Metal ceilings were another evidence of new technologies and national marketing that was rapidly replacing local traditions of craftsmanship.

The use of pressed metal ceilings began in the late 1860s—the earliest may have been the Gilbert Patent Corrugated Iron Arched Ceilings of 1868. They were never widely used in homes, for they remained more expensive than plain, flat plaster, but for several decades they were widely used in commercial and institutional buildings. Pressed metal was less expensive than ornamental plaster; it was reputed to be fireproof, was low maintenance, could be installed over deteriorating plaster, and it was available in a wide variety of patterns. In discussing the pattern he created for the central lobby, Frank Niernsee said the design allowed for the completion of the tower which his father had planned as the crowning element of the State House.[29]

Looking at Niernsee's ceilings and comparing them to those Neilson had done in the two legislative halls, a reporter described Neilson's work as "balderdash in comparison with the quiet dignity and refined taste displayed in Mr. Niernsee's work." Niernsee's design was based upon a systematic color theory. While he was planning his color scheme he told the reporter that "color gives life to form . . . and has a powerful influence on the mind . . .," and he ". . . laid down as a principle . . . that one color should dominate and that this dominating color should be a primary or secondary and the other colors must be subsidiary to it. In the majority of cases the most perfect and beautiful harmony . . . was produced by employing neutralized hues of color for large masses, and then giving freshness, cheerfulness and beauty to the whole by the introduction in small masses of the primary or secondary colors." Niernsee also said that all the primary colors must be present in some form if the eye was to be fully satisfied, and he noted that the color scheme must "emphasize or clearly express the constructive features of a building." These theories were put into practice in the main corridor and Senate lobby where "the coloring is most tastefully accomplished, the ceiling and cornices being . . . bronze, copper, old gold, leather, buff and maroon. All in all it is the finest piece of structural iron work in the South. . . ."[30]

In his summary of work for the year, Frank Niernsee lingered on the description of the library which was intended to be the most ornate room in the State House. As the repository of the law, the library symbolized accumulated legislative wisdom. Practically speaking, books and documents represented the key to orderly government based

DESIGN OF CAST IRON BRACKET FOR BALCONY IN HALL BY FRANK NIERNSEE, CIRCA 1890. COURTESY OF THE SOUTH CAROLINA ARCHIVES AND HISTORY CENTER

METAL WORK BY FRANK NIERNSEE, CIRCA 1890. COURTESY OF THE SOUTH CAROLINA ARCHIVES AND HISTORY CENTER

upon legal precedent. The State House library reflected the increasing architectural prominence of libraries in America as society accepted the idea that progress was necessarily based upon knowledge.

Because of the concentrated weight of book stacks, library interiors were among the earliest nonindustrial public spaces to make extensive, visible use of cast iron. An early, internationally famous use of exposed cast iron for the support of book stacks and balconies was found in the Bibliotheque Ste Genevieve in Paris (1843–1850) by Henri Labrouste. It was published in the *Revue generale de l' architecture* (1852) and influenced the similar use of cast iron in the British Museum Library Reading Room (1854–1856), the Copenhagen University Library (1856–1861), and Labrouste's second great library, the Bibliotheque Nationale (1865–1868).[31]

The use of iron in the library resembles William Strickland's design for the library in the Tennessee State Capitol. Both libraries are regional echoes of international developments. Frank Niernsee described the South Carolina library balconies as having German Renaissance ornament and medieval scrollwork. Oxidized silver ornaments emphasized the ends of the scrolls, and the cast and wrought iron stairs had a nickel plated rail with oxidized silver rosettes at the ends and panels of ornamental, punched Russian sheet iron. The library windows and doors were framed in salvaged Tennessee marble. The galvanized, pressed iron ceiling was painted in "warm grays, olives and gold. . . . Soft grays and olives will be the tints mainly used, with soft Tuscan reds and maroon to give warmth, while gold will be liberally employed to give richness and brightness to the whole. The walls will be in a tint of terra cotta."[32] Captain Charles Newnham was paid $1,500 for painting the ceiling and walls, and much of the ornamental work was executed by A. W. Hamiter.

Frank Niernsee introduced plumbing and electrical systems into the State House to match his up-to-date construction. Before planning the utilities he told the commissioners he needed to go to New York "for there everything of the newest and latest improvement in all Engineering and Building matters center. The new Mutual Life Ins. Building—Columbia College, Cander Hospital—Presbyterian Hospital—Hoffman House and the Randolph Apartment House in that city is said to have the most perfect plumbing arrangements in the world. I also desire to stop in Washington to inspect later improvements which the Government are adopting in plumbing, etc."[33]

There was no municipal sewerage system in Columbia in 1888; consequently, Frank Niernsee first had to complete a sewer line from the State House to the river, but this was simple compared to the installation of pipes through and beneath the massive walls built by his father. Reporting on this aspect of the work, Frank Niernsee wrote, "the construction of a sewerage system in a building such as our Capitol, with solid granite walls varying from six to seven feet in thickness, was quite a serious matter, especially when it became necessary to tunnel and arch with brick and cement the front founda-

LIBRARY. PHOTOGRAPH BY JET LOWE, 1995

Library stairs. Photograph by Jet Lowe, 1995

tion of the main building and portico extending outwards some sixty feet."[34] Toilets, urinals, and wash basins were located in the basement below and ventilated through the lobby stairs. Everyone recognized this was not ideal. The basement was a long way from the legislative halls, and it was impossible to ventilate properly. But all the rooms upstairs were occupied, and even after considerable debate nobody was able to propose a better place.

Frank Niernsee said and wrote more about color theory, or metal ceilings, plumbing or fireproof floor construction than he did about electricity. When electricity became available in the mid-1880s and early 1890s, few people recognized how profoundly it would alter life. Unlike the railroad, electricity was an unobtrusive, silent power, and no songs celebrated its coming. In fact, in 1884 the music stopped altogether when the lights flickered out during one of the first evening concerts on the State House grounds, and the newspaper declared that "As a success the electric lights so far have been a failure."[35]

Without noting the importance of what he was doing, Frank Niernsee offhandedly installed the first permanent electricity at the State House in 1888–1889. These first electric lights were viewed simply as a supplement to the inefficient, expensive gas lights and oil lamps which had been in use for thirty years. The Congaree Gas and Electric Company, the first company to distribute electricity in Columbia, was formed in December, 1887. By fall, 1888, they had put street lights along Main and Gervais streets, and the next session of the legislature approved running a line of wires into the State House so four arc lights could be placed in the Hall of the House of Representatives, and three arc lights installed in the Senate Chamber. The Secretary of State, who directed the architect's work, was authorized to proceed "provided, that the sum expended shall not exceed one thousand dollars. . . ."[36] Existing gas fixtures were adapted for electricity, and the wiring was probably a knob and pole system mounted on the wall below the cornice. In any case, the system was so cheap and simple that it was not discussed by the commissioners the way they talked about heating, ceilings and floors, bookcases, plumbing, etc. The use of gas lighting was discontinued in 1889 and in 1890 the Secretary reported that four additional electric lights had been placed on the grounds.

By October, 1890, Frank Niernsee was able to report that "nearly the whole interior of the State House has been completed." He urged the legislature to appropriate enough money for the coming year to finish interior details and begin work on the north portico. The latter he considered especially pressing, for its foundation—laid thirty years earlier—had "become endangered by softening of the clay soil on account of imperfect drainage and a want of protection from surface water. . . ." He estimated that an appropriation of $75,000 would maintain the momentum of the work and presented an estimate "based on absolute measurements and calculation of quantities" showing it would cost $171,277.32 to erect the north portico. The north portico was the essential first step toward finishing the exterior envisioned by Governor Manning, Henry Kirke Brown, and John R. Niernsee.

By appropriating only $4,500, the legislature emphatically rejected Frank Niernsee's recommendations. The commissioners promptly "made [an] agreement with Architect Mr. Niernsee to allow him $175 per month until April 1st—to plan and supervise all work. . . . No compensation to be allowed should the work be continued after April 1st."[37] The only major work undertaken that winter and spring was the completion of the main stairs in the central lobby. Numerous small interior projects continued (railings in the House, shelving in the library, building mantels, leveling doors, minor plastering, and painting), but taken all together, there was not enough work to engage an architect, and although Frank Niernsee remained in Columbia, of necessity he turned away from the State House, much as his father had returned to Baltimore.[38]

John Quitman Marshall and the Campaign to Complete the State House

Despite Neilson and Frank Niernsee's work on the interior, the exterior of the State House remained unfinished throughout the 1890s. Without porticos or any ornament on the roof it looked like "an old box-shaped barn, dark, dreary and unhealthful within, unsightly and unattractive without, leaky and poorly ventilated . . . a wreck of the war. . . ."[39] During the final efforts to complete the building, c. 1890–1902, John Quitman Marshall (1849–1911) became the most forceful advocate for maintaining the design and quality of construction begun by John L. Manning and John R. Niernsee.

For 18 years, first as Secretary of State, then as a Senator from Richland County, and as a member and chairman of legislative committees and commissions, Marshall argued against finishing the building cheaply. His unyielding insistence would precipitate a bitter public controversy about the dome, spark two legislative investigations, and prompt a law suit against Frank Pierce Milburn, the architect who followed Frank Niernsee. Like Cicero in the Roman Senate, Marshall stood alone repeatedly to warn against what he considered to be grave mistakes. He persisted despite the fact that he was overruled at every turn, and whatever the merits of his implacable rejection of the dome, much of his criticism concerning the quality of construction would prove prophetic.

Public service and the willingness to act decisively were central to Marshall's character. His father, Jehu Foster Marshall, like James Jones, had raised a company of volunteers and fought with the Palmetto Regiment. He had also participated in the first Secession Convention in Abbeville, South Carolina and had died at Second Manassas in 1863. His son, John Quitman Marshall, was named after General John Quitman under whom Jehu Foster Marshall had served in the Mexican War. John Quitman Marshall grew up in Abbeville where his grandfather, Dr. Samuel Marshall, owned White

Tennessee State Capitol Library, circa 1940. Historic American Buildings Survey, courtesy of the Library of Congress

Design for electroliers on main stairs by Frank Niernsee, circa 1890. Courtesy of the South Carolina Archives and History Center

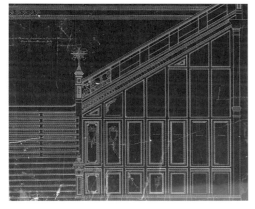

Design of principal stairway in cast and wrought iron by Frank Niernsee, circa 1890. Courtesy of the South Carolina Archives and History Center

Lobby stairway. Photograph by Jet Lowe, 1995

Hall Plantation, 2,742 acres, and, at his death in 1861, 147 slaves. After graduating from the South Carolina College in 1872, John Quitman Marshall was admitted to the bar and became politically active working for the Redemption movement which led to the Democratic victory in 1876. As part of the Democratic ticket, he was elected a trial judge in Columbia and administered the oath of office to Wade Hampton. Marshall resigned his judgeship in 1888 to accept appointment as Secretary of State, and as Secretary he automatically became a member of the commission supervising work on the State House and grounds. During four subsequent terms in the Senate (1899–1906) he served as chairman of the Public Buildings committee.[40]

Marshall took an intense interest in the work from the outset. In addition to managing the files during Frank Niernsee's term as architect, he pressed the implementation of E. O. Schwagerl's landscape plan which had been begun by R. M. Sims when he was Secretary a decade earlier. Marshall's landscaping contributions, 1888–1890, included repairing the fence, establishing outdoor lighting (the four electric lights mentioned above), and moving the statue of Washington, which stood in the lower corridor of the State House, outdoors "on a marble and granite pedestal in front of the East wing of the State House, so that now three monuments stand in triangular shape in front of the Capitol." He also put benches along the walks, and at the east end of the building built an ornamental mound crowned by a fountain using "pieces of refuse granite which were scattered over the grounds."[41]

Beautification of the grounds was one facet of Columbia's rapid growth during the 1890s.[42] The State House was at the center of the expanding web of trolley lines, and its unfinished exterior was said to be bad for business. The Columbia newspaper called the building "grand in its neglect," a symbol "should [it] ever be completed [that] will knit the people of South Carolina closer together, for they will have one common bit of grandeur over which they can boast." A chorus of smaller newspapers chimed in to urge a renewed building campaign: the Newberry *Observer,* the Abbeville *Medium,* the Greenville *Mountaineer,* the Manning *Times,* the Saluda *Advocate,* the Sumter *Item,* the Kershaw *Era,* and the Gaffney *Ledger* were unanimous in their support. The Gaffney *Ledger* summed up prevailing sentiment by observing "through all the days of good stealing, and through all the days of extravagant appropriations [the State House] has remained in its dilapidated condition, an eyesore and a disgrace to the whole state. Let it be completed now. The people of the State should have one building in which they can take a common pride."[43]

J. Q. Marshall entered the Senate in 1899 and was immediately appointed to a joint committee to prepare an estimate of the cost to completion the State House. At the first committee meeting (January 13, 1900), he was elected chairman; he obviously had an estimate ready, for the next day a report to the committee appeared in the newspaper by Gadsden E. Shand. Having been Frank Niernsee's assistant at the turn of the century, Shand was now working with W. B. Whaley and Company. He gave the estimate free and said it was predicated on respect for John R. Niernsee's original design and the use of modern technology. Shand estimated that it would cost $214,500 to complete the building, but this assumed several changes which Marshall would later find offensive. First, Shand proposed substituting a Portland cement dome for the original tower; secondly, he omitted steps on the south, or rear, portico. Shand also pointed out, as John R. Niernsee had in 1884, that $75,000 could be saved if the porticoes were made more shallow by having "one row of columns only, instead of two. . . ."[44] Marshall must have been concentrating upon securing an appropriation and thinking about the money, for he did not—initially at any rate—make an issue of the proposed changes.

ELEVATION WITH DOME, GADSDEN E. SHAND, CIRCA 1900. COURTESY OF THE SOUTH CAROLINA ARCHIVES AND HISTORY CENTER

Shand's estimate provided the basis for discussion in the legislature. Completion of the building was never in doubt; instead, debate centered on the appropriation and how to pay for it. On February 17, 1900, an "Act to Provide for Completion of the State House" was approved; it authorized the expenditure of $175,000 and created a commission to direct the work.[45] Marshall was appointed to the commission which was chaired by Governor M. B. McSweeney. By late March, 1900, they advertised "to invite architects to submit plans and specifications, with estimate of cost . . . stating or showing the departure from the original design for the building. . . ."[46]

Shand's estimate and the commission's advertisement show that changes to the original design were anticipated. In making the estimate, Shand suggested a dome. An undated drawing by him depicts an attenuated version of the U.S. Capitol dome, complete with a peristyle—a ring of freestanding columns—around its base. Whether or not this drawing illustrates his earliest suggestion, it is clear he proposed replacing J. R. Niernsee's tower with a dome months before F. P. Milburn—who has been blamed for the dome for a century—ever became involved.

Frank Pierce Milburn, Architect of the Completion of the State House

The commission received three responses to its advertisement. Predictably, Shand applied. Charles Coker Wilson (1864–1933) and William Augustus Edwards (1866–1939), architects, also applied and said if their application were successful, Shand could be paid for his earlier, gratuitous valuable services out of their fee.[47] The third applicant, Frank Pierce Milburn (1868–1926), won the competition and became responsible for the completion of the State House.[48]

In hindsight it is easy to see why the committee chose Milburn, but at the time Shand must have appeared likely to win, for he had prepared the estimate and had worked for Frank Niernsee. He also had the luster of New York training and was the scion of an old Columbia family. (His grandfather, Peter J. Shand, had been rector of Trinity Episcopal Church for fifty-two years.) Shand, however, was hobbled by the fact that in 1900 his experience was largely limited to industrial buildings.

Charles Coker Wilson also appeared to be a strong competitor.[49] He was then the most active architect in the midlands. Between 1892 and 1900 he was responsible for thirty residences, fourteen churches, eleven commercial buildings and three schools. Unfortunately, he had only worked on one governmental building—a $15,000 remodeling of the Sumter County Courthouse. Governmental construction was rare in late nineteenth-century South Carolina, and this put Wilson at a severe disadvantage, for Milburn already had designed public buildings in Kentucky, North Carolina, Virginia, Georgia, and South Carolina.

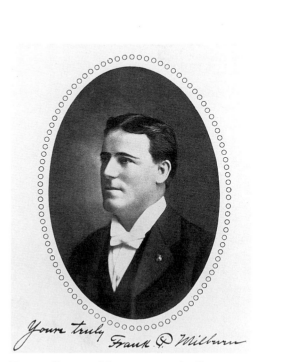

FRANK PIERCE MILBURN, 1906. COURTESY OF THE SOUTH CAROLINIANA LIBRARY

Milburn's reputation at the turn of the century rested upon a series of recent courthouses including the Clay County Courthouse in Manchester, Kentucky (1889); the Magoffin County Courthouse in Salversville, Kentucky (1892); the Forsyth County Courthouse in Winston, North Carolina (1893); the Mecklenburg County Courthouse in Charlotte (1896); the Anderson County Courthouse and jail in Anderson, South Carolina (1897); and the Glynn County Courthouse in Georgia (1897). Unlike Shand or Wilson, Milburn specialized in public buildings: by 1906 he had designed thirty-six courthouses, ten jails, eight Union Railroad stations, and fourteen smaller stations. His civic buildings stood in every southern state except Mississippi.

Milburn's regional practice was the result of a new level of self-promotion. By comparison, C. C. Wilson's professional life represented an earlier, more tranquil era. Wilson relied—as Frank Niernsee had—upon personal contact and word of mouth. Milburn, on the other hand, published booklets illustrating his work; he placed notices in trade journals, submitted attractive renderings in competitions, spent days on the train shuttling between jobs, and was quite prepared to relocate his office to exploit greener pastures. The energy he invested in public relations is suggested by booklets published in 1901, 1903, and 1905. They typically contain approximately seventy-five plates depicting his buildings and drawings. This type of advertising allowed Milburn to cast a wider net than his more traditional contemporaries. State borders meant nothing to him and the State House commission had every reason to believe that he offered the cosmopolitan professionalism of a John R. Niernsee. The commission, however, gave a simple, direct reason for having chosen Milburn: "Three plans were submitted and those of Mr. F. P. Milburn were adopted . . . as being the cheapest."[50]

To make his design feasible within the budget, Milburn reworked his competition presentation into plans and specifications and submitted these on June 29, 1900. Based upon them, a notice to potential contractors was published the following week. At a meeting on August 1, 1900, with Milburn in attendance, the following bids were opened: Gude and Walker, Engineers and Contractors, Atlanta ($212,000); W. A. Chesterman, Richmond ($177,000); J. W. Bishop Company, General Contractors, Worcester (Mass.), Boston, Providence, and Montreal ($184,676); Stewart Contracting Company, Columbia ($182,142); Nicholas Miner [?], Columbia ($169,472); and McIlvain Unkefer Company, Pittsburgh ($158,306). The committee accepted the low bid from McIlvain Unkefer and decided to prepare a contract stipulating that the work was to be completed on or before December 1st, 1901.[51]

Marshall immediately protested; he "wanted all bids handed back and the thing done over again." Due to illness, he had missed the previous meeting at which Milburn's plans and specifications had been accepted; now he saw that the competition drawings did not match those approved as a basis for the bids. He was forceful in explaining his objections to the commission, and "there was quite a spat between Col. Marshall and Architect Milburn." Marshall pointed out that the competition drawings "represented

LOWNDES COUNTY COURT HOUSE. FROM *DE-SIGNS FROM THE WORK OF FRANK P. MILBURN*, 1901, COURTESY OF THE SOUTH CAROLINIANA LIBRARY

ABBEVILLE, GEORGIA, COURT HOUSE. FROM *DESIGNS FROM THE WORK OF FRANK P. MILBURN*, 1901, COURTESY OF THE SOUTH CAROLINIANA LIBRARY

SOUTH CAROLINA STATE HOUSE. FROM *DESIGNS FROM THE WORK OF FRANK P. MILBURN,* 1901, COURTESY OF THE SOUTH CAROLINIANA LIBRARY

the front and rear porches . . . as originally designed," but the final specifications left out six columns on the north portico and reduced the depth of the south portico by removing an entire row of columns. Marshall believed that Milburn's competition drawing had been a ruse, that the architect had paraded a thoroughbred before the commissioners but now proposed to deliver a mule. Marshall felt the commissioners had been duped, and he was alarmed by their supine acceptance of Milburn's changes.[52]

Marshall never accepted the fact that the appropriation made modifications necessary. He would continue to criticize Milburn's reduction of the porticoes. The dome, however, was his main concern. With Milburn in the room, Marshall pointed out that

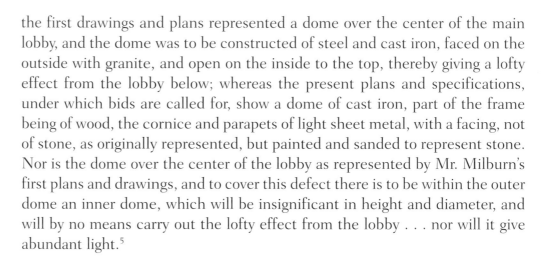

the first drawings and plans represented a dome over the center of the main lobby, and the dome was to be constructed of steel and cast iron, faced on the outside with granite, and open on the inside to the top, thereby giving a lofty effect from the lobby below; whereas the present plans and specifications, under which bids are called for, show a dome of cast iron, part of the frame being of wood, the cornice and parapets of light sheet metal, with a facing, not of stone, as originally represented, but painted and sanded to represent stone. Nor is the dome over the center of the lobby as represented by Mr. Milburn's first plans and drawings, and to cover this defect there is to be within the outer dome an inner dome, which will be insignificant in height and diameter, and will by no means carry out the lofty effect from the lobby . . . nor will it give abundant light.[5]

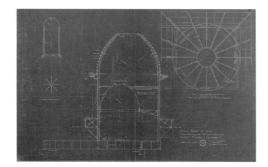

"STEEL FRAME OF DOME COMPLETION OF SOUTH CAROLINA CAPITOL BUILDING," BY FRANK P. MILBURN, CIRCA 1900. COURTESY OF THE SOUTH CAROLINA ARCHIVES AND HISTORY CENTER

Marshall had accepted—in lieu of John R. Niernsee's tower—the larger, more elaborate dome depicted in Milburn's competition drawing, but he felt the smaller, sheet metal domes defined in the specifications were an abomination. He also objected to the steeply pitched gravel roof specified by Milburn. Marshall asserted that the existing slate roof was superior and said "no change should be made in the present roof (except to repair it where it is found necessary) until the State is prepared to put on a first-class roof which will be fireproof." Things left undefined in the specifications troubled him as much as the treatment of the porticoes, dome, and roof. He considered the specifications "indefinite and incomplete" leaving "entirely too much . . . to the contractor to fill in as his judgment or interest may suggest. . . ." Milburn protested, and Marshall challenged him by asking one of the contractors present if the specifications were "full and perfect in all details." The contractor replied, "No . . . they did not cover all details."[54] (In fact, according to testimony during the subsequent investigation, there were no detail drawings at all.)

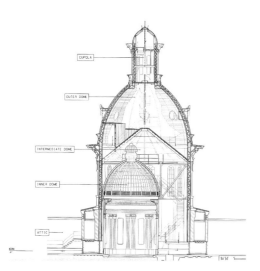

DOME STRUCTURE, BY STEVENS AND WILKINSON, 1995

Marshall urged the commissioners not to go forward: "To complete the building as proposed by the architect would, in my judgment, be a failure. The State of South Carolina has spent nearly two million dollars upon its State capitol and it would be better to let it remain in its unfinished state than to complete it as now proposed. Let it stand as a monument of what the State intended it should be, rather than finish it in a manner not intended by the people of the State."[55] The commissioners, led by Governor McSweeney, rejected Marshall's advice and authorized Milburn and McIlvain Unkefer and Company to proceed.

Using Milburn's approved plans, McIlvain Unkefer and Company quickly began work. The contract only allowed them sixteen months and they were to erect the steps, porticos and dome, replace the roof, move the toilets from the basement into new rooms under the portico steps, and complete "such renovating and repairs as . . . necessary to make the old and new work correspond in appearance."[56] They began removing the roof, laying brick foundations for the porticos and steps, bringing granite by rail for the steps and porticos from their quarry in Pacolet, South Carolina. They also took down Frank Niernsee's colorful ceiling in the main lobby so they could hoist girders up to frame the dome.

Before work had begun on the dome, seeing brick being used for the foundations of the porticos, Marshall convinced the commission to establish a subcommittee, with himself as chairman, to investigate the quality of the work. They were authorized to call expert witnesses and sought the testimony of four architects, a builder, a stone mason, and the Attorney General. After inspecting the foundations, the architects (Wilson and Edwards, Walter and Legare) reported that they were not plumb and their mortar joints were too thick, being 1/2" instead of the 1/4" called for in the specifications. The architects also said the stonework was inferior to the original, for here again the joints were too wide, "the faces of the adjacent stones not being in a true plane as in the old building" and the surface of the stone was not as smooth as the contract required. John Milady, the builder who testified, criticized the same points, but suggested the work, though flawed, was acceptable: "I find the foundation walls on the north side to be a little out of plumb and line, but not sufficient to impair the durability or appearance of the building, as this will be all underground, and is never shown the same care in any building as the outside or face work."[57]

The most damning comments came from the stone mason, J. W. Ethridge. He had considered bidding on the job initially, but did not "because the specifications made the old work on the State House the standard of work to be done." He knew from thirty-three years experience how difficult it was to achieve the quality of the antebellum stonecutting. Ethridge testified flatly that "the work is not of the same class of work that is on the old building in finish nor construction." The joints were too wide; the beds of the stones were too narrow; the surface was not smooth enough; the brick walls were not plumb or straight, and the wide mortar joints in the new brick foundations meant that they "will settle faster than the stone work, and therefore will not stand." He concluded, saying he would have bid on the job had he "known that this class of work would have been accepted."[58] Defending the work and his reputation, Milburn obtained testimonials from six contractors who inspected the work at his request. Each of them contradicted the assertions of Marshall and the critics, and their letters were made part of the record.[59]

The subcommittee addressed two issues beyond the quality of construction. First, a monolithic column had broken while being lifted into the north portico. Rather than requiring the contractor to make a replacement, the commission had approved simply deleting the pair of inner columns which were to have framed the main entry. Marshall protested that this was a structural loss to the building and a financial loss to the state. He also testified that the contractor was selling building materials salvaged from the dismantled roof and stone and iron stored on the grounds. He argued that, although the contract granted the contractor control of excess materials, this clause meant for reuse on the job.

Having heard testimony presented by the architects, contractors, and their colleague Marshall, the subcommittee could not agree on a recommendation. Two members, Robert J. Gantt and M. R. Cooper, issued a majority report declaring the work acceptable. Marshall, alone, issued a minority report unequivocally stating "that the work done . . . is seriously defective and falls far short of coming up to the proper requirements of the contract, plans and specifications." He submitted his minority report to the full legislature so "they may take such action as they may deem proper."[60]

Despite Marshall's continued criticism, the full commission once again overruled him, endorsed the subcommittee majority report, allowed work to proceed, and finally informed the legislature on February 4, 1903: "the work is satisfactory, and . . . the contract has been substantially performed."[61] The State House, they said, was completed.

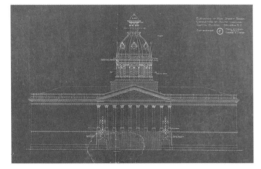

"Elevation of Main Street Facade, Completion of South Carolina State House," by Frank P. Milburn, circa 1900. Courtesy of the South Carolina Archives and History Center

The State of South Carolina vs. McIlvain, Milburn, et al.

As anticipated, Marshall filed yet another minority report restating earlier concerns and adding grave, new charges: Frank Niernsee's colorful, complex lobby ceiling, which had cost the state some ten thousand dollars had been replaced by "a cheap and common stamped ceiling, that cost some four hundred dollars . . ."; gas pipes had been removed from the House and Senate and not replaced. The roof and front portico were not watertight. In fact, the portico leaked so badly that the new bathrooms beneath the porticos could not be used. Finally, the contractor's $50,000 performance bond had been released by Governor McSweeney "without any action of the Board, and without my knowledge or consent."[62]

The legislature reacted by establishing two committees: the first, with Marshall as its chairman, was to examine the State House and recommend repairs; the second, chaired by Robert Aldrich, was to take testimony and investigate charges contained in Marshall's several minority reports.

In recommending repairs, Marshall's committee avoided problems being dealt with by the investigating committee. Marshall retained C. C. Wilson who itemized projects estimated to cost $40,269.69; these included interior painting, repairing ceilings in the library, House and main lobby, a new fireproof roof, a new heating plant, and exterior doors to secure the corridors and bathrooms beneath the porticos. An appropriation for this work was promptly approved.[63]

While C. C. Wilson was drawing up his list of proposed repairs, the investigating committee retained S. S. Hunt, a contractor based in Washington, D.C., who had worked extensively on federal buildings. They believed only an outside expert could provide an impartial critique. On May 25 and 26, 1903, the investigating committee convened to hear the results of Hunt's inspection. Milburn, whose office was still in Columbia, declined an invitation to testify at this meeting. Being requested to forward notice of the hearings to McIlvain and Unkefer, he said he no longer knew their address. Hunt was the principal witness, and he did not mince words.[64]

Starting with the observation that the specifications were vague and there were no detailed drawings, Hunt's analysis went from bad to worse. He said the pressed metal ceilings in the porticos showed "an entire disregard for . . . architectural beauty," that the new ceiling in the lobby "is unfinished. There was no effort made to connect [it to] the cornice [or the] dome." He considered the dome itself "done in a very crude and unworkmanlike manner." It was an insubstantial, sheet metal shell "full of kinks and crimps, with nothing to keep it up." Neither the inner nor the outer dome were braced as strongly as called for in the specifications. On the roof he found places where the sheet metal flashing and guttering had no backing at all; consequently, only a thin sheet of tin "1–32 part of an inch [stood] between the inner portion of the building and the wide, wide world." The gravel on the roof was too big; it didn't hold the tar, and everything was sliding down into the gutters. He said that deleting the inner columns weakened the structure and that to claim otherwise was "an insult to the intelligence of your committee." New capitals on the south portico made by McIlvain were not as good as the antebellum work: "the new capitals are roughly cut; not as shapely in form, do not agree in outline, nor in relief."[65] Hunt was professionally offended by the shoddy craftsmanship and concluded, emphatically calling Milburn's work "a parody upon the science of architecture, an insult to the fame of John R. Niernsee, and a disgrace to the State of South Carolina."[66]

Given Hunt's testimony, it is little wonder that the investigating committee concluded, "Senator J. Q. Marshall is fully sustained by the evidence taken and by the visible facts for all to see. . . ." They deplored "the botch-work palmed off on the State" and noted that "the testimony taken reveals a dark picture . . . but nothing short of an actual inspection of the work can convey an adequate idea of the monstrous swindle of which the State is the victim. . . ." They recommended "appropriate legal steps be taken to recover, if possible, from Frank P. Milburn and McIlvain Unkefer Company as much as possible of the damages the State as suffered. . . ."[67]

The reaction of Milburn, McSweeney, and the now-disbanded State House commissioners was vehement. Although he had declined to testify before the investigating committee, Milburn issued a statement calling their report unjust and a misrepresentation of the facts. He said that for the past eighteen years he had "erected creditable buildings in all of the southeastern states, varying in number from 35 to 55 buildings each year," and this was the first time his name had "been mentioned in connection with any irregular proceedings." He attacked Marshall "who told me the first time I ever met him and before he saw my plans and specifications, that he felt under obligations to support another architect, which he did with all his power and influence."[68]

McSweeney and the commissioners requested a formal hearing so they could compel witnesses to testify under oath. Their request was denied; consequently, they submitted an official thirty-page rebuttal denouncing Marshall, S. S. Hunt, and the "vicious attack . . . directed against the architect and the contractors . . . [and the suggestion] that the Commission was duped and bamboozled by these employees. . . ."[69] Without commenting on the rebuttal by McSweeney and the commissioners, the legislature directed a committee to file *The State of South Carolina, plaintiff, against E. J. McIlvain, John G. Unkefer, E. B. Goucher and James C. Johnson, under the firm name of McIlvain, Unkefer and Company, and Frank P. Milburn, defendants.* The State sought $200,000 in damages and alleged that Milburn had written the specifications "vague and ambiguous in many respects so as to enable him by collusion and confederacy with any contractor to cheat and defraud the State. . . ."[70]

No matter how confident he was about the quality of the work, while waiting for the trial, Milburn must have found the situation troubling. There was worse to come. During the examination to recommend repairs, C. C. Wilson concluded that the dome was not adequately supported. John R. Niernsee had placed piers and columns in the basement and intended to carry them up through each level to provide support for the original tower, but when the second and third floors were built, these interior piers and columns were omitted. When the time came to design the dome, lacking vertical support to the ground, Milburn had retained the American Bridge Company of Pittsburgh, and they had designed a steel support system and framework for the dome resembling a railroad bridge.[71] Consequently, Wilson found the dome perched above the lobby on several cantilevered steel beams which he calculated were not strong enough to support its weight safely.

Prompted by Wilson's warning, the new governor, Duncan Clinch Heyward, arranged for an inspection by Kert Berle, Chief Structural Engineer of the Office of the Supervising Architect of the U.S. Treasury Department. Berle's report (June 20, 1904) declared the dome safe and its "stresses well within the elastic limit."[72] Berle's certification of the dome's support was a welcome pretrial omen for Milburn. On December 7,

1905, *The State's* headlines summed up the litigation: "A Mistrial Results in State House Suit—Jurors Unable to Agree After Twenty Hours—Trial Lasted Nearly Two Weeks—Hard Legal Fight Ends With Neither Side Victorious." Although Milburn may have felt vindicated, the trial must have been a bitter experience, and with his career in South Carolina under a cloud, he moved to Washington, D.C., in 1907 where he practiced architecture successfully until his death in 1926. In retrospect, the charges against Milburn were ill founded and stemmed from his attempt to work within the budget. This brought him into conflict with Marshall who ignored financial constraints and was unyielding in his insistence on antebellum standards of craftsmanship.

In a happier day when Milburn had been getting underway, the newspaper reported that the State House was "at last nearing completion. Designed originally to cost $5,000,000 and intended, as some of the political patriarchs of the State aver, to serve as the capitol of the southern Confederacy. It is today but a semblance of the conception of John R. Niernsee, who designed it. As it stands, it has cost the State of South Carolina $2,500,000. It is intimately associated with many tragic incidents in the State's history, and has become already one of the historic structures of the country."[73]

Though it differed from John R. Niernsee's design of 1854, the State House was declared substantially completed in 1903. Institutional buildings, however, are rarely static, and even as was Milburn defending his work, C. C. Wilson, who was drawing up the list of repairs, observed, "it is only a question of a few years when important extensions will have to be considered, in order to provide for the growing needs of State Government."[74]

Chapter Five

Defining the Grounds

The first building called a *Capitol*—the Roman *Capitolium*—was built in the sixth century B.C. Its courtyard became so cluttered with statues, plaques, and memorials that in 179 B.C. "it was necessary to remove them en masse."[1] Despite this cleanup, it was soon crowded again, and all capitols since have been surrounded by monuments, for they attract statues like stars draw planets, or planets hold moons. Monuments express the *gravitas,* or importance, of governmental work.

In America the vogue for civic monuments reached its peak between 1880 and 1915, and in South Carolina during this period the monuments to Wade Hampton, the Women of the Confederacy, and the Revolutionary War Partisan Generals (Sumter, Marion, and Pickens, respectively) were all erected adjacent the State House as part of a nationwide phenomenon known as the City Beautiful Movement which favored a style called the American Renaissance.[2] This was the Golden Age of American public sculpture.

There are several explanations for the turn-of-the-century blossoming of public sculpture. First, historical consciousness, having been aroused by the Civil War, was successively stimulated by the national centennial, the four hundredth anniversary of Columbus's voyage, and the Spanish American War. Secondly, dramatic social changes made the concrete, emphatic expression of historic values seem especially desirable, and public monuments serve as fixed points of reference, like navigation buoys anchored against the tide. Finally, the emergence of America as an imperial power prompted many to endorse new levels of artistic grandeur to express a new self-image. Seeking appropriate images, American artists often turned to the Italian Renaissance, an age which saw the birth of nationalism, a new faith in reason, and the growth of international trade. According to Bernard Berenson, the Renaissance appealed to turn-of-the-century Americans "because of our faith in science and the power of work [we] are instinctively in sympathy with the Renaissance. . . . The spirit which animates us was anticipated by the spirit of the Renaissance, and more than anticipated. That spirit seems like the small rough model after which ours is being fashioned."[3]

Frederick W. Ruckstull and the Major Sculptural Monuments

FREDERICK WELLINGTON RUCKSTULL IN HIS STUDIO, CIRCA 1900, *METROPOLITAN MAGAZINE*. COURTESY OF THE GENERAL RESEARCH DIVISION, THE NEW YORK PUBLIC LIBRARY, ASTOR, LENOX, AND TILDEN FOUNDATIONS

With the State House substantially complete, attention turned to the condition of the grounds. The Wade Hampton monument was the first major project and it foreshadowed things to come. Frederick Wellington Ruckstull (1853–1942), the sculptor who made the Hampton monument, would later make both the Women of the Confederacy statue and the columnar memorial to the Revolutionary Partisan Generals. All would be in the American Renaissance Style; all were related to specific works of art elsewhere, and all expressed specifically local sentiments.

A legislative Commission to Provide for a Monument to the Memory of Wade Hampton was created in 1903. The commission was directed to select a sculptor and authorized to spend up to $20,000 after having raised $10,000 from private sources. John Quitman Marshall served as the commission's treasurer and then as its chairman. The commission sought recommendations, interviewed Ruckstull, and made a contract with him for a total price of $28,000. Ruckstull then went to Paris where he designed the statue and supervised its casting by A. Durenne.[4]

Hampton is presented mounted and reviewing his troops. Both horse and rider are virtually identical in posture and detail to Ruckstull's earlier (1897) equestrian bronze of Major General John F. Hartranft, created for the grounds of the Pennsylvania State Capitol in Harrisburg. The Hampton statue and its die (upper section of its base, made of Brussels gray granite quarried in the Vosges Mountains of Alsace) was shipped to Savannah, then loaded on a train and finally drawn by twelve mules up Gervais Street to the State House grounds. With Ruckstull in attendance, it was unveiled before a crowd of 10,000 people on November 20, 1906. The monument was well received and marked the beginning of a series of South Carolina commissions for Ruckstull.[5]

The commissioners had selected Ruckstull for many of the same reasons their predecessors had retained H. K. Brown and J. R. Niernsee. By 1903 Ruckstull had a national reputation based on European training. He had visited Paris in 1882 and returned there in 1885 and entered the Academie Julian. He was thirty-three years old

GENERAL JOHN F. HARTRANFT, BY F. W. RUCKSTULL. COURTESY OF THE PENNSYLVANIA CAPITOL PRESERVATION COMMITTEE

when he began studying in Paris; his taste was already formed, and he was offended by early hints of abstraction in Paris studios. He found the work of the young Rodin degrading and "a desecration of the world of art, an insult to the intelligence of mankind, and symbolic [of] sadism. . . ."[6] Rejecting Modernism, Ruckstull was attracted to the conservative Beaux Arts Style which drew upon the past for models of excellence. The Beaux Arts Style was favored by American Renaissance sculptors and architects. It promoted the use of historically sanctioned allegory as well as decorative forms. This use of the past was well suited to the elegiac focus of the Lost Cause movement. Ruckstull's three works at the State House reflect his melding of the Beaux Arts Style, the American Renaissance vogue for public sculpture, and the expression of local Lost Cause sentiment.

Ruckstull established himself quickly. His first major piece, an allegorical figure of Evening (now in the Metropolitan Museum), won an honorable mention at the Paris Salon of 1888. He set up a studio in New York in 1892 and the following year his Evening won a gold medal at the Chicago World's Fair. That year he was one of the founders of the National Sculpture Society (others included Augustus Saint-Gaudens, John Quincy Adams Ward, Daniel Chester French, and the architects Richard Morris Hunt and Stanford White). Two years later he won the competition for the General Hartranft monument, the predecessor of the Hampton Monument, and in 1899 he directed the sculptural program for the Dewey Triumphal arch in New York. In 1902 he served briefly as the Director of Sculpture for the World's Fair in St. Louis. His earliest major confederate memorial, Gloria Victis, was begun in Paris in 1887, cast in 1902, and installed in Baltimore and featured on the cover of the *Confederate Veteran* in 1903.[7] Thus when he was contacted by the Hampton Monument commissioners, Ruckstull, like H. K. Brown and J. R. Niernsee, was known nationally in his field.

As preparations began for the unveiling of the Hampton Monument, the newspaper called attention to "the grounds surrounding the State House. . . . They are positively a disgrace to the State. . . . Think of setting a three million dollar building and these beautiful monuments in the middle of an old field or of a cow pasture! The 'sidewalks' girding the grounds are nothing but uncurbed, unpaved footpaths. Paths bisect the grass plots; there are a few hundred feet of gas-pipe railing. The poorest county has not given less attention to its court house grounds than the State of South Carolina has bestowed on the setting to its most costly and imposing public building."[8]

The grounds were not manicured in time for the unveiling; consequently, criticism grew. The Columbia City Council, the Chamber of Commerce, and Civic Leagues around the state began to lobby, and in 1907 the legislature responded by creating a Commission on the State House and Grounds with an appropriation of $15,000 to begin work. The commission retained C. C. Wilson to coordinate the landscaping and directed him to "conform as near as possible to the original Niernsee plans." P. J. A. Berckmans Company of Augusta was awarded the planting contract. Fruitlands, Berckmans' historic nursery had been established in 1858. In 1932 Fruitlands would become the

Augusta National Golf Club, home of the Masters tournament, so ornamental trees on the State House grounds have "cousins" along historic fairways, much as Ruckstull's statues and Muldoon's soldier have "relatives" in other cities.[9] On a more down-to-earth note, the City of Columbia furnished crushed rock for the sidewalks, and these were laid by Frank Barker, a contractor from Savannah. The walks largely followed Schwagerl's 1878 plan and were finished in 1907. At the end of the year, Wilson reported that $51,000 would be needed to develop the raised terraces planned by J. R. Niernsee, and the commissioners noted that they did "not contemplate any work on the wings [the grounds east and west] of the capitol as this might conflict with the plans the legislature might have in view for the extension of the building."[10] They obviously knew that there was already an undercurrent of interest in expanding the State House to provide more office space.

STATUE OF WADE HAMPTON, CRATED, 1906. REPRINT FROM *THE STATE*, 1954

STATUE OF WADE HAMPTON BY F. W. RUCKSTULL, 1906. PHOTOGRAPH BY HUNTER CLARKSON, 1997

ADMIRAL DEWEY TRIUMPHAL ARCH, 1899.
COURTESY OF THE LIBRARY OF CONGRESS

GLORIA VICTIS, BY F. W. RUCKSTULL, 1903.
PHOTOGRAPH BY LINDA DE PALMA. COURTESY
OF THE COMMISSION FOR HISTORICAL AND
ARCHITECTURAL PRESERVATION, BALTIMORE,
MARYLAND

The Hampton Monument was created to honor one individual, and its history is straightforward. By contrast, the Women's Monument tries to summarize the multifaceted, historic role of a group, and Ruckstull designed it with another commission in mind; consequently, its history is interestingly convoluted. The idea of erecting monuments to the women who supported the Confederacy on the home front was discussed in Louisiana in 1895 and endorsed at the annual United Confederate Veterans meeting in Richmond in 1896. The following year at a meeting of the Camp Hampton Confederate Veterans in Greenville, the idea was proposed in South Carolina. The Greenville veterans determined to raise $10,000, but the project languished, probably for lack of money.[11] Their idea was revived and expanded in 1906 by General C. Irvine Walker, a Charlestonian, who proposed a regional campaign to raise $25,000 to fund the creation of a major original bronze. He pointed out that the southern states could pool resources and "invite the artists of the world to compete," then a committee would select the design most emblematic of "the magnificent lessons of the sublime heroism of our Confederate mothers" and reproduce the winning design at a modest cost for each state.[12]

Walker's proposal was approved at the 1906 convention of the USCV, and *The Confederate Veteran,* the official newsletter of the United Confederate Veterans, the United Daughters of the Confederacy, the Sons of Veterans, and other organizations publicized the project. As chairman of the Women's Memorial Committee, Walker received some eighty proposals. Among the unsuccessful entries was one by F. W. Ruckstull. The competition submissions do not survive, but Ruckstull's description, published in the *Veteran,* shows his design for the competition was later used as the South Carolina Women's Monument. Describing the competition sketch, Ruckstull wrote:

It shows a Southern woman of about forty-five with a face full of beauty and aristocracy and the refinement and strength of the perfect type . . . seated in a splendid Greek chair in a simple dress of the period . . . she will be looking straight ahead of her in a mood at once listless and pensive with a tinge of sadness as she reflects of the events of the past and as if saying with the poet:

> How fondly memory wanders
> Where the feet no more may tread
> Into vistas dim and haunted
> By the past's unquiet dead,
> With familiar phantoms trysting,
> Sad to stay, yet loath to part
> From spots o'errun by broken
> Trailing tendrils of the heart!

SOUTH CAROLINA WOMEN OF THE CONFEDERACY, BY F. W. RUCKSTULL, 1910. PHOTOGRAPH BY HUNTER CLARKSON, 1997

Back of her will be a splendid winged figure of Fame holding in her left hand a palm branch and a trumpet, and with her right hand holding over the head of the seated woman a wreath of laurel . . . she had just come down from the skies to honor the noble woman seated before her. By the left side of this figure of Fame will be a boy Cupid . . . by the right side will be a girl Cupid, more timidly walking along and bearing in her left arm a lot of flowers and in her right hand an open scroll with the State seal upon it and showing the name of the Governor who signed the bill passed by the Legislature ordering the erection of this monument.[13]

Before a final decision was reached in the regional competition, the South Carolina legislature established a commission "to Provide a Monument to the Heroism, Fidelity and Fortitude of the Women of South Carolina during the War Between the Confederate States and the United States." General Walker was appointed to the commission, and they contracted with Ruckstull to create the monument.[14] Once again, as he had done with the Hampton Monument, Ruckstull went to France, this time to St. Leu near Paris, where he spent the next two years preparing the full-sized model. The sculpture was cast in Brussels, then shipped via New York, and unveiled on the south side of the State House, facing south, on April 11, 1912.[15] In Columbia for the unveiling of the Woman's Monument, Ruckstull trimmed his sails to local conditions by adjusting the meaning of the figures. He told a local reporter:

> . . . there is a large symbolism in the group. The figure at the rear and the two smaller figures at the sides stand for the State of South Carolina coming joyfully to crown the noble womanhood of the Confederacy. The winged figure predominating is a Victory, the idea being that in her deeds the woman of the Confederacy was victor of every situation, whatever may have been the outcome of the armies.
>
> The figure of the Confederate matron is seated in a throne of State with the Bible, the main comfort and strength of the women of the Confederacy, in her lap. Her dress is of homespun of the plain character worn by the women during the war. She is looking out into space with a firm, serene and courageous look, meditating over the past and the future.[16]

The figure of the winged woman, called Fame in the description of the competition design, had been a standard personification since the sixth century B.C. She represented the goddess Nike, or Victory, and typically carried the laurel wreath as a crown of immortal fame and a palm frond as a symbol of triumph.[17] She often appears hovering protectively, crowning her mortal from behind. (In the Christian era she often becomes an angel; the wreath becomes a halo.) Ruckstull used Nike alone on the Soldiers' Monument (1896) in Jamaica, Long Island, as the central figure in a group on the Army Column of the Dewey Arch (1899), as the driver of a quadriga for the U.S. Government Building at the Pan American Exposition in Buffalo (1900), and as the major figure in Baltimore's Gloria Victis, dedicated in 1903. She also stands atop the column of his Revolutionary Partisan Generals, commissioned for the State House grounds by the Daughters of the American Revolution in 1909 and completed in 1913. He had earlier placed a look-alike cousin, if not a twin, atop the Defense of the Flag monument (1905) in Little Rock, Arkansas, and on the Confederate Monument in Salisbury, North Carolina (1909). This use of ancient symbols and allegory to express contemporary sentiment made

Ruckstull a prominent sculptor of public monuments during the American Renaissance, c. 1895–1915.[18]

REVOLUTIONARY PARTISAN GENERALS, F. W. RUCKSTULL, 1913. PHOTOGRAPH BY HUNTER CLARKSON, 1997

In Columbia on November 29, 1904, before going abroad to work on the Hampton statue, Ruckstull made an address in Columbia to the local Civic Improvement League.[19] The local league, active c. 1904–1924, was part of a nationwide movement of volunteer organizations which flourished c. 1895–1920. These clubs promoted parks, parkways, fountains, statuary, and, above all, city planning. But they did not advocate beauty for its own sake; instead, they lobbied for the systematic development of amenities as a means of improving the physical, psychological, and financial well-being of their communities. Across the country the leagues tried to give tangible form to ideals now characterized as the City Beautiful Movement.[20] Lewis W. Parker, a textile executive and Whaley's successor as president of the Olympia Mill, was instrumental in founding the Columbia Civic Improvement League. His brother, Thomas W. Parker, had retained Harlan P. Kelsey, a landscape architect from Boston, to create a plan for the Monaghan Mill in Greenville, South Carolina. Impressed by the result, Lewis W. Parker arranged for Kelsey to speak to the legislature about the State House grounds and in announcing the event the newspaper reported "at the conclusion of the lecture the women will organize a Civic Improvement society for Columbia."[21]

To the Columbians assembled at the first annual meeting of the league, Ruckstull presented an agenda then being considered—and in some cases implemented—across the nation. Development of a civic center was a central tenet of the City Beautiful Movement. Interest in ceremonial and functional urban focal points—landscaped groupings of public buildings—had been aroused by the success of the Columbian Exposition, the Chicago World's Fair, 1892–1893, and by the work of the MacMillan Commission then guiding the active development of federal offices, the Mall, and parkways along the Potomac. Ruckstull envisioned the State House as a logical civic center. He emphasized sculpture and described to the Civic League how the embellishment of the State House grounds might be extended into the cityscape:

> Suppose, now, you began with a fountain on the first street north of the Capitol in the middle of Main street, and two blocks away you put up a column twenty feet high with a fine bronze eagle or victory on top, and two blocks away another fountain. Then two blocks away a statue of Washington. Then another fountain, then another column, then a statue of Gen. Robert E. Lee, etc. Think of what a magnificent effect this would produce looking up from the steps of your Capitol! You could easily achieve all this in twenty years; and, by following this plan for one generation, your city would become so beautiful that it would be talked of all over the country and attract desirable settlers and capital from sources you do not now dream of.[22]

Warming to his audience, Ruckstull compared the potential of Columbia to that of Paris, Brussels, and New York, and he offered a series of specific, seemingly realistic steps to realize that potential. He said that if the city would consistently allocate one-tenth of one percent of its annual budget to his agenda, the cityscape would be transformed in two generations. Ordinances should be adopted restricting manufacturing to the lowlands and reserving the plateau for residential development; a building height limitation (exempting steeples and domes) of eighty feet should be established. As in Paris, architectural unity should be created by allowing the first building on each block to establish the stylistic norm for subsequent buildings erected on the block.

He recommended developing parks connected by parkways and addressed street design suggesting a fountain on every fourth block throughout the city, installing attractive street signs and lamp posts and curbs and sidewalks to improve conditions for pedestrian and vehicular traffic, drainage, and the health of the trees. "As soon as possible," he said, "pass a law that every telephone and telegraph wire must go under ground . . . put all the trolley wires under ground. . . . For nothing is more hideous in a city than ugly telegraph poles and overhead wires. Your city is entirely too full of telegraph poles, and they are an eyesore—and a danger to your trees." He devoted considerable attention to the existing trees: "You have the most magnificent trees of any city . . . a priceless heritage. I would make them the object of my most jealous care."[23] And he described a system of arbor culture and the advantages of an ordinance protecting trees.

Ruckstull claimed a beautification program would attract "capital and desirable settlers" and "act like a tonic . . . on your body as well as on your soul. For you would feel that you are pursuing patiently but steadily the noblest civic ideal possible . . . making a paradise of your earthly dwelling-place, even if you never realize that ideal."[24]

The State House as Civic Center

The year after Ruckstull's address, Kelsey and Guild, Landscape Architects, Boston, submitted a citywide plan commissioned by the same Columbia Civic Improvement League. In its private sponsorship and recommendations, the plan demonstrated civic interest in the State House as a focal point. Kelsey and Guild's suggestions for a civic center were never discussed by the legislature. Nonetheless, their plan is important as the first of a series of twentieth-century attempts to end the tradition of dealing with the site on an ad hoc basis. Working within the City Beautiful Movement idiom, they offered specific form to most of the ideas sketched verbally by Ruckstull. They reiterated the need for adopting "a systematic, well conceived scheme of improvement" administered by an on-going joint city and state commission which would be immune to passing whims. They stressed the financial benefits of planning, noting that outlying parks, parkways, and reservations along the Congaree and nearby swamps should be acquired before urban sprawl drove up the price of wild lands. Urging a network of park and parkways, they cited the experience of Albany, New York, where "the value of the ground contiguous to the parks has not only doubled, but quadrupled and sextupled." The Capitol Park was to be the center, "a valuable beginning of a park system."[25] The failure of the Kelsey and Guild plan was predictable, for South Carolinians—unlike New Englanders—had no tradition of village greens and commons.

Kelsey and Guild presented two plans for the State House grounds: both designs assumed that J. R. Niernsee's original plan would be retained and that architecturally compatible governmental offices would be grouped south of it. Similar civic centers were already underway, they observed, in Cleveland, St. Louis, Buffalo, St. Paul, Hartford, and Providence. Unlike Ruckstull, they did not emphasize sculpture; instead, they suggested new buildings be placed in a landscaped setting so each could be viewed—as J. L. Manning had said of the State House—from all points of the compass.

They criticized the new City Hall (designed by Milburn on the northwest corner of Main and Gervais opposite the State House) as "a striking example of the lack of both a scheme for grouping and the entire absence of an architectural motive for the city's public buildings. Its style, whether good or not in itself, is certainly in total discord with the dignified lines of the Capitol [and] its location directly across the street is unfortunate."[26] They must have concluded that the view to the north was beyond redemption, for their second civic center plan reoriented the State House so the south facade became the principal entry. This proposal would have created a vista framed by new government buildings along South Main. Landscaping surrounding the new offices would have merged into the university campus.

Apparently without reference to the Kelsey and Guild plan, during the 1960s the state acquired land along both sides of South Main. Plans for a governmental mall were begun, but several factors, including a change in leadership, the growth of government, the development of the interstate highway system, and new means of interoffice communication combined to make a central cluster of state offices obsolete.[27]

Kelsey's emphasis on green space came naturally. Although he was born in Pomona, Kansas, the family moved to Highlands, North Carolina in 1885 when he was twelve. His father, Samuel T. Kelsey, was instrumental in establishing the town and a nursery promoting native ornamental plants. The business was a success; its nurseries were moved to Linville, North Carolina, in 1895, and a sales office was opened in Boston in 1897. The scale of the operation is indicated by an order placed in 1890 by Frederick Law Olmsted for G. W. Vanderbilt's Biltmore Estate. From the Kelsey Nursery, Olmsted ordered thirty thousand native plants—four varieties of rhododendron, four varieties of ilex (*Leucothoe catesbaei*), and dwarf sand myrtle (*Leiophyllum buxifolium*). Harlan P. Kelsey was to start the plants at the nursery and deliver them to Biltmore for planting in the fall of 1891 and 1892.[28]

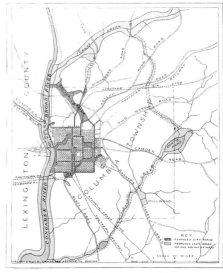

Plan Showing a Suggested System of Inner and Outer Parks and Reservations, and Connecting Roads and Driveways

"SUGGESTED SYSTEM OF INNER AND OUTER PARKS AND RESERVATION AND CONNECTING ROADS AND DRIVEWAYS," KELSEY AND GUILD, 1905. COURTESY OF THE SOUTH CAROLINIANA LIBRARY

"PROPOSED PARK AREAS," KELSEY AND GUILD, 1905. COURTESY OF THE SOUTH CAROLINIANA LIBRARY

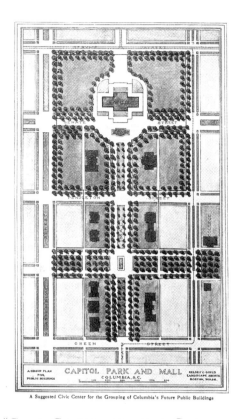

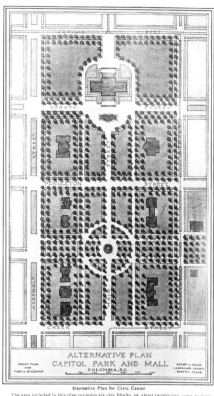

"CIVIC CENTER FOR THE GROUPING OF COLUMBIA'S FUTURE PUBLIC BUILDINGS," KELSEY AND GUILD, 1905. COURTESY OF THE SOUTH CAROLINIANA LIBRARY

"ALTERNATIVE PLAN FOR CIVIC CENTER," KELSEY AND GUILD, 1905. COURTESY OF THE SOUTH CAROLINIANA LIBRARY

Sometime prior to 1905, Harlan P. Kelsey moved to Boston. He first operated a nursery in Marblehead, Massachusetts and then, after 1912, established the Kelsey-Highlands Nursery in East Boxford, Massachusetts. He took an active part in professional and civic affairs, serving as president of the New England Nurserymen's Association, 1913–1914, president of the American Association of Nurserymen, 1923–1925, and president of the Massachusetts Nurserymen's Association, 1931–1932. He was president of the Appalachian Mountain Club, 1920–1921, and during the Hoover administration served as vice-chairman of the Southern Appalachian National Park Commission. As a consultant to the National Park Service, Kelsey played a role in defining the boundaries of the Shenandoah, the Great Smoky Mountain, and the Grandfather Mountain National Parks. He also served as a Trustee of Public Reservations, an influential citizens' board established in 1891 by the Commonwealth of Massachusetts to conserve wild lands for the public.

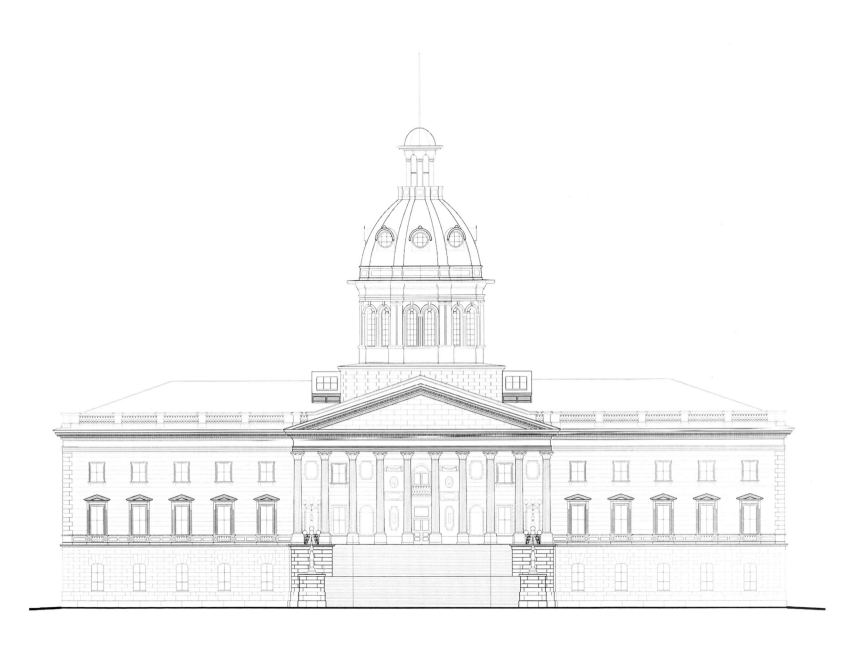

North elevation, Stevens and Wilkinson, Architects, 1995

PLASTER MODEL, A. W. TODD, 1911. COURTESY OF THE SOUTH CAROLINA ARCHIVES AND HISTORY CENTER

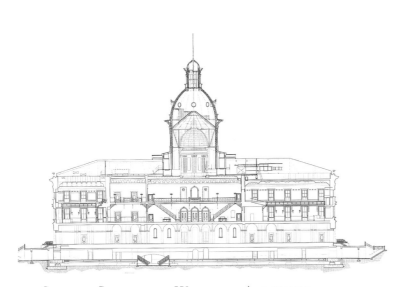

SECTION, STEVENS AND WILKINSON, ARCHITECTS, 1995

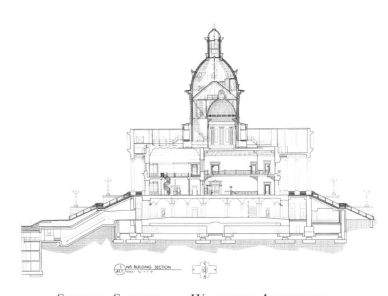

SECTION, STEVENS AND WILKINSON, ARCHITECTS, 1995

North Elevation, A. W. Todd, 1911. Courtesy of the South Carolina Archives and History Center

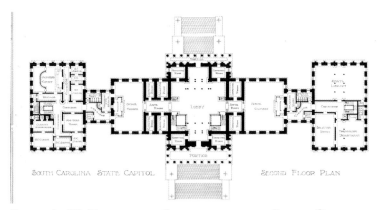

Plan, A. W. Todd, 1911. Courtesy of the South Carolina Archives and History Center

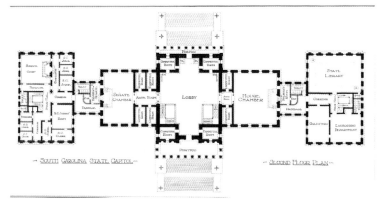

Plan, A. W. Todd, 1911. Courtesy of the South Carolina Archives and History Center

NORTH ELEVATION, A. W. TODD, 1911. COURTESY OF THE SOUTH CAROLINA ARCHIVES AND HISTORY CENTER

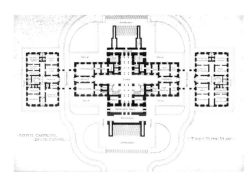

PLAN, A. W. TODD, 1911. COURTESY OF THE SOUTH CAROLINA ARCHIVES AND HISTORY CENTER

The Olmstedian elements of Kelsey's plan for Columbia—the parks linked by parkways, the development of existing water courses and shorelines, and the conservation of native flora—all reflect an intimate knowledge of Olmsted's Boston park system. Kelsey believed landscape design was a public service and should address more than recreation. He was yet another outside expert—like J. R. Niernsee, Neilson, Milburn, Schwagerl, and Ruckstull—who brought a breadth of professional sophistication to the State House grounds.[29]

Kelsey was a nurseryman without any academic training, but his partner, Irving Tracy Guild (1860–1936), had attended the MIT school of architecture in 1885–1886 and again in 1886–1887 as a nondegree candidate. Guild was probably responsible for the civic center proposal for the State House grounds. He also may have done the drawings, for the idea and its presentation reflect the French Ecole des Beaux Arts influence that dominated the architectural curriculum at MIT.[30]

In the French tradition the most monumental buildings were those housing the

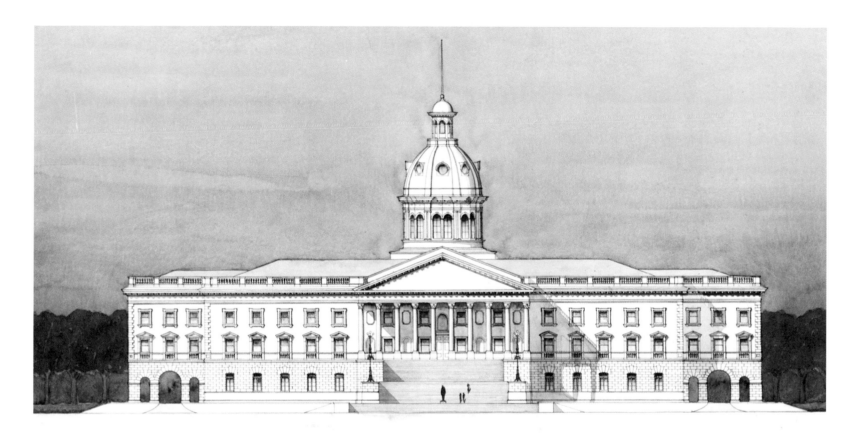

ELEVATION, A. W. TODD, 1911. COURTESY OF THE SOUTH CAROLINA ARCHIVES AND HISTORY CENTER

king, state, or church. Institutional permanence, authority, and dignity were expressed architecturally by visual prominence, prestigious classical ornament, proportion, and symmetry. The French academic tradition promoted by the Ecole des Beaux Arts favored groupings of buildings in formal landscapes which carried the message of social order beyond the offices and into the streetscape. These ideals were first promoted in America by Richard Morris Hunt who had spent six years in Paris at the Ecole as a student. Returning to America in 1855, he indoctrinated many young architects in his New York office. One of them, William R. Ware, became the director of the first academic architectural program in the United State, the program established at MIT in 1868. Hunt also bolstered the popularity of the Beaux Arts Style through his work as Chairman of the Board of Architecture at the Chicago World's Fair, 1892–1893. The other high-water mark of the Beaux Arts in America was the redevelopment of the Mall in Washington, D.C. by the MacMillan Park Commission. Their plans, 1901–1902, drew heavily upon the architectural advice of Charles Follen McKim, another graduate of the Ecole.[31]

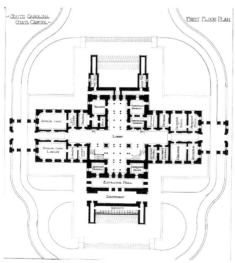

PLAN, A. W. TODD, 1911. COURTESY OF THE SOUTH CAROLINA ARCHIVES AND HISTORY CENTER

ENLARGEMENT OF STATE CAPITOL TO BE CONSIDERED

ELEVATION, C. C. WILSON, 1916, *THE STATE*. COURTESY OF THE SOUTH CAROLINIANA LIBRARY

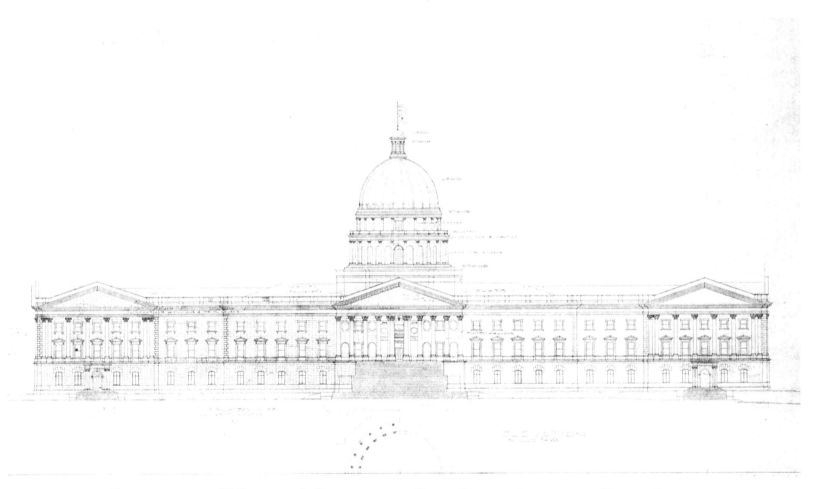

NORTH ELEVATION, W. BAKER, 1946. COURTESY OF THE SOUTH CAROLINA ARCHIVES AND HISTORY CENTER

Guild's second Civic Center plan, if it had been fully realized, would have created a governmental-university complex focusing upon the State House and echoing, in a minor key, the buildings decorously spaced along the mall in Washington. Although nothing came of Guild's plan per se, it may have played a role in siting subsequent office developments to the south, separating them from the State Capitol itself and saving the green landscape frame around J. R. Niernsee's building.

Proposals to Enlarge the State House

Those interested in preserving the grounds and the original State House inevitably came into conflict with politicians who experienced firsthand the need for additional space to house a growing government. The possibility of expanding J. R. Niernsee's plan had been suggested by J. C. Neilson in 1885 when he presented a design which added two stories to the central block. Neilson's proposal accomplished nothing beyond demonstrating the broad-based allegiance to the original plan; nonetheless, the need for more space was real, and by the early twentieth century, the problem became a refrain, often repeated by governors and committees in the House of Representatives.

ALTERATIONS & ADDITIONS TO THE STATE HOUSE OF SOUTH CAROLINA

END ELEVATION, W. BAKER, 1946. COURTESY OF THE SOUTH CAROLINA ARCHIVES AND HISTORY CENTER

In 1907 Governor Duncan Clinch Heyward noted in his address to the General Assembly that "the State House now is too small to meet the requirement of our Government. A number of State Officers now, including the Railroad Commissioners, the State Superintendent of Education, the Commissioners of Agriculture, Commerce and Immigration, and the State Bank Examiner, have no office in the State House." He added "I, of course, understand that the State House cannot be enlarged," so he suggested creating a separate building for the State Supreme Court and thought "this change would provide needed offices of every State official, and would meet the requirements of the situation." The newspaper agreed and wrote that the state needed not only a "a temple of justice," but also offices for the state geologist, the board of health, the board of education, and the state armory, in addition to the inadequately housed agencies cited by Governor Heyward.[32] No action was taken by the legislature in 1907.

The next governor, Martin F. Ansel, made the same point in his address to the General Assembly in 1908. Ansel recommended "a neat and commodious brick building . . . erected on the State House grounds near the corner of Assembly and Senate Streets" to accommodate the Supreme Court and its library.[33] C. C. Wilson, who had been directing repairs of the roof, dome, bathrooms, and heating plant, supported the governor and went a step further by advocating a civic center, or group of buildings, in keeping with the concept presented by Kelsey and Guild. Wilson said, "I can not too strongly urge that the State pause in the work for a year, and have a thorough study of the problem made, and the results submitted to the next legislature with definite plans and estimates and a plaster model of the completed building and grounds." He suggested separate pavilions, or buildings, sited east and west of the State House, preserving J. R. Niernsee's design and providing the much needed accommodations.[34] The legislature did not act on these recommendations in 1908, but Ansel persisted and repeated his suggestion in 1909 and 1910.[35] Ansel's suggestions roused protests from the Civic League "against any cheap building on [the] capitol grounds," for the league did not trust the state to build something fitting adjacent the capitol. They sent copies of the Kelsey and Guild plan to the governor, legislators, and "all the civic leagues in South Carolina, urging the members . . . to use their influence . . . for the preservation of the

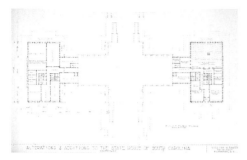

PLAN, W. BAKER, 1946. COURTESY OF THE
SOUTH CAROLINA ARCHIVES AND HISTORY
CENTER

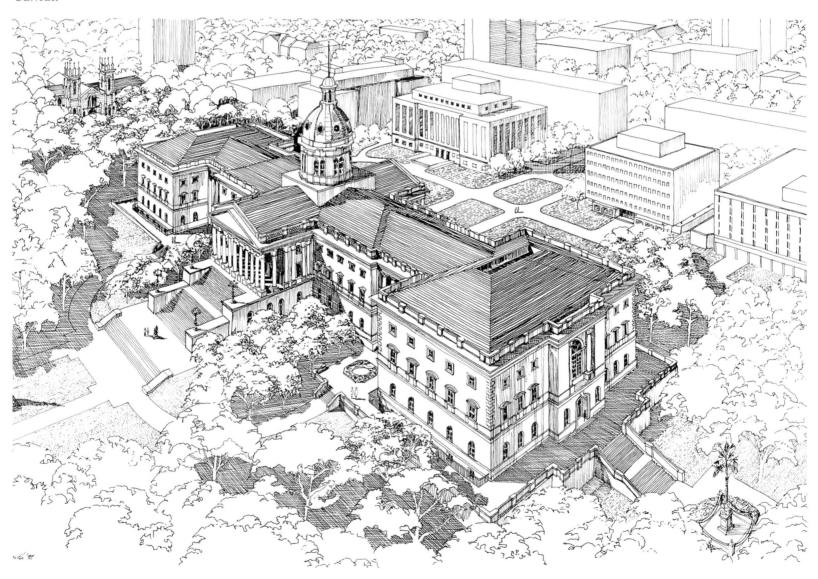

NORTH ELEVATION WITH PROPOSED WINGS, STEVENS AND WILKINSON, ARCHITECTS, 1992

capitol grounds."[36] The following year the Committee on State House and Grounds appointed a subcommittee to study the problem, and this subcommittee authorized A. W. Todd, architect, "to prepare plans to carry out the suggestions contained in the Message of His Excellency, the Governor."[37] Todd's plan (1911) was an outgrowth of C. C. Wilson's proposal. Like the earlier plans by Neilson and Wilson, Todd's plan produced a great deal of controversy, but no construction. (See pages 136–40.)

Albert Whitner Todd (1856–1924) was born in Anderson, South Carolina. He studied architecture by correspondence and practiced in Anderson and Augusta, Georgia, before moving to Charleston about 1899. He entered politics and represented Charleston in the South Carolina House of Representatives continuously, 1907 through 1914; he was reelected to the House for the 1921–1922 session and elected to the Senate 1923–1924. During his first stint in the House, he served on the Public Buildings Committee (1907–1912) and was its chairman during the 1911–1912 session.[38]

In his report to the House and Grounds Subcommittee (September 25, 1911), Todd proposed a $1,000,000 project rearranging the interior of the existing State House and adding substantial wings to the east and west. He also suggested "a new dome . . . in design and keeping with the dignity of the State Capitol." He criticized the "abominable toilet arrangements, which are not only a disgrace to a civilized community, but wholly inadequate" and called the "interior arrangement on the ground floor . . . a great big bluff, for there are a number of . . . offices that are badly lighted, ventilated and illy [*sic*] heated, and are only fit for storage of plunder. . . ." The wings Todd proposed were each 83 by 131 feet; they were to be connected to the existing building by a link 38 by 48 feet. Each of the new segments was to be three stories high with exteriors matching J. R. Niernsee's building. The east wing would house the Governor, Secretary of State, and Attorney General on the first floor, the Supreme Court on the second floor, and its library on the third floor. The west wing would house a variety of agencies and officials (Agricultural Commissioner, Insurance Commissioner, Bank Examiner, Historical Commission, Adjutant General, and Commissioner of Lands or Deeds) and legislative offices. Both wings were to have electric elevators, numerous bathrooms, and fireproof vaults adjacent the offices.[39]

The subcommittee endorsed the concept and so did the whole Committee on State House and Grounds. They authorized their secretary to sign a contract with Todd and directed the secretary "to formulate a bill to present to the next session." They granted Todd $900 to make a model and even provided him $1,000 to "visit as many of the members as possible, and use any means in his power to acquaint them of the contemplated work."[40] After getting off to a good start with the committees, Todd, like a short-winded sprinter in a long race, ran into nothing but trouble.

The Civic League lobbied energetically: "Let Capitol Alone Says Civic League" were the headlines when the League spoke against "the dreaded destruction of the symmetry and beauty of the present State House grounds."[41] The Ways and Means Committee recommended that the House reject the House and Grounds report and disallow a $13,500 payment to Todd. Lowndes J. Browning, Chairman of Ways and Means, said that the original charge—to explore ways to improve the entrances and bathrooms of the existing building—"affords no sufficient pretext for the enormous project of enlargement of the Capitol and dome. . . ."[42] Browning was incensed by the attempt to pay Todd $1,000 to "educate" legislators. On the floor he said "this is the first instance in American history where a subcommittee has attempted to appropriate State funds for influencing members of a general assembly. Speaking even plainer, the subcommittee has made an effort . . . to bribe and debauch the members . . . into adopting the plans. . . ."[43]

An investigation was launched by the House. Todd claimed the governor had approved everything verbally; the governor denied having done so. The Attorney General ruled that the subcommittee had exceeded its charge, and that Todd's contract was therefore invalid. The newspapers reveled in the controversy and pointed out "there is no evidence that any other architect was consulted." In the House and in the press the subcommittee was censured for having proceeded "with an absolute disregard of all methods of business procedure and without any effort to keep any proper record of their proceedings." Todd's claim was stricken out of the appropriation bill. The controversy completely overshadowed his design: its architectural merits were never seriously discussed.[44]

C. C. Wilson, who had proposed detached flanking buildings (and a plaster model) in 1908, published an illustrated version of his proposal in 1916. This time his report had been prepared for the House Commission on Extra Office Room. In 1916 the State was paying approximately $8,000 rent for office space in Columbia. (The Department of Agriculture and the Railroad Commission were in the Union National Bank Building; the State Board of Health, the Board of Charities, Tax Commission, Insurance Department, Game Warden, and Department of Corrections were in the Palmetto Building. The Warehouse Commissioner and bank examiner had no offices.) Placing office buildings on the university campus had been considered, but the Extra Office Room Commission ultimately endorsed Wilson's plan showing L-shaped, freestanding buildings east and west of the State House.

The buildings were designed to front on Sumter and Assembly Streets, and to "be of granite and of the same general character and design as the State House, with corresponding story heights and cornice line." The eastern building would house a state museum on the ground floor, and the departments of agriculture, commerce, and industries on the second and third floors. The western building would have offices on the first and second floors and the Supreme Court, on the third floor. The report noted the plan was developed "with profound reverence for the genius of Major Niernsee, the original designer of the State House, and with all possible regard for the preservation of the dignity and beauty of the building and the setting."[45]

C. C. Wilson's proposal may have been a casualty of the First World War; in any event, with public attention diverted to more pressing issues, it sank quietly into oblivion. The Wilson plan was significant only as one more example of the on-going unsuccessful attempts to add to the State House. Two more efforts to erect wings were made. In 1946, hoping to obtain federal funds, a joint legislative committee retained William W. Baker, an architect from Florence, South Carolina, to prepare "preliminary plans, estimates and the filing of applications. . . ." Assisted by James E. Hunter of Columbia, Baker did "a tentative layout to determine space requirements," made estimates and drew an elevation "so the General Assembly and the public can judge for themselves of the appearance of the building when completed." He estimated it would cost $3,500,000 to complete the State House by renovating the existing building, add wings, and erect "a new dome to replace the present dome which is ill- proportioned and often condemned as unsafe."[46] Federal funds were not obtained, and Baker's proposal, like C. C. Wilson's vision of flanking pavilions, survives only in the archives.

More recently (1995) at the outset of the most recent renovation, Stevens and Wilkinson, architects, suggested the advantages of wings. They pointed out that extensions would minimize the alteration of J. R. Niernsee's original plan, for necessary new mechanical systems and safety code requirements could be located in the new construction.[47] Concerns were expressed about cost and the integrity of the historic building and grounds, and once again the possibility of adding wings was rejected.

The idea of additions resurfaces persistently in part because it had been done at other state capitols and—most prominently—at the U.S. Capitol. To provide space for an expanding federal government, Thomas U. Walter, a Philadelphia architect, designed extensions in 1851 which were judged to be in harmony with the original design. Walter also enlarged the dome and made it more sculptural to visually balance the increased horizontal mass of the building.[48] Proponents of enlarging the South Carolina State House were inevitably aware of the federal precedent, but it was not a politically useful model to cite in South Carolina.

The State Office Building

By 1923 state agencies were using sixty-eight offices outside the State House and paying $29,000 per year for rent. This cost was cited as a major justification for the construction of South Carolina's first modern governmental office building. Begun in 1924, and dedicated January 5, 1927, the building is historically important in relation to the State House for several reasons. First, being located southeast of the capitol, it ended for twenty years all talk of adding wings to the State House. It also initiated a

STATE OFFICE (CALHOUN) BUILDING, H. TATUM, 1927. PHOTOGRAPH BY HUNTER CLARKSON, 1997

cluster of governmental buildings to the south. With formal facades facing both east and west the new building appeared for a moment to be the first step toward realization of the City Beautiful civic center as proposed by Kelsey and Guild. Finally, it is important to note that the State Office was removed from the State House architecturally and psychologically as well as physically, for the new building was designed like a large bank or insurance company. It expressed a twentieth-century view of bureaucracy rather than the ceremonial view of government embodied in J. R. Niernsee's design for the capitol.[49]

The Sinking Fund commissioners initiated the project in 1923 when they recommended an act be passed authorizing them to acquire a site and erect an office building to accommodate officials inadequately housed in the State House and those paying rent in commercial buildings in Columbia. To substantiate the need for a state-owned office, the commissioners obtained a report from George E. Lafaye, architect, of Columbia. Lafaye's report did not even address the visual character of the proposed building. Instead, he compared the per-square-foot cost of existing rented office space to the cost of new construction. He visited all state offices and found (January, 1924) that the state was renting 23,236 square feet throughout the city. The annual cost of space in fireproof buildings averaged $1.44 per square foot; overall, office rental was costing the state $1.20 per square foot per year. Comparing these rents to the cost of construction, Lafaye estimated a six-story, fireproof building with 58,173 square feet of space, including the cost of the land, could be obtained for $450,000 and concluded that by constructing its own building, the state would recoup the cost in fifteen years through a savings in rent.[50]

Accepting the logic of Lafaye's report, the legislature passed (February 29, 1924) the *Act to Authorize and Empower the Sinking Fund Commission of South Carolina to Acquire a Site and Erect a State Office Building*. In its initial form the Act allowed the commissioners to spend up to $500,000 for a site and fireproof office building, and they quickly received letters from twelve architects seeking the job. More South Carolinians competed for this commission than for any of the campaigns associated with the original State House. Their keen competition indicated the growth of the architectural profession during the prosperous early twentieth century.

Looking back to the turn of the century, C. C. Wilson recalled, "the architects of the State were widely scattered and little known to each other, and their relations were characterized by dislike, jealousy and distrust."[51] He had tried to cultivate a sense of professionalism by organizing the South Carolina Association of Architects in 1901. In 1912, with Wilson as president and thirty-four out of thirty-seven architects residing in the state attending, the association had adopted the constitution, bylaws, and professional standards of the American Institute of Architects (A.I.A.). The following year a state chapter of the American Institute of Architects was established with Wilson again serving as president. In 1917, largely through the efforts of A. W. Todd, the state had established a licensing board, and by 1924 there were forty-five registered architects in South Carolina, thirty-three of whom were members of the American Institute of Architects, the South Carolina Association of Architects, or both.

The officers of the state A.I.A. chapter, Albert Simons, Secretary Treasurer; Nat Gaillard Walker, Director; and J. D. Newcomer, President, met with the commissioners and requested a competition restricted to architects residing in the state and judged by a qualified outside expert. They suggested Warren Powers Laird, Dean of the School of Architecture, University of Pennsylvania, as a judge. They pointed out that a judge could serve as a disinterested advisor to the commission; that a competition would avoid any appearance of favoritism; and that the choices presented would ensure the best possible building. The commissioners thanked them, but decided to chose an architect themselves based on a series of interviews.[52]

James J. Baldwin and C. Gadsden Sayre from Anderson applied; so did Harold Tatum, J. Carroll Johnson, George Lafaye, and James B. Urquhart from Columbia. Hobart Upjohn of New York (then building the Trinity Church Parish Hall across Sumter Street) requested an interview, and Albert Ten Ecyk Brown, architect, of Atlanta, who had recently completed the Federal Land Bank in Columbia had seventeen letters sent to the commissioners to reinforce his application. Having designed fifteen banks, fifteen office buildings, seven courthouses, and four municipal buildings, Brown had more relevant experience than any of his competitors; nonetheless, he did not get the job. Nor did George Lafaye, who lobbied actively and emphasized his knowledge acquired through the survey of state agencies.[53] The surviving files do not indicate why, after voting eighteen times, the commissioners settled upon Harold Tatum (1887–1958).[54] It was his first major commission.

Tatum was born in Woodbury, New Jersey; studied architecture at the University of Pennsylvania; and for nine or ten years worked as a draftsman in Philadelphia before moving to Columbia in 1919. Between 1920 and 1923, he designed eight residences and one school (for Monarch Mills, Union, South Carolina).[55] Tatum's contract was signed on April 22, 1924. He proposed, and the commissioners ratified, Milton B. Medary of Philadelphia as consulting architect.[56] Medary's participation suggests a consciousness of the City Beautiful civic center ideal, for he was appointed by President Warren Harding to serve on the Commission of Fine Arts and by President Calvin Coolidge as a member of the National Capital Park and Planning Commission, both boards being charged with implementing the MacMillan Plan for Washington, D.C.

Preliminary plans were ready for the commissioners by June 6, 1924; during the initial examination of the drawings, "it was decided to provide quarters in the new building for the Supreme Court."[57] The court, then located in the State House, needed a larger courtroom, library, and offices. The Supreme Court was potentially a major tenant and accommodating it meant expanding the square footage projected by Lafaye. This decision made the original budget inadequate; it was only the first of many design changes, for even after construction began decisions were made to add and delete floors. Predictably, this on-again-off-again process produced upper stories which resemble a disjointed, off-center layer cake.

Anticipating problems with the budget ($500,000), the commissioners directed Tatum to prepare alternative designs for a four- and a five-story building. The revised plans were presented and approved in November, and bids were opened on December 22, 1924. Unfortunately, the low bid for the general contract was $608,000; to this initial cost the commissioners had to add bids for plumbing ($20,915), heating ($33,300), and elevators ($35,000). They negotiated with the low-bidding general contractor, George A. Fuller, "with a view of so eliminating and modifying the plan . . . as to bring the same within the amount advertised."[58] A major savings could be realized by eliminating the two top stories and minimizing the use of bronze and marble. Tatum was directed to alter the plans again.

During the summer work began on the scaled-down version, but the commissioners still hoped to erect a building capable of accommodating all the agencies listed by Lafaye plus the Supreme Court. They informed the legislature that they would save money by enlarging the new State Office Building during construction, thus avoiding the cost of on-going rents and the disruption that would be caused by any expansion after the building was occupied. The commissioners also pointed out that an enlarged office building could supply steam through an underground tunnel to heat the entire State House. The 1926–1927 legislature agreed and increased the appropriation by $300,000. Tatum was instructed to add two stories and develop plans for the heating plant and tunnel.[59]

As the building neared completion in the winter of 1927, the Supreme Court informed the commissioners that they had decided not to move out of the State House. The commissioners expressed regret, for they viewed the court as a desirable tenant and had spent some $30,000 customizing the entire fifth floor to the court's needs. Unable to compel the court to move, the commissioners had Tatum redesign the fifth floor into space suitable as offices for the State Bank Examiner.[60]

The new State Office Building was dedicated on January 5, 1927. The Sinking Fund Commissioners offices were on the first floor along with the offices of the Departments of Agriculture, Commerce and Industries, the Railroad Commission, and the Chief Game Warden. The Highway Department was located primarily on the second floor, but its motor vehicle division was on the ground floor, accessible to the public. The Tax Commission and the Department of Education shared the third floor, and the fourth floor housed the Warehouse Commissioner, the Board of Health, the Insurance Commissioner, and several of Clemson College's extension services, including the livestock sanitary department.[61]

The growth of government represented by the tenants of the new State Office Building accelerated during the decades following the Great Depression, and the area south of the State House (bounded by Pendelton, Senate, Sumter, and Assembly streets) was filled over the next half century by five more state office buildings.[62] These are uniformly gray, rectangular, and, except for isolated details on the Wade Hampton Building, without ornament. The twentieth-century state office buildings reflect an era that values efficiency rather than ceremony; they appropriately resemble elephantine filing cabinets. Their angular style shapes the landscape between them. Schwagerl's looping, curving walks have no place here. Remnants of the green mall envisioned by Kelsey and Guild survive; so too does the view from the south of J. R. Niernsee's State House, but seen through the frame of modern offices it is clearly a glimpse into another era.

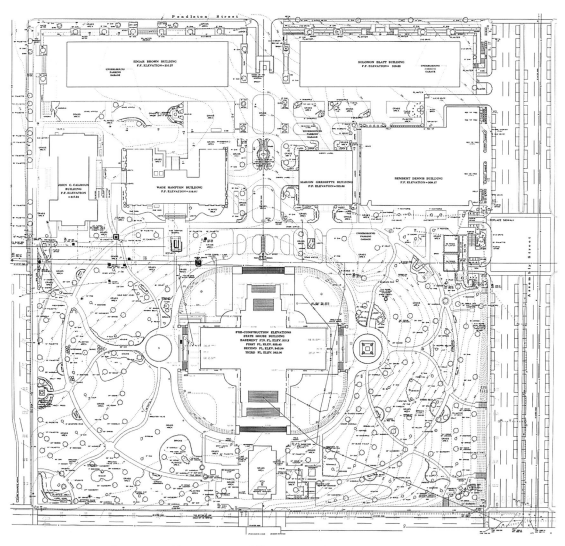

SITE PLAN, STEVENS AND WILKINSON, ARCHITECTS, CIRCA 1995

Chapter 6

The Renovation of 1992–1998

In several ways the creation of the State House reflects the values of the planters who dominated South Carolina prior to the Civil War. In 1854 Governor John L. Manning reoriented the plan to face north; John C. Calhoun's climactic address on state's rights occupied the place of honor beneath the cornerstone, and ornament was prepared to portray beliefs expressed in the speech. Association of the site with local and regional ideals has been reaffirmed periodically through symbolic sculpture, emblems, and a reverence for the original plan. It is important to remember, however, that locally significant symbols are embedded in a larger pattern which is distinctly national. For example, the design of the current State House is based upon a building type which developed in America following the Revolution; the major creators of the building, sculpture, and grounds were professionally established elsewhere before they came to South Carolina. Construction techniques also reflected national standards.

The Civil War dramatically affected both the design and construction of the State House. The unfinished exterior walls suffered only minor damage, but stockpiled materials were destroyed, and the state could not afford to finish the building as John R. Niernsee had planned. Work continued intermittently from 1868–1903, but changing standards of plumbing, heating, and fire protection combined with the growing need for legislative committee rooms and office space to make the State House seem increasingly inadequate. It is not surprising that expansions and additions were proposed in 1885, 1908, 1911, 1916, 1946, and 1995. The estimated cost and a loyalty to the historic exterior repeatedly prevented any major changes.

The State House was declared to be substantially completed in 1903, but throughout the twentieth century a series of interior changes have been made in an attempt to make the historic plan meet modern needs. The Senate was renovated in 1915. In 1937 J. Carroll Johnson and James E. Hunter redesigned the interior of the House. In 1959–1960 air conditioning was installed and the heating plant was modernized. The lobby was refurbished in 1962; the governor's office was redesigned in the west wing in 1966. Despite numerous projects, no thorough remodeling or renovation was attempted, and renovation was long overdue, for by 1990 critical parts of the building had simply worn out. The copper sheathing of the dome, for example, and the felt and flashing beneath the roofing slate had long passed their expected useful life and leaked badly. The mechanical systems, wiring, and plumbing, which had been installed, repaired, and added to for a century needed to be organized and brought up to date. Equally important, precisely because the building was historic, it did not meet modern, legally mandated standards concerning hazardous materials, fire safety, handicap accessibility, or seismic (earthquake) protection. In 1992, recognizing that virtually every part of the State House was affected by one or more of these problems, the legislative Committee on the State House commissioned Stevens and Wilkinson, Inc. Architects and Engineers, to conduct an analysis of the building as a whole.

Since 1941 the committee had been responsible for designating work to be done. For half a century they continued the tradition of addressing one problem at a time; consequently, the interior and its support systems evolved by accretion.[1] Throughout much of this period the roof and dome were an on-going source of concern; both leaked, and even worse, they presented an alarming fire hazard. In the 1950s Columbia's fire chief, A. McC. Marsh, actually condemned the attic and dome and identified numerous problems in the basement, corridors, the library, Supreme Court, and Governor's office. His 1957 report resulted in the installation of a sprinkler system in the attic, but most of the problems he pointed out were not addressed.[2] He could not close the building, for state law removed it from the jurisdiction of local fire, zoning, and building officials. This dubious protection was reinforced in 1976 when the State House was designated a National Landmark because landmarks are potentially exempt from portions of the National Fire Protection Association Life Safety Code, the Standard Building Code, and the Americans with Disabilities Act—the national standards relevant to life and safety issues in public buildings.

The committee wisely decided not to use historic status as an excuse to limit the work. Under the leadership of Senator Verne Smith and the advice of E. Cecil Mills, Manager of Construction and Planning for the state, they committed the project to the highest current standards in structural matters involving life and safety issues. By accepting national standards, the committee guaranteed that the renovation of 1995–1998 would be thorough.

The Stevens and Wilkinson analysis presented a daunting array of structural and functional problems.[3] It documented the need to replace the heating and air conditioning systems. Antiquated wiring, plumbing, and elevators needed renewal. Handicap access did not meet modern standards. Hazardous substances were identified including asbestos, lead in the water system, and radon in the basement. The fire alarm and sprinkler systems did not meet code requirements. Finally, the whole building fell short of earthquake safety provisions stipulated for public buildings by the Standard Building Code.

Prior to the architects' report, few people were conscious of serious structural deficiencies. Many, however, knew that the historic interior was poorly suited for modern office use. The spacious nineteenth-century lobby, open staircases, and wide halls took up forty-six percent of the 76,000 square foot interior. The Senate (4,452 square feet) and House (6,405 square feet) chambers deducted another fourteen percent. This left only 29,546 square feet for administrative and executive offices. The State House Committee wanted to make the building more functional as well as safer. They were also determined to respect the historic character of John R. Niernsee's design, and like others before them, they found these goals difficult to reconcile. New construction needed to meet life safety codes would consume 4,600 square feet of the interior, and much of this new work would necessarily be visible in the historic interior.

Stevens and Wilkinson—like the earlier architects C. C. Wilson, A. W. Todd, and W. Baker—recommended adding east and west wings. They also suggested developing rooms underground in the angles between the porticos and the facade. They pointed out that much of the construction needed to meet current codes could be located in the new areas; therefore, expansions would provide efficient office space while minimizing the impact on the historic building.

However, there was little legislative or public support for expansion, and the committee elected to restrict the work to renovation of the historic building. The architects estimated that this approach would cost $33 million dollars, take two years to complete, and result in 24,966 square feet of office space with the building adjacent the restored public spaces and legislative halls. In August, 1995, four bids were submitted by general contractors. These initial bids ranged from $43.6 to $46.4 million dollars due to a nationwide construction boom and the complexity of the seismic work. After a second round of bidding and negotiations, Caddell Construction of Montgomery, Alabama was retained as general contractor for $40,265,192.[4]

Approximately one-third of the construction cost was attributable to the decision to follow current seismic codes. Predictably, questions were immediately raised about the wisdom of spending money to earthquake proof the building, a decision which stemmed from the committee's determination to adhere to high national standards. The need for protection against earthquakes is assessed by the U.S. Geological Survey. After studying historic earthquakes and monitoring seismic activity, the Survey periodically publishes maps showing the likelihood and probable magnitude of earthquakes across the country. South Carolina is designated an area of moderate seismic activity, and the Survey suggests that within the next 100 years there is a 70 percent chance of another earthquake similar to the one which devastated Charleston in 1886.

Having examined the State House, Stevens and Wilkinson informed the committee that such an earthquake might cause a sudden, catastrophic collapse of the dome, roof, and floors. In addition to the geologic survey's assessment and the architects' evaluation, the committee knew that the intersection of the Woodstock and Ashley faults—the source of the 1886 earthquake—was not the only earthquake site in the state. On the contrary, prior to the beginning of scientific seismic monitoring in 1974, forty-eight additional earthquake sites were reported across South Carolina. The largest earthquake known to have originated in the Piedmont occurred in Union County in 1913. It is estimated to have been moderately severe—a category 7–8 event (on a scale of 10). The Union earthquake was felt in Columbia, as were tremors originating south of the Lake Murray dam in 1945 and another small earthquake centered in Bowman, fifty miles southeast of Columbia, in 1971.[5] These data prompted the committee to follow national guidelines promoting protection against sudden structural collapse in the event of an earthquake.

Preparations for the work began in 1994 with the renovation of assembly halls and office space in the Carolina Plaza, a nearby former hotel owned by the University of South Carolina. When the legislative session ended in June, 1995, occupants of the State House moved into their temporary quarters, and the asbestos abatement program and interior demolition began. By the following September the general contractor was on site orchestrating (on a typical day) 200 craftsmen representing many trades. (Thirty-two subcontractors ultimately participated in the project.) The work was scheduled to be completed in twenty-six months. Excavations for the seismic work began in the fall of 1995; simultaneously, on the upper floors, decorative details were encased for protection and the interior demolition got underway.[6]

The nature of the historic construction made protection against earthquakes a difficult task. As a first line of defense, a system known as base isolation was adopted. This entailed a series of precise excavations to permit a continuous reinforced concrete beam to be cast in place directly beneath the five–ten foot thick base of the granite walls. The new concrete beam rests upon 127 isolators, or shock absorbers, which in turn rest upon concrete pads, also cast in place. The isolators look like giant sandwiches, with steel plates for bread and heavy black rubber and lead cylinders for filling. They support the new concrete beam which ties the base of the walls together; the isolators can deflect up to eight inches to compensate for any movement of the earth beneath them. The base isolation system is designed to allow the building to move as a single unit in the event of an earthquake. In addition to the new foundation, the seismic protection included the installation of flexible connections for all the incoming new wiring and plumbing, reinforcing of the openings within the walls, strengthening the roof and dome against lateral movement, constructing a moat to allow the walls to move laterally, and reinforcing the floors and parapet.[7]

Artifacts were unearthed during the digging. Major finds included Civil War cannon balls, broken granite balusters, marble fragments, and a large wrought iron entrance door lock bearing evidence of fire—probably from the burned first State House. The excavations also uncovered things and conditions which delayed the work. First, the base of the walls proved to be thicker in places than had been anticipated; second, two historic wells were found beneath the foundations of the State House. These wells required archaeological examination and, because they were directly in the path of the seismic beams and footings, additional engineering; finally, soil beneath the east wall lacked the compressive strength required for the seismic footings. Encountering surprises was inevitable, for exploratory digging and probing had been impossible while the building was occupied.

Additional discoveries were made inside the building when added walls, ceilings, and floor coverings were stripped away. Interior walls adjacent the south portico were found to be out of vertical alignment from floor to floor; this caused laborious rerouting of wiring and ductwork. Defects in the original construction of the porticos required engineering adjustments. The north portico proved to be four inches out of square, and the slope of the roof of the south portico was found not to match the angle of its gable. As work progressed, it was found that the drum, or base, of the dome is not a true circle, and the new braces and exterior copper sheathing had to be custom fitted to its irregularities.

Most visitors will never see the structural improvements. Few people will be aware of the sophisticated wiring or alarm systems. However, everyone will notice the dramatic vaulted hallway in the east and west wings where additions have been removed. Restored marble floors in the lobby and Governor's office are impressive, as are the skylights in the lobby and marble walls on the first floor. These obvious renovations represent only a fraction—perhaps twenty-five percent—of the work. The ultimate success of the 1995–1998 renovation lies precisely in the fact that from foundation to dome the State House is in better condition and is more serviceable than ever, but it appears essentially unchanged.

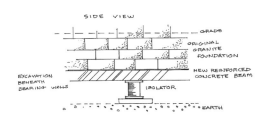

SEISMIC TREATMENT OF FOUNDATION, DRAWN BY JOHN M. BRYAN, 1997

EXCAVATION AND INSTALLATION OF SEISMIC BEAM AND ISOLATORS. PHOTOGRAPH BY ROB BRYAN, 1996

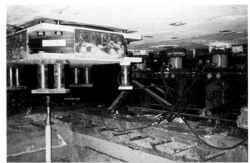

EXCAVATION AND INSTALLATION OF SEISMIC BEAM AND ISOLATORS. PHOTOGRAPH BY ROB BRYAN, 1996

EXCAVATION AND INSTALLATION OF SEISMIC BEAM AND ISOLATORS. PHOTOGRAPH ROB BRYAN, 1996

CIVIL WAR CANNON BALLS FOUND DURING EXCAVATIONS. PHOTOGRAPH BY HUNTER CLARKSON, 1997

FRAGMENT OF GRANITE BALUSTER FOUND DUR-ING EXCAVATION. PHOTOGRAPH BY HUNTER CLARKSON, 1997

FRAGMENT OF MARBLE ORNAMENT FOUND DURING EXCAVATION. PHOTOGRAPH BY HUNTER CLARKSON, 1997

Wrought-iron lock and key found during excavation. Photograph Hunter Clarkson, 1997

Interior during renovation, boxed ornament, first floor corridor. Photograph by Rob Bryan, 1996

157

INTERIOR DURING RENOVATION, HOUSE CHAMBER. PHOTOGRAPH BY ROB BRYAN, 1997

INTERIOR DURING RENOVATION, SENATE CHAMBER. PHOTOGRAPH BY ROB BRYAN, 1997

Restoration of dome. Photograph by Rob Bryan, 1997

Exterior view of finished dome. Photograph by Hunter Clarkson, 1997

State House lobby. Photograph by Hunter Clarkson, 1998

State House lobby from balcony. Photograph by Hunter Clarkson, 1998

163

HALLWAY. PHOTOGRAPH BY HUNTER CLARKSON, 1998

SENATE CHAMBER ROSTRUM WITH PAINTING BY ALBERT CAPERS GUERRY OF JOHN C. CALHOUN. PHOTOGRAPH BY HUNTER CLARKSON, 1998

PAGES 166–67: VIEW OF THE HOUSE CHAMBER. PHOTOGRAPH BY HUNTER CLARKSON, 1998
THIS PAGE: STATE HOUSE LIBRARY. PHOTOGRAPH BY HUNTER CLARKSON, 1998

CAPITOL LOBBY DOME. PHOTOGRAPH BY HUNTER CLARKSON, 1998

NORTH FACADE OF STATE HOUSE WITH CONFEDERATE MONUMENT. PHOTOGRAPH BY HUNTER CLARKSON, 1998

South facade of State House. Photograph by Hunter Clarkson, 1998

Oblique view of south facade. Photograph by Hunter Clarkson, 1998

South portico, east view. Photograph by Hunter Clarkson, 1998

Notes

Preface

1. *The State*, December 18, 1901.
2. *House Journal*, I (1938), 784, and (1962), 458, 962; *Senate Journal* (1956), 1184–85; *The State*, April 8, 1961.

Chapter One: A False Start

1. Helen Kohn Hennig, *William Harrison Scarborough, Portraitist and Miniaturist* (Columbia: R. L. Bryan, 1937), 118, entry number 228.
2. *Journal of the House of Representative of the State of South Carolina: Being the Annual Session of 1853* (Columbia: R. W. Gibbes, State Printers, 1853), 16–30.
3. For brief biographical sketches of J. L. Manning, see Robert Sobel and John Raimo, eds., *Biographical Directory of the Governors of the U.S., 1789–1978* (Westport, Conn.: Meckler Books, 1978), 4: 1408; also see the *National Cyclopedia of American Biography* (New York: James T. White, 1904), 7: 171.
4. David Duncan Wallace, *South Carolina, A Short History, 1520–1948* (Columbia: Univ. of South Carolina Press, 1969), 614, 703–7. Also see Helen Kohn Hennig, *Great South Carolinians of a Later Date* (Chapel Hill: Univ. of North Carolina Press, 1940–1949), 3–36, 245–68. J. L. Manning's father, Richard I. Manning, had served as governor (1824–1826), as had his mother's relatives, Burchell Richardson (1802–1804) and John P. Richardson (1840–1842), the father of Manning's young secretary, who himself would serve two terms as governor, 1886–1888 and 1888–1890. J. L. Manning's distant in-law, Wade Hampton, served two terms, 1876–1878 and 1878–1879, as did one of his nephews, Richard. I. Manning, who was governor 1915–1917 and 1917–1919.
5. Ralph Wooster, *South Carolina Historical Magazine* 55, no. 4 (October, 1954): 185–97.
6. Gene Waddell and Rhodri Windsor Liscombe, *Robert Mills's Courthouses and Jails* (Easley, S.C.: Southern Historical Press, 1981); also see John M. Bryan, ed., *Robert Mills, Architect* (Washington: American Institute of Architects, 1989).
7. Mills Lane, *Architecture of the Old South: South Carolina* (Savannah: Beehive Press, 1984), 198–203.
8. Ibid.; also see Kenneth Severens, *Charleston: Antebellum Architecture and Civic Destiny* (Knoxville: Univ. of Tennessee Press, 1988), 100–105; and Beatrice St. Julien Ravenel, *Architects of Charleston* (Charleston: Carolina Art Association, 1964), 177–81.
9. Minard Lafever, *Beauties of Modern Architecture* (New York: D. Appleton, 1839).

10. Transcriptions of "The Milford Papers" appear in the *Victorian Society Newsletter* 1974: 1–4, and are quoted by Lane, *Architecture of the Old South, South Carolina*, 200–203.

11. Examples of J. L. Manning's patronage are found in the Williams-Chesnut-Manning Papers, Box 7, 1845–1859, South Caroliniana Library, Univ. of South Carolina; see April 29, 1840, Henry Inman to JLM; December 14, 1841, Bishop Stephen Elliott to JLM; and July 23, 1843, J. A. Binda to JLM.

12. Arnold Blumberg, "The Strange Career of Joseph Binda," *South Carolina Historical Magazine* 67, no. 3 (July, 1966): 155–65.

13. Transcription of an undated letter by JLM in the collection of the Columbia Museum of Art, Columbia. The analysis by Professor Eric R. Varner, Emory University, of one of the Manning-Binda marbles, a copy of a cult image from the temple of Jupiter Optimus Maximus Capitolinus in Rome, is also an unpublished letter, October 7, 1992, in the files of the Columbia Museum of Art.

14. John Drayton, *A View of South Carolina* (Charleston: W. P. Young, 1802); also see Anna Wells Rutledge, *Artists in the Life of Charleston* (Columbia: Univ. of South Carolina Press, 1980), 127.

15. A. S. Salley, "Origin and Early Development," in Helen Kohn Hennig, *Columbia, Capital City of South Carolina, 1786–1936* (Columbia: R. L. Bryan, 1936), 1–12; Edwin L. Green, *A History of Richland County* (Columbia: R. L. Bryan, 1932), 146–66; and John Hammond Moore, *Columbia and Richland County, A South Carolina Community, 1740–1990* (Columbia: Univ. of South Carolina Press, 1993), 37–57.

16. Rosemarie Zagarri, "Representation and the Removal of State Capitals, 1776–1812," *Journal of American History* 71 (March, 1988): 1239–56.

17. Jos[eph] A. Hoskins, comp., *President Washington's Diaries, 1791–1799* (Greensboro, Tenn.: Golden Rule Press, 1921), 36.

18. Edwin L. Green, *A History of Richland County* (Columbia: R. L. Bryan, 1932), 153. Green may have relied upon Glenn Brown, *History of the U.S. Capitol* (Washington: Government Printing Office, 1900), 1: 94.

19. Ravenel, *Architects of Charleston,* 77. Also see Samuel Lapham in Walter Petty, ed., *Architectural Practice in South Carolina* (Columbia: S.C. AIA, 1963), 4.

20. Lane, *Architecture of the Old South,* 97.

21. Henry-Russell Hitchcock and William Seale, *Temples of Democracy* (New York: Harcourt Brace Jovanovich, 1976), 50–51.

22. GW to Commissioners of the District of Columbia, 8 June 1792, BLC 04474, Washington Papers, Univ. of Virginia

Gentlemen,

The bearer of this, Mr. James Hoban, was strongly recommended to me by Col. Laurens and several other gentlemen of South Carolina when I was there last year, as a person who had made architecture his study, and was well qualified, not only for planning or designing buildings, but to superintend the execution of them. He informs me that he intends to produce plans of the two buildings next month, agreeably to the advertisement of the Commissioners, and is now on his way to view the ground on which they are to stand. I have given him this letter of introduction in order that he might have an opportunity of communicating his views and wishes to you, or of obtaining any information necessary for completing the plans. But, as I have no knowledge of the man or his talents, further than the information which I received from the gentlemen in Carolina, you must consider this letter merely as a line of introduction, for the purposes mentioned.

With esteem and regards
I am Gentlemen,
your most obedt. Servant,
GWashington.

23. *Statutes at Large of South Carolina*, Acts, 751–52.

24. Edward Hooker, *Diary of Edward Hooker, 1805–1808* (Washington: Government Printing Office, 1897), 853, and are quoted by Lane, *Architecture of the Old South*, 200–203.

25. *American Beacon and Commercial Diary* (Norfolk, Va.), May 29, 1816.

26. Edwin J. Scott, *Random Recollections of a Long Life, 1806–1874* (Columbia: Charles A. Calvo, 1884), 39–40.

27. SCDAH, GA, 10 6 869, December 3, 1803.

28. SCDAH, GA, 10 4 1833, Committee Report, December 10, 1833.

29. *Charleston Morning Post and Daily Advertiser*, March 3, 1786.

30. David Kohn, ed., *Internal Improvement in South Carolina, 1817–1828* (Washington: Privately printed, 1938), 5.

31. Ibid., 34.

32. Robert Mills, "Autobiography," 12 pp., D. Microfilm Papers of Robert Mills, Smithsonian Institution; Bryan, *Robert Mills, Architect,* 182. In 1810 Mills had unsuccessfully submitted a proposal for the State Capitol in Harrisburg, Pa. These two unrealized plans for state capitols foreshadow his later concentration upon governmental buildings.

33. "Report of the Board of Public Works on Fire proof offices connected with a future State house." GA Papers 10 17 n.d. 117. SCDAH. Although the document is undated, it is signed by Herbemont as president of the Board, an office he held only in 1822. Since he died in 1836, the drawings he describes clearly antedate the Lopez or Hammarskold plans, 1844 and 1851 respectively, discussed below.

34. Bryan, *Robert Mills, Architect,* 28. Nicholas Michel Laurent Herbemont tutored French at South Carolina College, c. 1805–1817, and had a local reputation as a vintner and horticulturalist. See Hollis, 1: 43, 48; *The State,* March 2, 1924; Green, *A History of Richland County,* 311.

35. Kohn, *Internal Improvement in South Carolina,* 108.

36. *Reports and Resolutions of the General Assembly of South Carolina, 1842* (Columbia: A. H. Pemberton, 1843), 103–4.

37. *Journal of the House of Representatives of the State Of South Carolina, 1846* (Columbia: Summer & Carroll, 1846), 32.

38. SCDAH, GA, 10 4 1848, Committee Report, December 14, 1848.

39. *Reports and Resolutions of the General Assembly of South Carolina, 1848* (Columbia: I. C. Morgan, 1848), 201–2.

40. SCDAH, GA, 10 4 1849, Committee Report, December 11, 1849.

41. *Charleston Daily Courier,* August 18, 1847, quoted by Ravenel, *Architects of Charleston,* 77.

42. SCDAH, GA, Misc. Communications 10 17 1844 16, November 27, 1844. Lopez was later General Superintendent of State Works. See MS Collection, South Caroliniana Library, University of South Carolina, Lopez to Jas.* Tupper, March 9, 1863. For information on Lopez, see Lane, *Architecture of the Old South,* 100, 204; Ravenel, *Architects of Charles-*

ton, 157, 218, 225; and Gene Waddell, "An Architectural History of Kahal Kadosh Beth Elohim, Charleston," *South Carolina Historical Magazine* 98, no. 1 (January, 1997): 24, n. 28, 58. Lopez was a member and the builder of the synagogue which "initiated Reform Judaism in the United States." Waddell, 6.

43. *Daily South Carolinian,* October 17, 31, 1844.

44. *Journal of the House of Representatives, 1846* (Columbia: Summer & Carroll, 1846), 32.

45. *Reports and Resolutions of the General Assembly, 1850* (Columbia: I. C. Morgan, 1850), 157–58.

46. SCDAH, GA, Committee Report 10 4 1851 143, December 15, 1851 and Misc. Communications GA 10 17 1852 23.

47. *Charleston Daily Courier,* August 26, 1851.

48. U.S. District Court, Charleston, S.C., Journal, Book 6, 1849–1860, Petition for Citizenship, 7.

49. For a brief biographical sketch of Hammarskold, see Ravenel, *Architects of Charleston,* 241–43.

50. SCDAH, GA, Committee Report 10 4 1851 143, December 15, 1851; *Charleston Daily Courier,* January 15, 1852.

51. *Charleston Daily Courier,* March 24, 1853.

52. Broadus Mitchell, *William Gregg: Factory Master of the Old South* (Chapel Hill: Univ. of North Carolina Press, 1928), 42–55; Ernest McPherson Landes, *The Textile Industry in Antebellum South Carolina* (Baton Rouge: Louisiana State Univ. Press, 1969), 54–62. Mr. Billy Brewer, forester, and Mr. Ira E. Coward, engineer, Avondale Mills, interviews and tour, December, 1997.

53. SCDAH, GA, 10 4 1854 72, Committee Report, December 21, 1854.

54. SCDAH, GA, 10 17 1852 23, Misc. Communications.

55. *Charleston Daily Courier,* December 19, 1853.

56. Ibid.

57. SCDAH, GA, 104 1853 145, December 16, 1853.

58. *The Daily South Carolinian,* January 30, 1854.

59. Ibid., January 5 and 19, 1854.

60. *Daily South Carolinian,* April 9, 1854. Hammarskold claimed to have directed the relocation (SCDAH, GA, 10 3 1854 72, Petitions, December 6, 1854). The 1854–1855 legislative session opened in the relocated building on November 28, 1854. *Journal of the House of Representatives, 1854,* 20.

61. SCDAH, GA, 10 3 1854 72, Petition, December 6, 1854. Little is known about Hammarskold's life or work following his dismissal. In 1859 and 1860 he advertised as an architect, surveyor, and engineer in Memphis, Tenn. Tanner, Halpin & Co., *Memphis City Directory, 1859,* 91; *Williams' Memphis Directory,* 1 (1860): 183; *John L. Mitchell's Tennessee State Gazetteer and Business Directory (1860–1861),* no. 1: 85). He died of pneumonia at the age of 43 on February 16, 1861, in Shelby County, Tenn. *Shelby Co., Tenn. Vital Records. Register of Deaths, 1860–1875,* Tennessee State Library and Archives.

62. George E. Walker, *Exposition of the Proceedings of Commissioners of the New State Capitol* (Columbia: R. M. Stokes, n.d.), 7.

63. Emma Josephine Niernsee, "Recollections for her Grandchildren," an irregularly paginated manuscript, Maryland Historical Society, MS 2 45 7, 3.

64. For brief biographies of Niernsee see Francis W. Kervick, *Architects in America of Catholic Tradition* (Rutland: Charles E. Tuttle, 1962), 102; H. F. and E. R. Withey, *Biographical Dictionary of American Architects (Deceased)* (Los Angeles: Hennessey & Ingalls, 1970), 442. Withey gives 1831 as Niernsee's date of birth.

65. Kenneth Hafertepe, *America's Castle* (Washington, D.C.: Smithsonian Press, 1984), 107.

66. SCDAH, GA, 10 17 1854 62, Misc. Communications, June 19, 1854; also see "the Joint Report of Messres. Niernsee & Kay," June 19, 1854, Papers of John L. Manning, from the Chesnut-Miller-Manning Papers, South Carolina Historical Society.

67. *The Daily South Carolinian*, June 21, 24, July 1, 12, 22, and August 2, 1854.

68. SCDAH, GA, 10 3 1854 70, Petition, 1854.

69. Kenneth Severens, *Charleston: Antebellum Architecture and Civic Destiny* (Knoxville: Univ. of Tennessee Press, 1988), 167–76.

70. For a brief biography of Walker see Ravenel, *Architects of Charleston*, 244–48. White had applied for the job of consulting architect at the State House, but withdrew when he learned Niernsee already had been appointed.

71. Papers of George Edward Walker, microfilm, Univ. of South Carolina, South Caroliniana Library, August 4–November 11, 1854.

72. Ibid., August 5, 1854.

73. Ibid., August 12, 13, 1854.

74. Ibid., August 31, September 1, 1854.

75. Ibid., August 21, 1854.

76. Ibid., 18.

77. SCDAH, GA, 10 4 1854 72, Committee Report, December 21, 1854.

78. Ibid.

79. Ibid. These quotations are taken from Walker's final report, December 8, 1854.

80. Walker, *Exposition*, 16.

81. Ibid., 17.

82. Ibid.

83. *Journal of the House of Representatives, 1854*, 19–20.

84. Walker, *Proceedings*, 21.

85. Ibid., 21–23.

86. Ibid.

87. Ibid., 25.

88. Ibid., 40, 26

89. Ibid., 28. "A digression to mention especially the connection of Prof. McCoy [sic] with the board may be of interest. He was probably selected as particularly suited for the position from his knowledge of mathematics and of the principles of architecture, wherein he was of great assistance, no doubt, to the lay members of the commission. But candor compels one relating history to state that on account of his unfortunate manners and disposition the professor was the main cause of much of the dissensions that crept into the counsels of those in charge of the State's business. . . . It may be mentioned, in way of corroboration of this view, that Prof. McCoy secured through his ambition the position of president of the college . . . in a short while so stirring up ill feeling among the faculty and insubordination among the students . . . whereby the institution became much weakened in public estimation and suffered irreparable harm. The matter was not settled until the trustees received the resignation of the entire staff of professors, and reorganized the faculty with the same corps of officers, President McCoy being the sole exception." *The State*, January 13, 1901.

90. Walker, *Proceedings*, 28–29.

91. Ibid., 32–33.

92. Ibid., 36.

93. Ibid., 37.

94. Ibid., 38.

95. Commissioners of the New State House . . . Changes Made in the Building Plans. n.d. [c. November, 1855] Misc. Communication. 0010 017 n.d. 00 00344 00. SCDAH.

96. Ibid.; also see *Daily South Carolinian,* September 10, 1855.

97. Walker, *Proceedings,* 38.

98. Ibid., 30–31.

99. Ibid., 42.

100. Ibid., 49–50.

Chapter Two: Getting Started

1. SCDAH, GA, 10 4 1854 73, Committee Report, 1854.

2. For petitions by Daly see SCDAH, GA, 10 3 1854 175, Petition, and 10 4 1855 14Z, Committee Report. For McCulloch see SCDAH, GA, 10 3 1854 70, Petition, and 10 4 n.d. [c. 1856] 2667, Committee Report; also see 10 4 1857 80, Committee Report; 10 4 1859 4, Committee Report, and 10 16 1857 17, Resolution.

3. SCDAH, GA, 10 16 n.d. 509, Resolution, c. 1856. Also see GA 10 16 1855 9, Resolution, December 5, 1855; and GA 10 16 1855 10, Resolution, December 17, 1855. Commissioners of the New State House . . . Changes Made in the Building Plans. n.d. Misc. Communication. 0010 017 n.d. 00 00344 00. SCDAH.

4. SCDAH, GA, 10 4 n.d. 2378, Committee Report.

5. John A. Chapman, *History of Edgefield County* (Newberry: n.p., 1897), 54; also see M. M. Cohen, *Notices of Florida and the Campaigns* (Gainesville: Univ. of Florida Press, 1964), 140–48; anon., *Sketches of the Seminole War* (Charleston: Dan[iel] J. Dowling, 1836), 114–15; and the *South Carolina Historical Magazine* 48 (January, 1947): 86; and 59 (1958): 96–112. For Jones's role at Vaucluse and Graniteville, see Broadus Mitchell, *William Gregg* (Chapel Hill: Univ. of North Carolina Press, 1928), 14, 40, 245.

6. James Jones, *Letter Book, 1855–1861,* South Caroliniana Library, JJ to JRN, February 6, 1856.

7. JRN, *Journal of J. R. Niernsee, c. 1851–1856,* MS 2 45 7, Manuscripts Division, Maryland Historical Society.

8. Ralph W. Chalfant, "Building List: Niernsee and Neilson, Architects of Baltimore," typescript, American Institute of Architects Archives, Record Group 804.

9. BHL to JRN, August 15, 1839, Manuscripts Division, Maryland Historical Society, MS 2457.

10. JRN, *Continuation of My Diary from May 1st, 1838 till–,* trans. E. Albrecht, VF, Manuscripts Division, Maryland Historical Society.

11. J. F. Williams, *Old and New Columbia* (Columbia: Epworth Orphanage Press, 1929), 75.

12. Ibid., 44.

13. SCDAH, Report of the Commissioner of New State House, November, 1856.

14. Ibid., 105.

15. Ibid., 169.

16. MS Population Schedules for Richland District, South Carolina, U.S. Federal Census, 1860.

17. SCDAH, GA, 10 17 1856 2, Misc. Communications, December 16, 1856.

18. Williams, 41.

19. Report of the Commissioner of the New State House, November, 1856, 170–71.

20. Henry-Russell Hitchcock and William Seale, *Temples of Democracy: The State Capitols of the USA* (New York: Harcourt Brace Jovanovich, 1976), 76.

21. Ibid., 65–67, 93–96.

22. Ibid., 112–33, from State House Commissioners, *Report* (Columbia: December 28, 1839).

23. *South Carolina Reports and Resolution, 1868–1900,* Estimates for Completion of the State Capitol, 1884, 1: 819–35, roll 13, frame 424–32.

24. Agnes Gilchrist, *William Strickland, Architect and Engineer, 1788–1854* (New York: Da Capo, 1969), 106–12; Hitchcock and Seale, 114–17.

25. *Journal of the House of Representatives, 1854,* 19–20.

26. SCDAH, GA, 10 4 n.d. 5890, Committee Report, and 10 3 n.d. 5692, Petitions, c. 1836.

27. J. F. Williams, *Old and New Columbia,* 25; E. J. Scott, *Random Recollections,* 41; E. T. H. Shaffer, *Carolina Gardens* (Chapel Hill: Univ. of North Carolina Press, 1939), 212.

28. *Daily South Carolinian,* April 29, 1853 and December 29, 1853.

29. SCDAH, GA, 10 4 1845 187, Committee Report, December 8, 1846; SCDAH, GA, 10 3 1854 132, Petition, November 27, 1854.

30. *Daily South Carolinian,* April 29, 1853 and December 29, 1853. In the census of 1850 Russell was listed as being 58 years old and living with Sarah, 36; Mary, 11; James, 9; Zephrona, 7; Jeroline, 5; and Peter S., 2. *Seventh Census of the US, 1850,* Nat. Archives, Microcopy 432, roll 858, City of Columbia, Richland District, 45.

31. Commissioners of the Fire Proof Building to C. Werner, c. 1853; ibid., June 23, 1852–October 19, 1853, both South Caroliniana Library, MS P 10509. The other two German iron workers were J. A. W. Iusit and Frederick Julius Ortmann; see Alston Deas, *Early Ironwork of Charleston* (Columbia: Bostick & Thornley, 1941), 30–31.

32. Wylma Anne Wates, *A Flag Worthy of Your State and People: The History of the South Carolina State Flag* (Columbia: SCDAH, 1990), 8.

33. *Journal of the House of Representatives . . . 1851* (Columbia: State Printer, 1851), 18–19.

34. SCDAH, GA, 10 16 1856 61, Resolution, November 9, 1856; ibid., 10 4 1856 286, Committee Report, December 13, 1856; ibid., 10 16 n.d. 943, Resolution, c. 1856; and ibid., 10 16 n.d. 525, Resolution, c. 1858.

35. Ibid., 10 4 1858 292, Committee Report, December 8, 1858.

36. Annual Report of the Commissioner of the New State House, 1859, 125–26.

37. *James Jones Letter Book, 1855–1861,* South Caroliniana Library, March 2, 1857; December 3, 1857; December 28, 1857; December 31, 1857; December 28, 1858; and February 22, 1859.

38. Anne King Gregorie, ed., "Micajah Adolphus Clark's Visit to South Carolina in 1857," *South Carolina Historical Magazine* 54, no. 1 (January, 1953): 17.

39. Annual Report of the Commissioner of the New State House . . . 1862, 153–54.

40. Facts and figures in the following review of construction, 1857–1863, are found in the Annual Report of the Commissioner of the New State House and the annually appended Architect's Report. SCDAH.

41. *Annual . . . Architect's Report, 1857,* 7.

42. *Columbia Daily Register,* November 29, 1896.

43. Ibid., 1859, 132. Using the tram line, Niernsee figured that the twenty-six ton columns cost $412 apiece delivered to the site.

44. Ibid., 1860, 226; also see 1862, 153.

45. Some of the decorative stone carving was done in Baltimore, probably in the shop of

Sisson. George A. Frederick, a Baltimore architect, writing his memoirs "recalls the large temporary stone cutters sheds on the W. side of North, between Center and Monument Streets, where now stands one of the largest of the N.C.R. freight depots, where all the heavy interior marble work for the State Capitol of South Carolina, at Columbia, was prepared and where he oft with eager attention, watched the skillful carvers at their artistic labors on the Corinthian caps and column shafts." "Recollections of George A. Frederick," October 10, 1912. Typescript, Vertical File, Maryland Historical Society, 13.

46. Annual Report of the Commissioner of the New State House, 1860, 226.

47. Ibid.

48. Vertical Files, Archives of American Art, Smithsonian Institution. John F. Kensett of New York and James R. Lambdin of Philadelphia served with Brown on the commission.

49. Charles Sumner, *Art in the National Capitol, Speech in the Senate of the US, July 17, 1866* (Boston: Wright & Potter, 1866), 8. For brief biographical sketches of Brown, see Milton Rugoff, ed., *Encyclopedia of American Art* (New York: E. P. Dutton, 1981), 88; George C. Groce and David H. Wallace, *New York Historical Society's Dictionary of American Artists* (New Haven: Yale Univ. Press, 1957), 86; and Matthew Baigell, *Dictionary of American Art* (New York: Harper & Row, 1979), 51.

50. HKB to Lydia, November 7, 1856, Henry Kirke Brown Papers, reel 1.

51. Ibid.

52. *Daily Journal,* Newburgh, New York, August 2, 1886. Henry Kirke Brown Papers, Archives of American Art, Smithsonian Institution, Microfilm reel 2771.

53. Ibid.

54. Kirk Savage, *Standing Soldiers, Kneeling Slaves* (Princeton: Princeton Univ. Press, 1997), 16.

55. Ibid., 32–35.

56. HKB to Morris, January 27, 1856, Henry Kirke Brown Papers, reel 1.

57. Ibid. The soldiers mentioned here do not appear in the only known photograph of the model.

58. HKB to Morris, November 27, 1856, Henry Kirke Brown Papers, reel 1.

59. Anon., *Graham's Magazine* (April, 1854), 428.

60. Henry K. Bush-Brown Papers, the Library of Congress; the letter is transcribed in an unpublished manuscript entitled "Henry Kirke Brown: The Father of American Sculpture," 5: 1270–72; cited hereafter as Bush-Brown. For Brown's arrival in Columbia, also see "Brown, H. K., sculptor, bds nw cor Richardson and Pendleton," Julian A. Selby, *Columbia Directory* (Columbia: R. W. Gibbes, 1860), 9. Brown is not listed in the 1859 directory.

61. JMM to MEM, February 20, 1861, Univ. of South Carolina, South Caroliniana Library.

62. Bush-Brown, 5: 1289–91; HKB to Mr. Maynard, May 13, 1860.

63. Ibid., 1368–69.

64. Ibid., 1363.

65. *Home Journal,* March 15, 1876, a clipping found in Henry Kirke Brown Papers, reel 2771: "Just before our civil war, Mr. Brown was engaged in ornamenting, from his own design, in marble, the State House at Columbia, S.C." Also see JRN to HKB, April 2, 1859, Bush-Brown, 1268. Niernsee, writing Brown about the medallions of Hayne and McDuffie (discussed below), added, "I much desire to consult you for some more extensive sculpture for the Tympanum of the northern Portico, which may be not only a very large work—but also more worthy of your chisel."

66. The statue of Washington is one of six casts taken from the original made by Jean Antoine Houdon (1741–1828) for Virginia. The South Carolina legislature approved the purchase on December 20, 1858. *The State,* November 25, 1906 and March 20, 1936;

Christie Zimmerman Fant, *The State House of South Carolina, an Illustrated Historic Guide* (Columbia: R. L. Bryan, 1970), 116–18.

67. The Christian hope rationalization is concisely expressed by Robert W. Shand (1840–1915), in "Incidents in the Life of a Private Soldier in the War Waged by the United States Against the Confederate States," MS vol. bd., 1908–1909, Papers of R. W. Shand, Univ. of South Carolina, South Caroliniana Library: "I once thought that slavery was ordained by God in perpetuity; that a dissolution of the Union between North and South was inevitable and desirable; that the Southern States could not prosper if indeed they could exist, with the Negroes emancipated. I now think that Negroes were brought from Africa to this country (the only part of the world into which they could have been brought in large numbers,) by Divine Decree to be here held in slavery until sufficiently advanced in civilization and Christianity to be changed into freedmen; then to remain here until they had thrown off the habits of slavery and acquired the knowledge of liberty and its restraints, and to go gradually back to Africa for the betterment of their race there. . . ." Shand, 5.

68. John C. Calhoun, "On the Slavery Question, delivered in the Senate, March 4, 1850," Richard K. Crallé , ed., *The Works of John C. Calhoun,* 6 vols. (New York: Appleton, 1883), 6: 542.

69. Papers of George E. Walker, Architect's Diary, October 14, 1854, South Caroliniana Library.

70. *Charleston Daily Courier,* June 11, 1856.

71. Ibid.

72. Brown's model and the unfinished work was destroyed in the fire of February 17, 1865.

73. David C. Roller and Robert W. Twyman, eds., *Encyclopedia of Southern History* (Baton Rouge: Louisana State Univ. Press, 1979), 584, 786.

74. Bush-Brown, 1268, 1272A, 1272B and especially 1373, where it is noted that the presence of the stars "tends to sustain the hypothesis, that the building was intended for the Capitol of the Confederacy, then hopefully (to the builders) looming on the political horizon."

75. The HKB party received a South Carolina passport "to travel through on their way to Washington without molestation," see Bush-Brown, 1333–34.

76. Henry Kirke Brown Papers, reel 2771.

77. JJ to Governor Pickens, April 28, 1861, *James Jones Letter Book, 1855–1861.* South Caroliniana Library. Also see SCDAH, GA, 10 4 n.d. 1344, Committee Report; 10 4 1861 13, Committee Report, December 21, 1861; and 10 16 n.d. 733, Resolution, c. 1862.

78. SCDAH, Annual Report of the Commissioner of the New State House, for the Year 1861, 169–72.

79. SCDAH, Annual Report of the Commissioner of the New State House, for the Year 1862, 162.

80. Emma Josephine Niernsee, "Recollections for Her Grandchildren," Maryland Historical Society, MS 2 45 7, 13.

81. Unless noted otherwise, information concerning JRN's work as a military engineer is based upon dated entries in JRN, untitled, unpaginated MSS journal, c. 1862–1863, Maryland Historical Society, MS 2 45 7. JRN was appointed Major of Engineers "in the State service" on October 29, 1862. See Charles E. Cauthen, ed., *Journals of the South Carolina Executive Councils of 1861 and 1862* (Columbia: S.C. Archive, 1956), 281.

82. George E. Walker also worked as a military engineer. He was responsible for planning and directing the construction of Battery Bee in Charleston Harbor; worked on fortifications in Mobile; and sickened and died (September 9, 1863) while serving as Captain of Engineers, CSA, in Columbus, Georgia. *Charleston Daily Courier,* September 19, 1863; and *Charleston Mercury,* September 22, 1863. For JRN's report on the river surveys see Gov. Milledge L. Bonham Papers, Letters Received, Box 1, Folder 15, SCDAH; also see P. G. T.

Beauregard to M. L. Bonham, June 25, 1863. *War of the Rebellion: A Compilation of the Official Records of the Union and Confederate Armies* (Ann Arbor: Edwards Brothers, 1890; reprint, 1985), series 1, 28: pt. 2. Correspondence, 163, and P. G. T. Beauregard to James Chesnut, November 10, 1862; ibid., series 1, 14: 673–74.

83. William Dougherty to the Committee on State House and Grounds, SCDAH, GA, 10 17 1861 15, Misc. Communication, December 20, 1861.

84. SCDAH, Annual Report of the Acting Commissioner and Architect of the New State House for the Fiscal Year 1863, 109–10; 114.

85. *Columbia Tri-Weekly South Carolinian*, August 18, 1864, quoted by Marion Brunson Lucas, *Sherman and the Burning of Columbia* (College Station: Texas A&M Press, 1976), 29.

86. J. F. Williams, *Old and New Columbia*, 46, 47.

87. Ibid., 107; also see Lucas, *Sherman and the Burning of Columbia*, 22–29.

88. A. R. [Anna Wells Rutledge], "Statues' Curious History," *Charleston News and Courier*, March 29, 1942.

89. Lucas, *Sherman and the Burning of Columbia*, 29. See Lucas, 30–50, for a concise recapitulation of the fall of Columbia. For the storage of records from Charleston, see SCDAH, GA, 10 16 n.d. 1245, Resolution; and 10 16 1862 13, Resolution, December 16, 1862; and 10 4 1863 93, Committee Report, December 17, 1863.

90. J. F. Williams, *Old and New Columbia*, 44.

91. Lucas, *Sherman and the Burning of Columbia*, 30.

92. Keith E. Davis, *George N. Barnard, Photographer of Sherman's Campaign* (Kansas City: Hallmark Cards, 1990), 63–94. Also see *Photographic Views of Sherman's Campaign* published by Barnard and republished by Dover, 1977, edited by Beaumont Newhall.

93. Mary Boykin Chesnut, *A Diary from Dixie*, ed. Ben Ames Williams, (Boston: Houghton Mifflin, 1949), 488; or C. Vann Woodward, ed., *Mary Chesnut's Civil War* (New Haven: Yale Univ. Press, 1981), 680, 694.

94. Chestnut, 456–57.

95. Chestnut, 465–66.

96. Marli F. Weiner, ed., *Heritage of Woe: The Civil War Diary of Grace Brown Elmore, 1861–1868* (Athens: Univ. of Georgia Press, 1997), 88–89. Also see Moore, *Columbia and Richland County*, 198–200.

97. *The Daily South Carolinian*, January 18, 1865; also see ibid., January 1, 17, 19, and 20, 1865; and SCDAH, GA, 10 16 1864 7, Resolution, December 8, 1864.

98. *War of the Rebellion: A Compilation of the Official Records of the Union and Confederate Armies*, series 1, 44: 797, quoted by Lucas, *Sherman and the Burning of Columbia*, 30–31.

99. JRN to AGM, April 20, 1865, photostatic copy. South Caroliniana Library. This appears to be the only surviving detailed account of the defensive perimeter and of Niernsee's role in that work.

100. Ibid. Andrew Gordon Magrath Papers, 1864–1865, Letter Book, 1: 52, AGM to JRN, December 20, 1864, microfilm roll 1, SCDAH.

101. Ibid.

102. Ibid.

103. Lucas, *Sherman and the Burning of Columbia*, 36.

104. JRN to AGM, April 20, 1865.

105. Ibid.

106. Ibid.

107. J. F. Williams, *Old and New Columbia*, 121–22.

108. Emma Josephine Niernsee, "Recollections for her Grandchildren," Maryland Historical Society, MS 2 45 7. Pagination is irregular as extra pages have been inserted. The narrative concerning the fall of Columbia begins on "extra page 13/2."

Chapter Three: The Hiatus

1. E. P. Burton, *Diary of E. P. Burton* (Des Moines: Historical Records Survey, Works Progress Administration, 1939), 62–63.

2. Fenwick Y. Hedley, *Marching Through Georgia* (Chicago: Donahue, Henneberry, 1890), 365–66. Hedley's description is clearly subjective and may be apocryphal, for it is not confirmed by other sources.

3. Melvin Grigsby, *The Smoked Yank* (privately printed, 1888), 235–36.

4. Wilfred W. Black, ed., "Marching Through South Carolina: Another Civil War Letter of Lieutenant George M. Wise," *Ohio Historical Quarterly* 66 (April, 1957): 192.

5. Hedley, 380–81.

6. Shelby Foote, *The Civil War, A Narrative* (New York: Vintage, 1986), 3: 794; Lucas, *Sherman and the Burning of Columbia,* 127–28.

7. The inscriptions and bronze stars concerning the shelling were authorized in 1937 and 1938. See the *Journal of the House of Representatives, First Session of the 82nd General Assembly* (Columbia: Joint Committee on Printing, 1937), 578, and *Second Session, 1938,* 358.

8. SCDAH, Annual Report of the Commissioner and Architect of the New State House, 1865. James Jones "died at Graniteville So. Ca. Oct. 19, 1865. Apoplexy." Brent Holcomb, *Record of Deaths in Columbia S.C. and Elsewhere as Recorded by John Glass 1859–1877* (privately printed, 1986), 72.

9. SCDAH, Annual Report of the Commissioner and Architect of the New State House, 1865.

10. Ibid.

11. Ibid.

12. Ibid.

13. On October 25, 1865 the session opened in Longstreet (then called Carolina Hall) with the House upstairs and the Senate in the basement; shortly thereafter, the House moved to the Clariosophic Hall and the Senate began meeting in the South Caroliniana Library. Daniel W. Hollis, *University of South Carolina,* vol. 2, *College to University* (Columbia: Univ. of South Carolina Press, 1956), 8–9.

14. *Acts of the General Assembly, Regular Session, 1866* (Columbia: F. G. de Fontaine, 1866), iv.

15. Conversations with Robert Stockton and Daisy Mullett-Smith, January, 1997.

16. SCDAH, Gov. James L. Orr Papers, Letters Received, Box 1, JRN to JLO, February 9, 1866. The state cleared its account with Niernsee by paying him $3000 on January 1, 1866, SCDAH, *Ledger.*

17. Emma Niernsee, 23; Chalfant, "Building List," and S. Allen Chambers, Jr., *Lynchburg, An Architectural History* (Charlottesville: Univ. of Virginia Press, 1981), 223–25.

18. *Journal of the House . . . Special Session 1868* (Columbia: John W. Denny, 1868), 33–34.

19. Clare M. McCall, *History of Richland Lodge No. 39 Ancient Free Masons of South Carolina* (Columbia: Richland Lodge No. 39, 1991), 121; Julian A. Selby, *Columbia Directory* (Columbia: R. W. Gibbes, 1860); J. T. Hershman, comp., *Columbia City Directory* (Columbia: R. W. Gibbes, 1859).

20. McCall, 122.

21. Ravenel, *Architects of Charleston,* 202, 219, 229; also see Samuel Lapham, "Architectural Practice in South Carolina, 1680–1890," in Petty, *Architectural Practice in South Carolina,* 6.

22. *Journal of the House of Representatives . . . Special Session of 1868* (Columbia: John W. Denny, 1868), 33–34.

23. Ibid.

24. *Acts and Joint Resolutions of the General Assembly, 1868–1869* (Columbia: John W. Denny, 1869), 286–87.

25. South Carolina Reports and Resolutions, 1868–1900, Report of the State-House Keeper and Librarian, November, 1869, 301–3, roll 2, frames 507–8 (Sc-ArM-13).

26. Report of the Joint Investigating Committee on Public Frauds . . . 1877–1878 (NP),1201–2.

27. For a thorough, recent account of the period 1865–1876, see Richard Zucek, *State of Rebellion* (Columbia: Univ. of South Carolina Press, 1996). For 1877–1890, see William J. Cooper, Jr., *The Conservative Regime: South Carolina, 1877–1890* (Baltimore: The Johns Hopkins Press, 1968). For the most detailed portrait of the black leadership during Reconstruction, see Thomas Holt, *Black over White, Negro Political Leadership in South Carolina during Reconstruction* (Chicago: Univ. of Illinois Press, 1977).

28. *Charleston News and Courier,* April 28, 1877.

29. Report . . . Frauds, 1019.

30. Report of the Joint Investigating Committee, 1182.

31. Ibid., 1157–58.

32. Ibid., 1020.

33. Report of the Joint Investigating Committee, 1026.

34. Henry T. Thompson, *Ousting the Carpetbagger From South Carolina* (New York: Negro Universities Press, 1962; reprint, 1926), 66; also see *War of the Rebellion: Official Records of the Union and Confederate Armies* (Washington: Government Printing Office, 1880–1901), series 1, 14: 28, 36.

35. Report of the Joint Investigating Committee, 1201.

36. Ibid., 1036, 1026.

37. Ibid., 1036.

38. Ibid., 1035, 1212-13, 1210-11.

39. Francis Butler Simkins and Robert Hilliard Woody, *South Carolina During Reconstruction* (Chapel Hill: Univ. of North Carolina Press, 1932), 204; *Stat. S.C.* 14: 388; *Reports and Resolutions, 1877–1878,* Fraud Report, 1580.

40. Simkins and Woody, 204–8.

41. *Columbia Register,* July 28 and 30, 1875; August 3, 4, 7, 1875; September 7, 10, 1875, etc.; May 14, 1879.

42. Michael Kammen, *Mystic Chords of Memory, The Transformation of Tradition in American Culture* (New York: Alfred A. Knopf, 1991), 101.

43. John E. Kleber, ed., *Kentucky Encyclopedia* (Lexington: Univ. Press of Kentucky, 1992), 660.

44. *Columbia Register,* January 26, 1876.

45. Simkins and Woody, *South Carolina during Reconstruction,* 497; *Charleston News and Courier,* October 10 and 19, 1876.

46. Benjamin R. Tillman, *The Struggles of 1876 . . . Speech at the Red-Shirt Reunion at Anderson* (privately printed, 1909), 13–15, 33–39; also see Simkins and Woody, 499.

47. *Columbia Register,* October 13, 1876; cited by Simkins and Woody, 499.

48. Tillman, 29. The straight out campaign refers to those Democrats who refused to consider working with or supporting even the most reform-minded of the Republicans.

49. John G. Guignard, "How the Wallace House Met in Carolina Hall" (privately printed, signed 1912), a pamphlet in the collection of the South Caroliniana Library.

50. Simkins and Woody, *South Carolina during Reconstruction,* 523.

51. *Columbia Register,* November 28, 29 and December 1, 1876.

52. Ibid., April 9, 11, 13, 1877; also see Wallace, 605–6; Walter Allen, *Governor Chamberlain's Administration in South Carolina* (New York: G. P. Putnam's Sons, 1888), 472–73.

53. *Columbia Register,* April 13, 1877.

54. *Acts and Joint Resolutions . . . South Carolina, 1877–1878* (Columbia: Calvo and Patton, 1878).

55. *Columbia Register,* March 21, 1878. The earliest mention of Schwagerl's plan is *Columbia Register,* March 16.

56. *Columbia Register,* April 2, 1878.

57. John M. Bryan, ed., *Robert Mills, Architect* (Washington: AIA Press, 1989), 88.

58. Norman T. Newton, *Design on the Land* (Cambridge: Harvard Univ. Press, 1971), xxi–xxii.

59. For biographical information concerning Schwagerl, see David A. Rash, "Edward Otto Schwagerl," a biographical essay in Jeffrey Karl Ochsner, ed., *Shaping Seattle Architecture* (Seattle: Univ. of Washington Press, 1994), 52–57. Phil Lapsansky, Library Company of Philadelphia, checked the Philadelphia City Directories, and Lindsay Smith pointed out the surviving plan in the SCDAH and directed me to Schwagerl's work in the Northwest. The year after the State House plan was done, Schwagerl moved to Portland, Oregon, where he was retained to design Riverview Cemetery (1879–1881). The remainder of his career was spent in the Pacific Northwest. In Tacoma he designed Wright Park (1890) and Point Defiance Park (1890–1892), and in Seattle, Kinnear Park (1892–1894) and Denny Park (1894–1895). He served as Superintendent of Public Parks for Seattle and developed a proposal for a system of parks and parkways which anticipated the plan by the Olmsted Brothers ultimately adopted by the city. Schwagerl's work on Seattle's parks and his executed plans for subdivisions justify his reputation as the city's most important pioneer landscape designer. Schwagerl's success in the Northwest was based on his brief training in Paris, the work with Weidenmann, and twenty years of practice in various cities.

60. Swansford Lunsford (1755–1799), a native of Virginia and member of Lee's Legion during the Revolution, was buried on the State House grounds at the request of his daughter, Mrs. John Douglas of Chester, S.C. See *Columbia Register,* January 21, 1876; December 28, 1897. "Map of Columbia, S.C. and Suburbs," by Niernsee & Lamotte, City Engineers, 1895 (Baltimore: William A. Flamm & Co., 1895). The Schwagerl drawing is in the collection of the SCDAH.

61. *Columbia Register,* February 4, 1879; also see May–July, 1879; and August 20, 1881.

62. Ibid., March 21, 1879.

63. Ibid., May 14, 1879.

64. Lee Longstreth, Muldoon Memorials, to Dan Vivian, February 26, 1997; *Civil War Monuments in Kentucky, 1865–1935* (Kentucky Heritage Council: State Historic Preservation Office, 1997).

65. Reports and Resolutions, Report of the Secretary of State, 1874–1875, 669–70, roll 5, frames 954–55, (Sc-ArM-13).

66. Ibid., 1877, 351–52, roll 7, frame 195–96.

67. *Journal of the House of Representatives South Carolina, 1877–1878* (Columbia: Calvo & Patton, 1878), 35.

68. *Columbia Register,* February 21, 1878; September 9, 1881; January, 1884.

69. Governor Hugh S. Thompson Papers, SCDAH, Letters Sent, Letter Book B, 479–80.

70. Reports and Resolutions, 1868–1900; Estimates for Completion of the State Capitol, 1884, 1: 819–35, roll 13, frames 424–32.

71. Ibid.; for Niernsee's accident, see *Columbia Register*, February 9 and 21, 1883.

72. For biographical information concerning G. T. Berg, see *Statutes at Large of South Carolina*, Acts, 23: 501, *Minutes and Letter Book, 1900–1903,* Commission for the Completion of the State House. SCDAH, 50–53; McCall, 236–38; Petty, *Architectural Practice in South Carolina,* 8; John E. Wells and Robert E. Dalton, *The South Carolina Architects, 1885–1935: A Biographical Directory* (Richmond: New South Architectural Press, 1992), 13; *1870 Federal Census, Richland County, Columbia,* roll 1227, 41B, line 28; History of Synod Committee, *History of the Lutheran Church in South Carolina* (Columbia: R. L. Bryan, 1971), 345; Gilbert Voigt, *History of Ebenezer Lutheran Church* (Columbia: n.p., 1930), 31–32, 89–90; SCDAH, Inventory and Appraisement, Probate Court, Richland County, Book C, 53–54.

73. *Columbia Register,* June 9, 10, 1885; *Atlanta Constitution,* June 11, 1885. Niernsee died without a will: "departed this life intestate on or about the 7th of June 1885 possessed of a small personal estate of the value of about Five hundred dollars. . . ." *Estate Papers, Probate Court Richland County, South Carolina,* box 121, package 3147, Niernsee, J. R . His daughter Emma recalled "Father had just gotten his old offices fixed & we had taken a lease on the Nagel House [and] had only been there a few months when father died very suddenly. He left practically nothing, after paying off the funeral & the household expenses, we were fall [?] to face with the world, & not a weapon to fight it. We went over to Helen's (they were back in Columbia). Mother, Bro. Charlie, Lill & myself. Everything of value we sold. The silver service, was bought by a family in Charleston, by the name of Ryan. . . ." Emma Niernsee, Maryland Historical Society, MSS 2 45 7, 23.

Chapter Four: Substantial Completion

1. Report of the Commission for the Completion of the State House . . . 1887, 167.

2. SCDAH, RG 215, Records of the Commission to Complete the State House, 13, Hugh S. Thompson, Governor and Chr to JCN, June 15, 1885.

3. Ibid., 15, June 23, 1885.

4. *Columbia Register,* August 22, 23, 1885; Annual Report of the Commission for the Completion of the State House, 1885.

5. Annual Report . . . 1885.

6. Ibid., 832.

7. Ibid., 834.

8. *Columbia Register,* November 22, 25, 1885.

9. *Columbia Register,* July 2, 1886.

10. S.C. Reports and Resolutions, 1868–1900, Report of the Secretary of State, 1889, misc. reference, Sc-ArM-13, 1: 50–51, 269–71, roll 18.

11. Report of the Commissioners for the Completion of the Main Building . . . 1886, SCDAH, n.p.

12. Report of the Commission for the Completion of the State House . . . 1887, SCDAH, 168–73.

13. Ibid.

14. *Columbia Register,* August 10, 1886; August 21, 22, 1886.

15. *New York Times,* September 2, 1886.

16. *Columbia Register,* October 27, 1887.

17. Ibid.

18. Ibid.

19. Commenting on the residency requirement, the *Columbia Register* (January 5, 1888) reported, ". . . the motive thereof was plainly to prevent the continuance of the present arrangement, by which Mr. Neilson, of Baltimore, draws some $3,000 a year for an occasional visit of a day or two once in a month or two."

20. *Columbia Register,* February 4, 1888.

21. Records of the Commission to Complete the State House, SCDAH, February 3, 1888, 87–90.

22. Report of the State House Commission, 1888, n.p.

23. *Columbia Daily Register,* June 22, 1894.

24. Excepting the date given in the obituary, there no evidence indicating that Frank Niernsee was residing or active in Columbia as early as 1882. It is worth noting that his son, Frank McHenry Niernsee, was born in Bedford County, Virginia, June 25, 1883. *Official Roster of S.C. Soldiers, Sailors, and Marines in the World War, 1917–1918* (Columbia: Joint Committee on Printing, n.d.), 751.

25. J. Tracy Power, "'The Brightest of the Lot': W. B. Smith Whaley and the Rise of the South Carolina Textile Industry, 1893–1903," *South Carolina Historical Magazine* 93, no. 2 (April, 1992): 127–38.

26. Wells and Dalton, *The South Carolina Architects,* 156–58.

27. Although marble and granite do not burn, the heat of an intense fire causes moisture within the stone to expand, and this causes the stone to crack. That is apparently what happened to stone stored in wooden sheds or stacked near the Old State House.

28. *State House Commission Minutes,* 1884–1891, February 25, 1890.

29. Mary Dierickx, "Metal Ceilings in the U.S.," *Association for Preservation Technology* 7, no. 2 (1975): 83–84; Report of the State House Commission, 1889, 697.

30. *Columbia Register,* November 26, 1889; August 18, 1889; November 9, 1889.

31. Nikolaus Pevsner, *History of Building Types* (Princeton: Princeton Univ. Press, 1976), 107–10.

32. Report of the State House Commission, 1889; *Columbia Register,* May 7, July 18, August 10, October 20, 30, 1888.

33. *State House Commission Minutes, 1884–1891,* June 26, 1888, 337–41.

34. Report of the State House Commission, 1888, 894.

35. *The State,* November 13, 1884.

36. *House Journal, December 22, 1888,* 392; South Carolina Reports and Resolutions, 1868–1900, 1: 615, roll 17, frame 322; Moore, *Columbia and Richland County,* 241.

37. *State House Commission Minutes,* January 29, 1891, 22.

38. Frank Niernsee died in Columbia on May 28, 1899. *The State,* May 29, 1899.

39. *The State,* March 16, 1900.

40. Louise Bailey, et. al., *Biographical Directory of the South Carolina Senate, 1776–1985* (Columbia: Univ. of South Carolina Press, 1986), 2: 1058–60. *The State,* August 12, 1908. Conversation with Jane Mays, Granddaughter of JQM, March, 1997.

41. South Carolina Reports and Resolutions, 1868–1900, Report of the Secretary of State, October 31, 1889, roll 18, 1: 213–14, frame 115–16, Sc-ArM-13.

42. Moore, *Columbia and Richland County,* 277, 241; John M. Bryan and Associates, *Citywide Architectural Survey and Historic Preservation Plan, Columbia, South Carolina* (Columbia: SCDAH, 1993), 2.

43. *The State,* July 11, 1899; July 6, 7, 1899.

44. Ibid., January 14, 1900.

45. *First Annual Report of the Commission for the Completion of the State House, 1900* (Columbia: The State Co., 1901); for the debate about funding see *The State,* February 2, 15, 17, 22, 28, 1900.

46. *Manufacturers' Record* (Atlanta), March 29, 1900, 170.

47. SCDAH, RG 215, Commission to Complete the State House, Misc. Records, 1884–1903, 1 Flat File Box: GES to Committee, March 15, 1900; CCW & WAE to Commission, March 15, 1900.

48. For biographical information on Milburn, see Wells and Dalton, *The South Carolina Architects,* 122–27; Lawrence Wodehouse, "Frank Pierce Milburn, Architect," *North Carolina Historical Review* 50, no. 3 (July, 1973): 289–303; Mary Kathryn Frye, "Frank Pierce Milburn, Architect, 1868–1926" (M.A. thesis: Univ. of South Carolina, 1978).

49. For biographical information on C. C. Wilson, see Wells and Dalton, *The South Carolina Architects,* 209–19; also see C. C. Wilson, supplement by Samuel Lapham, *History of the Practice of Architecture in the State of South Carolina* (privately printed, 1938).

50. *First Annual Report of the Commission for the Completion of the State House, 1900* (Columbia: State Printers, 1901), 1733. Frank Pierce Milburn, *Designs from the Work of Frank P. Milburn, Architect* (Columbia: State Company, 1901), 6 pages of text and 55 plates; ibid. (1903), 7 pages of text and 76 plates; and *Frank P. Milburn and Company . . . Washington, D.C.* (Washington: Bibson Bros., n.d. [c. 1906]), c. 150 plates.

51. SCDAH, RG 215, Records of the Commission to Complete the State House; *The State,* August 3, 1900.

52. *The State,* August 3, 1900; also see *Second Annual Report of the Commission for the Completion of the State House, 1901* (Columbia: State Printers, 1902), Minority Report, 2125–35.

53. *The State,* August 3, 1900. The final outer dome (see dome structure, p. 118) is centered on the outside of the building, but because the south portico is not as deep as the north portico (see North Elevation, p. 137), an offset inner dome was necessary to adjust the interior view of the dome to the lobby.

54. Ibid.

55. Ibid.

56. *Second Annual Report of the Commission for the Completion of the State House, 1901,* 2115.

57. Ibid., 2125–39. Joseph O. Rogers III, manager-architect of the 1995–1998 renovation, notes that the masonry foundations of the porticos is "rubble work," the granite drum at the base of the dome is "crummy and cheesy" and the dome in plan is not a true circle; it was "apparently done by eye without templates." Interview with the author, September, 1997.

58. Ibid., 2128–29.

59. SCDAH, Book of Minutes of the Commission for Completion of the State House, Exhibit F, 87. It is worth noting that the renovation of 1995–1998 found that the only serious settling in the State House occurred on the east cheek wall of the north portico as a result of the brick foundations criticized by Marshall. During the renovation, architects also discovered that the slope of the roof over the south portico did not coincide with the pitch or angle of the portico gable. The wide mortar joints pointed out by Marshall are evident on the west cheek wall of the north portico. Structurally, the dome was found to be stable, but the lightly framed sheet metal flexed and leaked so badly that it was necessary to erect an intermediate dome, like an umbrella, between the inner and outer domes. The intermediate dome is visible in the illustration of the dome structure, p. 118.

60. Ibid., 2136, 2139.

61. *Reports and Resolutions of the General Assembly, 1904* (Columbia: State Printers, 1904), 2: 306.

62. Minority Report of Senator J. Q. Marshall of the Commission for the Completion of the State House, January 1, 1902–February 4, 1903, 1261–64.

63. *Report of the Commission for the Repairs of the State House, 1903* (Columbia: State Printers, 1904), 717–31; also see *The State,* November 26, 1903.

64. For Hunt's testimony see Report of the Joint Committee . . . on the Completion of the State House and Facts Relating Thereto, in *Reports and Resolutions of the General Assembly, 1904,* 2: 316–28.

65. William O. Wolfe, the father of the novelist Thomas Wolfe, was among the stone carvers who worked on these capitals. John Chandler Griffin, "Look Homeward, My Brother, a Chat With Fred Wolfe of Spartanburg," *Carologue* (Summer 1996): 14–17, 22–23.

66. *Reports and Resolutions of the General Assembly, 1904,* 2: 328.

67. Ibid., 308, 310, 315–16.

68. *The State,* February 13, 1904.

69. *Reports and Resolutions of the General Assembly, 1904,* 2: 922.

70. *The State,* June 14, August 31, 1904; February 10, July 11, December 7, 1905.

71. American Bridge Co. was one the largest, if not the largest, steel fabricators in America "with a capital of $70,000,000, and . . . reported to control about 90 per cent of the bridge tonnage of the country." Victor S. Clark, *History of Manufactures in the U.S.* (New York: Peter Smith, 1949), vol. 3, 1893–1928, 121.

72. *The State,* June 5, 15, 25, 27, September 29, February 12, 14, 1904. Berle was correct. The renovation of 1995–1998 found the supporting structure of the dome intact; however, its light metal sheathing leaked so badly—as predicted by Wilson—that during the 1980s it became necessary to erect an intermediate cone-shaped turret between the outer and inner dome to catch and divert incoming water.

73. *The State,* December 18, 1901.

74. *Report of the Commission for the Repairs of the State House* (Columbia: State Printers, 1903), 731.

Chapter Five: Defining the Grounds

1. Samuel B. Platner, *Topography and Monuments of Ancient Rome* (Boston: Allyn and Bacon, 1904), 282.

2. For a well-illustrated review of the American Renaissance see Richard Guy Wilson, *The American Renaissance: 1876–1917* (Brooklyn: Brooklyn Museum, 1979); also see Richard Guy Wilson, "American Architecture and the Search for a National Style in the 1870s," *Winterthur Portfolio* 18, no. 1 (1983): 69–87.

3. Bernard Berenson, *The Venetian Painters* (New York: G. P. Putnam's Sons, 1894), reprinted in *Italian Painters of the Renaissance* (Cleveland, 1957), iii.

4. *Report of the Commission to Provide for a Monument to the Memory of Wade Hampton, Reports and Resolutions, 1904,* 2: 951–56, and *Supplemental Report of the Hampton Monument Commission, Reports and Resolutions, 1907,* 3: 387–94. Also see *The Confederate Veteran* 14 (December, 1906): 12, 534; and 15 (March, 1907): 3, 134–35.

5. In addition to the three monuments on the State House grounds, Ruckstull would create a 7'2" marble figure of John C. Calhoun (1909) and a 7'6" marble figure of Wade Hampton (1929). Both were commissioned by the State of South Carolina for display in the U.S. Capitol.

6. F. W. Ruckstull, *Great Works of Art and What Makes Them Great,* a reprint of articles published in *The Art World Magazine, 1916–1918* (New York: G. P. Putnam's Sons, 1925), 20–21.

7. *Confederate Veteran* 2, no. 3 (March, 1903): 133. For biographical details see Ruckstull, 517–42; also see Wayne Craven, *Sculpture in America* (Newark: Univ. of Delaware Press, 1984), 477–81; and obituaries in the *New York Times* and *Herald Tribune,* both May 27,

1942. Also see vertical file, Archives of American Art, Smithsonian Institution; and New York Public Library, *The Artists File* (Alexandria: Chadwyck-Healy, 1989), microfiche.

8. *The State*, October 29, 1906.

9. Clifford Roberts, *The Story of the Augusta National Golf Club* (New York: Doubleday, 1976), 12–39; Charles Price, *A Golf Story, Bobby Jones, Augusta National and the Masters Tournament* (New York: Athenaeum, 1986), 59–62; Willard Range, *A Century of Georgia Agriculture, 1850–1950* (Athens: Univ. of Georgia Press, 1954), 27; James C. Bonner, *A History of Georgia Agriculture, 1732–1860* (Athens: Univ. of Georgia Press, 1964), 173; *Augusta Daily Herald,* November 8, 1910. Although no documents identify specific trees, given the treeless photographs of 1865 and the fact that Berckman had the only turn-of-the-century major planting contract, the older trees must have came from Fruitlands.

10. *Augusta Daily Herald,* February 3, 1908; January 9, 1906; February 15, 1907.

11. *Columbia Register,* November 11, 1897.

12. *The State,* January 23, 1906.

13. *Confederate Veteran* 17, no. 8 (August, 1909): 372. After much debate, Belle Kinney was declared the winner of the competition in 1910. Her Monument to Confederate Women was erected in Jackson, Mississippi, in 1912. Concerning Kinney and the competition see Elise L. Smith, "Belle Kinney and the Confederate Women's Monument," *The Southern Quarterly* 32, no. 4 (Summer 1994): 6–31.

14. *Reports and Resolutions of the General Assembly, January 11, 1910* (Columbia: Gonzales and Bryan, 1910), 1223.

15. *The State,* March 21, 1936.

16. *Daily Record,* January 1, 1912.

17. For Roman examples of Nike see Phyllis Pray Bober and Ruth Rubinstein, *Renaissance Artists and Antique Sculpture* (London: Harvey Miller Publishers, 1986), 200–202, plates 167–71.

18. Ruckstull described the sentiment and symbolism of Gloria Victis saying: "My conception was this: the Confederacy is symbolized by the dying soldier who having decided to fight to a finish throws away his hat and coat and rolls up his sleeves. Though his clothes are worn and full of bullet holes he continues fighting even when his gun is shot to pieces—until the fatal bullet hits him. . . . Fame then swoops down and clasps him to her breast while she holds aloft a crown and seems to say: 'Hold! Enough, he belongs to me!'" *Art World* (September, 1917): 504.

19. Frederick W. Ruckstuhl, "The Value of Beauty to a City," *Civic Improvement League, Bulletin No. 1* (Columbia, 1905), 12 pp. (Ruckstull Anglicized his name by dropping the *h* after the sinking of the Lusitania.)

20. For a history of the movement nationally see William H. Wilson, *The City Beautiful Movement* (Baltimore: The Johns Hopkins Univ. Press, 1989); John W. Reps, *The Making of Urban America* (Princeton: Princeton Univ. Press, 1965), 497–525.

21. *The State,* January 25, 1904; also see December 3, 1906. Thomas F. Parker (1861–1927) was instrumental in establishing a Municipal League in Greenville and hired Kelsey and Guild to prepare a city plan (1907) which proposed boulevards, public art, a civic center, and a park along the Reedy River. Thomas F. Parker described the benefits of planning in a mill village in "The South Carolina Mill Village—A Manufacturer's View," *The South Atlantic Quarterly* 9, no. 4 (October, 1910): 349–57. Concerning the Parker brothers and their contributions to the city beautiful movement, see Mary G. Ariail and Nancy J. Smith, *Weaver of Dreams, The Parker District* (Columbia: R. L. Bryan, 1977), 13; Archie Vernon Huff, *Greenville: The History of the City and County in the South Carolina Piedmont* (Columbia: Univ. of South Carolina Press, 1995), 245, 260; J. C. Hemphill, *Men of Mark in*

South Carolina: Ideals of American Life (Washington: Men of Mark Publishing Company) 1 (1907), 296–97; 2 (1908), 305.

22. Ruckstull, "The Value of Beauty to a City," 10.

23. Ibid., 10, 8.

24. Ibid., 11.

25. Kelsey & Guild, *The Improvement of Columbia, South Carolina: Report to the Civic League* (Harrisburg, Penn.: Mount Pleasant Press, [1905]), 64. Kelsey also prepared plans for Greenville and Marion, S.C., and Salem, Mass.

26. Ibid., 19.

27. Interview with E. Cecil Mills, Jr., September, 1997.

28. John M. Bryan, *G. W. Vanderbilt's Biltmore Estate* (New York: Rizzoli, 1994), 100.

29. Richard P. White, *From a Century of Service* (Washington, D.C.: American Association of Nurserymen, 1975), 402–4. Sheila Connor, The Arnold Arboretum of Harvard University, to the author, April 9, 1997. For the Massachusetts Trustees of Public Reservations (Kelsey recommended the creation of reservations in the Columbia plan), see Norman T. Newton, *Design on the Land* (Cambridge: Harvard Univ. Press, 1971), 320.

30. Lois Beattie, MIT Institute Archives, to the author, April 12, 1997.

31. For Hunt and the Ecole see Richard Chafee, "Hunt in Paris," an essay in Susan Stein, ed., *The Architecture of Richard Morris Hunt* (Chicago: Univ. of Chicago Press, 1986); for the methods and ideals of the Ecole des Beaux Arts see Donald Drew Egbert, *The Beaux-Arts Tradition in French Architecture* (Princeton: Princeton Univ. Press, 1980); also see Henry Hope Reed, *The Golden City* (New York: W. W. Norton, 1971), 76; and Wilson, *American Renaissance,* 21.

32. *Reports and Resolutions of the General Assembly, January 8, 1907* (Columbia: Gonzales and Bryan, 1907) 1: 716–17. *The State,* February 5, 1907.

33. *Reports and Resolutions of the General Assembly, January 14, 1908* (Columbia: Gonzales and Bryan, 1908) 2: 10–11.

34. *The State,* February 8, 1908.

35. *Reports and Resolutions of the General Assembly, January 12, 1909* (Columbia: Gonzales and Bryan, 1909), 1: 1034; and *Reports and Resolutions of the General Assembly, January 11, 1910* (Gonzales and Bryan, 1910), 2: 1223.

36. *The State,* February 8, 1910.

37. *House Journal, 1912,* 992. The largest surviving set of drawings, twenty-five plans and elevations, for the State House has erroneously been attributed to Frank P. Milburn. Although Milburn proposed alternative designs for the dome and tentatively explored the addition of wings, none of the surviving legislative papers or newspaper accounts indicate he presented detailed plans for the addition of wings shown in this set of drawings. A. W. Todd, on the other hand, advocated wings and was paid for a plaster model of the State House with the wings he proposed. The unsigned set of drawings matches Todd's model and must have been produced by Todd to guide the model-maker. The model itself is known only through photographs, for it appears to have been lost. The twenty- five drawings and the photograph of the model are in the collections of the SCDAH.

38. For biographical information on Todd see N. Louise Bailey, et. al., *Biographical Directory of the South Carolina Senate 1776–1985* (Columbia: Univ. of South Carolina Press, 1986), 3: 1623–24; David Duncan Wallace, *History of South Carolina* (New York: American Historical Society, 1934), 4: 520–21, Wells and Dalton, *The South Carolina Architects,* 180–83; and an obituary in the *Columbia Record,* December 30, 1924.

39. *Journal of the House of Representatives, 1912* (Columbia: Gonzales and Bryan, 1912), 484–89.

40. Ibid.

41. *The State,* January 25, 1912.

42. *Journal of the House of Representatives, February 6, 1912,* 586.

43. *The State,* February 8, 1912.

44. Ibid., February 10, 1912; also see February 7, 9, 1912; February 22, 1912; February 14, 1913. Todd based his claim for payment upon a standard American Institute of Architects contract which provided payment of 1.2 percent ($12,000) of projected costs for the preparation of preliminary drawings. He also claimed he was owed $900 for the model and $650 for the educational presentations. On Todd's behalf, colleagues continued to insert his claim, plus accrued interest, in appropriation bills as late as 1923. The claim was never paid. For a transcript of the inquiry, see *Journal of the House, 1912,* 996–1054. For the final veto in 1923, see Papers of Gov. T .G. McLeod, Legislative Matters, Box 30, "Todd Veto," SCDAH.

45. *The State,* December 10, 1916.

46. *Journal of the House of Representatives . . . Second Session of the 86th General Assembly . . . Regular Session Beginning Tuesday, January 8, 1946 and the Extra Session Beginning Tuesday, April 2, 1946* (N.p: Joint Committee on Printing, n.d.), 535–37.

47. Thomas O. Ramsey to Bobby Lyles, et. al., September 22, 1992, 7.6–7.6.15.

48. Pamela Scott, *Temple of Liberty, Building the Capitol for a New Nation* (New York: Oxford Univ. Press, 1995), 95- 106.

49. Rebecca G. Fulmer, "The Life and Times of the Calhoun Building: A Brief History of the First State Office Building," SCDAH, typescript, 1989.

50. SCDAH, RG 112, Records of the Budget and Control Board, Sinking Fund Commission Minutes, January 26, 1916 to May 15, 1926; see December 14, 1923, 184. *Journal of the House, February 23, 1923,* 504–5; *Statutes at Large of South Carolina,* Acts, 1924, 1840–42; and Acts, 1926, 1673–74. For Lafaye's report see SCDAH, Gov. Thomas McLeod Papers, Box 47, State Office Building.

51. Charles C. Wilson, supplement by Samuel Lapham, *History of the Practice of Architecture in the State of South Carolina* (privately printed, 1938), 10.

52. Ibid. Also see Petty, *Architectural Practice in South Carolina,* 9. SCDAH, Gov. Thomas McLeod Papers, Box 47, State Office Building; NGW to S. M. Wolfe, March 12, 1924; AS to WPL, March 12, 1924.

53. SCDAH, McLeod Papers, Box 47. The cornerstone of the Federal Land Bank in Columbia bears the date 1934, but R. H. Welch, General Counsel to the bank, writing to Gov. McLeod on March 14, 1924, refers to Brown as "the architect who designed the Federal Land Bank building of Columbia."

54. SCDAH, RG 112 Records of the Budget and Control Board, Sinking Fund Commission Minutes, 191–92.

55. Wells and Dalton, *The South Carolina Architects,* 176–77; Fulmer, "The Life and Times of the Calhoun Building," 6.

56. *Reports and Resolutions of the General Assembly, 1925,* 2: 9. Sinking Fund Minutes, 193. Fulmer, "The Life and Times of the Calhoun Building," 7–8.

57. Sinking Fund Minutes, 194.

58. Ibid., 195, 201, 218–19.

59. Ibid., 225–39; ibid., 9 June 1926–11 June 1940, 3–10.

60. Ibid., 15.

61. Fulmer, "The Life and Times of the Calhoun Building," 15.

62. The Wade Hampton Building, 1939–1940, by Lafaye, Lafaye, and Fair, Architects; the Rembert Dennis Building, by Hopkins, Baker & Gill, 1950, rebuilt in 1979 by McNair, Gordon, Johnson & Karasiewicz; the Edgar A. Brown Building, 1971–1973, by Lyles,

Bissett,Carlisle & Wolfe—Wilbur Smith & Associates; and the Solomon Blatt Building, 1975–1978, also by Lyles, Bissett, Carlisle & Wolfe and Wilbur Smith; the Marion Gressette Building, 1977, also by Lyles, Bissett, Carlisle & Wolfe.

Chapter 6: The Renovation of 1992–1998

1. *Acts and Joint Resolutions, Regular Session, 1941,* Act No. 261, 520. Major repairs and renovations prior to 1995 are listed by Judith M. Andrews, ed., *A History of South Carolina's State House* (Columbia: South Carolina Department of Archives and History, 1994), 29–50.

2. A. McC. Marsh, et. al., to The Chairman and Members of the House Ways and Means Committee, December 31, 1957, Archives of the Columbia Fire Department; *The State,* January 20 and 22, 1958; interview with John G. Reich, Fire Marshal, City of Columbia, September, 1997.

3. Thomas O. Ramsey to Bobby Lyles, Mike Frick, et. al., September 22, 1992, Stevens & Wilkinson, Inc. files.

4. *The State,* August 23, 1995.

5. Pradeep Talwani, *South Carolina Earthquakes, 1698–1995* (Columbia: South Carolina Emergency Preparedness Division, Office of the Adjutant General and Federal Emergency Management Agency, July, 1996). A summary of the data appears in *The State,* February 20, 1996. For the architect's report see Stevens & Wilkinson, "Seismic Investigation for the State House Structure," May 12, 1993.

6. Project Flow Chart, courtesy Joseph O. Rogers III, Manager-Architect, S.C. General Services.

7. Conversations with Mike Frick, Rob Bryan, and Wayne Redfern, project architects, 1996–1997.

Selected Bibliography

Books and Articles

Allen, Walter. *Governor Chamberlain's Administration in South Carolina*. New York: G. P. Putnam's Sons, 1888.

Andrews, Judith M., ed. *A History of South Carolina's State House*. Columbia: South Carolina Department of Archives and History, 1994.

Bailey, N. Louise, et. al. *Biographical Directory of the South Carolina Senate, 1776–1985*. Columbia: University of South Carolina Press, 1986.

Bober, Phyllis P. and Ruth Rubinstein. *Renaissance Artists and Antique Sculpture*. London: Harvey Miller Publishers, 1986.

Bonner, James, C. *A History of Georgia Agriculture, 1732–1860*. Athens: University of Georgia Press, 1964.

Brown, Glenn. *History of the United States Capitol*. Vol. I, *The Old Capitol - 1792–1850*. Washington, D.C.: Government Printing Office, 1900.

Bryan, John M. *G. W. Vanderbilt's Biltmore Estate*. New York: Rizzoli, 1994.

———, ed. *Robert Mills, Architect*. Washington, D.C.: American Institute of Architects, 1989.

———. *An Architectural History of the South Carolina College, 1801–1855*. Columbia: University of South Carolina Press, 1976.

Burton, E. P. *Diary of E. P. Burton*. Des Moines: Historical Records Survey, Works Progress Administration, 1939.

Cauthen, Charles E., ed. *Journals of the South Carolina Executive Councils of 1861 and 1862*. Columbia: S.C. Archives, 1956.

Chambers, Allen, Jr. *Lynchburg, An Architectural History*. Charlottesville: University of Virginia Press, 1981.

Chapman, John A. *History of Edgefield County*. Newberry: n.p., 1897.

Chesnut, Mary Boykin, *A Diary from Dixie*, ed. Ben Ames Williams. Boston: Houghton Mifflin, 1949.

Clark, Victor S. *History of Manufactures in the U.S.* New York: Peter Smith, 1949.

Cohen, M. M. *Notices of Florida and the Campaigns*. Gainesville: University of Florida Press, 1964.

Cooper, William J. *The Conservative Regime: South Carolina, 1877–1890.* Baltimore: The Johns Hopkins Press, 1968.

Craven, Wayne. *Sculpture in America.* Newark: University of Delaware Press, 1984.

Davis, Keith E. *George N. Barnard, Photographer of Sherman's Campaign.* Kansas City: Hallmark Cards, 1990.

Deas, Alston. *Ironwork of Charleston.* Columbia: Bostick & Thornley, 1941.

Drayton, John. *A View of South Carolina.* Charleston: W. P. Young, 1802.

Egbert, Donald Drew. *The Beaux-Arts Tradition in French Architecture.* Princeton: Princeton University Press, 1980.

Foote, Shelby. *The Civil War, A Narrative.* New York: Vintage, 1986.

Frary, Ihna Thayer. *They Built the Capitol.* Freeport, N.Y.: Books for Libraries Press, 1940.

Gallagher, Helen Mar Pierce. *Robert Mills, Architect of the Washington Monument, 1781–1855.* New York: Columbia University Press, 1935.

Gilchrist, Agnes. *William Strickland, Architect and Engineer, 1788–1854.* New York: Da Capo, 1969.

Green, Edwin L. *A History of Richland County.* Columbia: R. L. Bryan, 1932.

Gregorie, Anne King, ed. "Micajah Adolphus Clark's Visit to South Carolina in 1857." *South Carolina Historical Magazine* (January, 1953).

Grigsby, Melvin. *The Smoked Yank.* Privately printed, 1888.

Hafertepe, Kenneth. *America's Castle, The Evolution of the Smithsonian Building and Its Institution, 1840–1878.* Washington, D.C.: Smithsonian Institution Press, 1984.

Hazelton, George C. *The National Capitol, Its Architecture, Art, and History.* New York: J. F. Taylor & Co., 1914.

Hedley, Fenwick Y. *Marching through Georgia.* Chicago: Donahiue, Henneberry, 1890.

Hennig, Helen Kohn, ed. *Columbia, Capital City of South Carolina, 1786–1936.* Columbia: The State Printing Company, 1966.

Hitchcock, Henry Russell and William Seale. *Temples of Democracy, the State Capitols of the USA.* New York: Harcourt Brace Jovanovich, 1976.

Hollis, Daniel W. *University of South Carolina.* Vol. 2, College to University. Columbia: University of South Carolina Press, 1956.

Holt, Thomas. *Black over White: Negro Political Leadership in South Carolina during Reconstruction.* Urbana: University of Illinois Press, 1977.

Hooker, Edward. *Diary of Edward Hooker, 1805–1808.* Washington, D.C.: Government Printing Office, 1897.

Hoskins, Jos[eph] A., comp. *President Washington's Diaries, 1791–1799.* Greensboro: Golden Rule Press, 1921.

Kammen, Michael. *Mystic Chords of Memory: The Transformation of Tradition in American Culture.* New York: Alfred A. Knopf, 1991.

Kelsey, Harlan P. and Irving T. Guild. *The Improvement of Columbia, South Carolina: Report to the Civic League.* Harrisburg: Mount Pleasant Press, n.d. (c. 1905).

Kervick, Francis W. *Architects in America of Catholic Tradition.* Rutland: Charles E. Tuttle, 1962.

Kleber, John E., ed. *Kentucky Encyclopedia.* Lexington: University Press of Kentucky, 1992.

Kohn, David and Bess Glenn, eds. *Internal Improvement in South Carolina, 1817–1828.* Washington, D.C.: Privately printed, 1938.

Lafever, Minard. *Beauties of Modern Architecture.* New York: D. Appleton, 1839.

Lane, Mills. *Architecture of the Old South: South Carolina.* Savannah: The Beehive Press, 1984.

Lapham, Samuel. *History of the Practice of Architecture in the State of South Carolina.* Privately printed, 1938.

McCall, Clare M. *History of Richland Lodge No. 39 Ancient Free Masons of South Carolina.* Columbia: Richland Lodge No. 39, 1991.

Milburn, Frank P. *Designs from the Work of Frank P. Milburn, Architect.* Columbia: State Company, 1901.

Mitchell, Broadus, *William Gregg.* Chapel Hill: University of North Carolina Press, 1928.

Moore, John Hammond. *Columbia and Richland County: A South Carolina Community, 1740–1990.* Columbia: University of South Carolina Press, 1993.

Newton, Norman T. *Design on the Land, the Development of Landscape Architecture.* Cambridge: Harvard University Press, 1971.

Ochsner, Jeffrey Karl, ed. *Shaping Seattle Architecture.* Seattle: University of Washington Press, 1994.

Petty, Walter F., Charles Coker Wilson, and Samuel Lapham. *Architectural Practice in South Carolina, 1913–1963.* Columbia: The State Printing Company, 1963.

Pevsner, Nikolaus. *History of Building Types.* Princeton: Princeton University Press, 1976.

Power, J. Tracy. "The Brightest of the Lot: W. B. Smith Whaley and the Rise of the South Carolina Textile Industry, 1893–1903." *South Carolina Historical Magazine* (April, 1992), 127–38.

Range, Willard. *A Century of Georgia Agriculture, 1850–1960.* Athens: University of Georgia Press, 1954.

Ravenel, Beatrice St. Julien. *Architects of Charleston.* Charleston: Carolina Art Association, 1964.

Reed, Henry Hope. *The Golden City.* New York: W. W. Norton, 1971.

Reps, John W. *The Making of Urban America, A History of City Planning in the United States.* Princeton: Princeton University Press, 1965.

Roper, Laura Wood. *FLO, A Biography of Frederick Law Olmsted.* Baltimore: The Johns Hopkins University Press, 1983.

Ruckstull, Frederick W. *Great Works of Art and What Makes Them Great.* New York: G. P. Putnam's Sons, 1925.

Savage, Kirk. *Standing Soldiers, Kneeling Slaves: Race, War, and Monument in Nineteenth-Century America.* Princeton: Princeton University Press, 1997.

Scott, Edwin J. *Random Recollections of a Long Life, 1806–1874.* Columbia: Charles A. Calvo, 1884.

Scott, Pamela. *Temple of Liberty, Building the Capitol for a New Nation.* New York: Oxford University Press, 1995.

Selby, Julian A. *Columbia Directory.* Columbia: R. W. Gibbes, 1860.

Severens, Kenneth. *Charleston, Antebellum Architecture and Civic Destiny.* Knoxville: University of Tennessee Press, 1988.

Simkins, Francis Butler and Robert Hilliard Woody. *South Carolina during Reconstruction.* Chapel Hill: University of North Carolina Press, 1932.

Smith, Elise. "Belle Kinney and the Confederate Women's Monument." *The Southern Quarterly* (Summer, 1994), 6–31.

Stein, Susan R., ed. *The Architecture of Richard Morris Hunt.* Chicago: University of Chicago Press, 1986.

Sumner, Charles. "Art in the National Capitol." Speech in the Senate of the U.S., July 17, 1866. Boston: Wright & Potter, 1866.

Thompson, Henry T. *Ousting the Carpetbagger from South Carolina.* New York: Negro Universities Press, 1962.

Tillman, Benjamin R. *The Struggles of 1876.* Privately printed, 1909.

Waddell, Gene and Rhodri Windsor Liscombe. *Robert Mills's Courthouses and Jails.* Easley: Southern Historical Press, 1981.

Waddell, Gene. "An Architectural History of Kahal Kadosh Beth Elohim, Charleston." *South Carolina Historical Magazine* (January, 1997), 6–55.

Wallace, David Duncan. *South Carolina, A Short History, 1520–1948.* Columbia: University of South Carolina Press, 1969.

Weiner, Marli F., ed. *Heritage of Woe: The Civil War Diary of Grace Brown Elmore, 1861–1868.* Athens: University of Georgia Press, 1997.

Wells, John E. and Robert E. Dalton. *The South Carolina Architects, 1885–1935: A Biographical Directory.* Richmond: New South Architectural Press, 1992.

White, Richard P. *From a Century of Service.* Washington, D.C.: American Association of Nurserymen, 1975.

Williams, J. F. *Old and New Columbia.* Columbia: Epworth Orphanage Press, 1929.

Wilson, Charles C. *History of the Practice of Architecture in the State of South Carolina.* Privately printed, 1938.

Wilson, Richard Guy, et al. *The American Renaissance.* New York: The Brooklyn Museum, 1979.

Wilson, William H. *The City Beautiful Movement.* Baltimore: The Johns Hopkins University Press, 1989.

Withey, H. F. and E. R. *Biographical Dictionary of American Architects (Deceased).* Los Angeles: Hennessey & Ingalls, 1970.

Wodehouse, Lawrence. "Frank Pierce Milburn, Architect." *North Carolina Historical Review* (July, 1973), 289–303.

Woodward, C. Vann and Elisabeth Muhlenfeld, eds. *The Private Mary Chesnut: The Unpublished Civil War Diaries.* New York: Oxford University Press, 1984.

Zagarri, Rosemarie. "Representation and the Removal of State Capitals." *Journal of American History* (March, 1988), 1239–56.

Zuczek, Richard. *State of Rebellion: Reconstruction in South Carolina.* Columbia: University of South Carolina Press, 1996.

Unpublished Sources

Chalfant, Ralph W. "Building List: Niernsee and Neilson, Architects of Baltimore," typescript, American Institute of Architects Archives, Record Group 804.

Chesnut-Miller-Manning Papers, South Carolina Historical Society, Charleston.

Ford Farewell Mills and Gatsch, Architects, Princeton, "Historic Documentation Report on South Carolina State House," March 31, 1993.

Frye, Mary Kathryn. "Frank Pierce Milburn, Architect, 1868–1926." M.A. Thesis, University of South Carolina, 1978.

Fulmer, Rebecca G. "The Life and Times of the Calhoun Building: A Brief History of the First State Office Building," typescript, South Carolina Department of Archives and History, 1989.

Jones, James. Letterbook, South Caroliniana Library, University of South Carolina.

Niernsee, Emma J. and John R. Niernsee Papers. Maryland Historical Society, MS 2457.

Walker, George Edward, Walker Papers, South Caroliniana Library, University of South Carolina.

Williams-Chesnut-Manning Papers, South Caroliniana Library, University of South Carolina.

Records of the General Assembly, South Carolina Department of Archives and History, including:
Acts and Resolutions
Annual Reports of the Commissioners of the New State House

Committee Reports
House of Representatives Journal
Miscellaneous Communications
Petitions
Reports and Resolutions
Senate Journal

Index

Italic page numbers indicate illustrations.

Aldrich, Robert, 120
Allen, James M., 78
Ansel, Martin F., 141
Armstrong, A. J., 102

Baker, William W., *140, 142,* 145, 152
Baldwin, James J., 147
Barker, Frank, 127
Barlett, B. J., 102
Barnard, George N., 61
Basshor, Thomas C., 100
Beauregard, P. T. G., 59, 63
Bedon, R. H., 14, 27
Berckmans, P. J. A., 126
Berenson, Bernard, 125
Berg, Caroline Muller, 93
Berg, Gustavus Theodore, 93, 103
Berle, Kert, 122
Berry, M. H., 80
Binda, Joseph Guiseppe, 3
Bishop, J. W., 116
Blanding, Abram, 11
Bonaparte, Joseph, 3
Brown, Albert Ten Ecyk, 147
Brown, Henry Kirke, 47–51, 52, 55, 56, 89,
    111, 125, 126
Brown, Joseph E., 34, 63
Browning, Lowndes J., 144
Buchanan, James, 47
Bulfinch, Charles, 36, 37
Bull, William Izard, 14, 16, 17
Bullett, Charles, 83
Butler, Pierce M., 40

Cain, Lawrence, 81
Calhoun, John C., 55, 60, 69, 150, *165*
Chamberlain, Daniel W., 85, 86
Chesnut, Mary Boykin, 61
Chesterman, W. A., 116
Clark, Micajah Adolphus, 42, 44, 45
Clinton, DeWitt, 48
Coolidge, Calvin, 147
Cooper, Edward, 105
Cooper, M. R., 120
Crane, H. M., 100
Cummings, Thomas S., 3

Daly, Joseph D., 17, 22, 23, 31, 34
Davis, William Morris, 54
Dennis, John B., 79, 80, 85
Denson, J. F., 102
DeVeaux, James, 3
Douglas, James, 8
Drayton, John, 4, 33
Drayton, William Henry, 40

Edwards, William Augustus, 115, 119
Elliott, Stephen, 91
Elmore, Grace, 62
Ethridge, J. W., 119

French, Daniel Chester, 126
Fuller, George A., 148

Gantt, Robert J., 120
George, J. Z., 84
Gibbes, James W., 46

Gibbes, L. R., 102
Gillon, Alexander, 9
Goodwyn, Thomas Jefferson, 26, 28, 64
Goucher, E. B., 122
Grant, Lewis, 79
Grant, Ulysses S., 63, 66
Green, Edwin L., 6
Green, Halcott Pride, 17, 36
Green, John S., 83
Gregg, William, 15, 32
Guignard, John G., 97
Guild, Irving Tracy, 138, 140, 141

Hamiter, A. W., 107
Hammarskold, Peter Hjalmar, 14–18, 19, 22, 23, 26–31, 35, 39, 45, 55, 75
Hampton, Richard, 9
Hampton, Wade, 3, 57, 63, 81, 82, 84, 86, 91, 113, 124, 125, 126, 128, 131, 149
Harding, Chester, 47
Harding, Warren, 147
Hartranft, John F., 125, *126*
Haydon (Hayden), I. A., 64
Hayes, Rutherford B., 86
Hayne, Robert Y., 56, 56
Herbemont, Nicholas, 11, 12
Hewitson, Ralph E. B., 75, 91, 93, 103
Hewitt, Abram S., 105
Heyward, Duncan Clinch, 122, 141
Hoban, James, 2, 6–8
Hooker, Edward, 9, 10, 33
Hunt, Benjamin F., 13, 14
Hunt, Richard Morris, 126, 139
Hunt, S. S., 121, 122
Hunter, James E., 145, 151

Inman, Henry, 3

Jefferson, Thomas, 2, 36
Johnson, J. Carroll, 147, 151
Johnson, James C., 122
Jones, A. O., 79
Jones, Clara, 32
Jones, Edward C., 32, 75
Jones, James, 31, 32, 34, 35, 36, 40, 42, 56, 59, 69, 86, 96, 111
Jones, Lewis, 32
Jones, Mathias, 32

Kay, John A., 18, 19, 21, 32, 35, 75, 91, 93, 103
Kay, Mary Hewitson, 75
Keitt, L. M., 14
Kelsey and Guild, 132, *133, 134,* 146, 149
Kelsey, Harlan P., 131, 133, 134, 138, 141
Kelsey, Samuel T., 133
Kimpton, H. H., 81
Kraft, Goldsmith, Kraft, 60

Labrouste, Henri, 107
Lafaye, George E., 104, 146, 147, 148
Lafever, Minard, 3
Laird, Warren Powers, 147
LaMotte, Ashbury Gamewell, 98, 103, 104
Latrobe, Benjamin Henry Jr., 2, 33, 38
Leconte, Joseph, 60
Lee, Francis D., 75
Lee, Robert E., 63, 131
Lopez, David, 13, 14
Lovell, Gene M., 64
Lucas, Marion Brunson, 61
Lundsford, Swanson, 90

Mackey, E. W. M., 85, 86
Magrath, Andrew Gordon, 63, 64, 66
Manning, John L., *1*–4, 18, 21, 25, 27, 38, 39, 78, 111, 133, 150
Manning, Susan Hampton, 2
Marsh, A. McC., 151
Marshall, Jehu Foster, 111
Marshall, John Quitman, 96, 111–15, 116, 118, 119, 120, 121, 122, 123, 125
Marshall, Samuel, 111
Martin, Isabella D., 91
Martin, William, 82
McCullock, Charles, 15, 17, 19, 31, 34
McDuffie, George, 56
McIlvain, E. J., 122
McIlvain Unkefer Company, 116, 119, 121, 122
McKim, Charles Follen, 139
McRae, John, 57
McSweeney, M. B., 115, 119, 120, 122
Means, John H., 40
Medary, Milton B., 147
Middleton, Arthur, 40
Milady, John, 119

Milburn, Frank Pierce, 111, *115–20*, 121, 122, 123, 133, 138
Mills, E. Cecil, 151
Mills, Robert, 2, 7, 11, 12, 15, 88
Mills, Robert G., 11
Moses, F. J., 80
Mulat, Mons, 88
Muldoon, Michael McDonald, 82, 83, 127
Mullet, A. B., 74
Munday, Johnson M., 50, 51, 54, 55
Munday, Mary E., 51

Neilson, James Crawford, 18, 33, 74, 94–102, 106, 111, 138, 141, 143
Newcomer, J. D., 147
Newnham, Charles, 107
Niernsee, Charlie, 66
Niernsee, Emily Bradenbaugh, 33, 69
Niernsee, Emma Josephine, 66, 74
Niernsee, Francis McHenry (Frank), 57, 74, 102–7, 110, 111, 113, 115, 116, 119, 120
Niernsee, Helen, 32
Niernsee, John Rudolph, 18–19, 20, 21, 22, 23, 24, 25–28, 29, 30, 31, 32–45, 46, 47, 49, 55, 56, 57–59, 61, 63–66, 69, 73, 74–75, 81, 88, 89, 91, 92, 93, 94, 95, 103, 104, 105, 111, 113, 114, 115, 116, 118, 121, 122, 123, 125, 126, 127, 133, 138, 140, 141, 143, 144, 145, 146, 149, 150, 152
Niernsee, Lill, 66
Niernsee, Rudolph, 32, 57

Oakshott, Thomas, 74
Olmsted, Frederick Law, 88, 133, 138
Orr, James L., 74, 75, 78, 85

Parker, Lewis W., 131
Parker, Thomas W., 131
Parker, William, 47
Pendleton, Henry, 9
Phyfe, Duncan, 3
Pinckney, Charles, 6
Poinsett, Joel R., 11
Pope, J. J., 57
Potter, Nathaniel F., 2, 3
Powers, Hiram, 60

Purcell, Pierce, 7
Purgin, Byron A., 102

Quattlebaum, Paul, 32
Quitman, John, 111

Ravenel, Beatrice St. Julien, 7
Reichardt, Charles F., 88
Renwick, James, 18
Reynolds, J. L., 55
Rhett, Robert Barnwell Jr., 40
Richardson, John P., 1, 10
Rodin, Auguste, 126
Ruckstull, Frederick Wellington, 89, *125–132*, 138
Russell, Robert E., 39, 87, 88
Rutledge, Edward B., 10, 102

Saint-Gaudens, Augustus, 126
Sayre, C. Gadsden, 147
Scarborough, William H., 34
Schmidt, T. J., 95, 96, 97, 98, 100, 102
Schramm, Charles, 104
Schwagerl, Edward Otto, 88, 89, 113, 127, 138, 149
Schwagerl, Hermann J., 88
Shand, Gadsden E., 104, 105, 113, 114, 115, 116
Shand, Peter J., 115
Sherman, William T., 59, 61, 62, 63, 66
Simons, Albert, 147
Sims, R. M., 86, 88, 90, 91, 113
Sisson, Hugh, 33, 46, 56
Sisson and Dougherty, 56, 57, 59, 69
Smith, Vern, 151
Solomon, Hardy, 79
Stevens and Wilkinson, *135, 136, 142*, 145, *149*, 151, 152, 153
Strickland, William, 38, 107
Suder, Peter, 22
Sumner, Charles, 48
Sumter, Thomas, 3

Tatum, Harold, *143*, 147, 148
Taylor, Thomas, 9
Thompson, Hugh S., 92
Thornton, William, 37
Tillman, Benjamin R., 84

Todd, Albert Whitner, *137, 138, 139*, 143, 144, 147, 152
Turnbull, William, 18

Unkefer, John G., 122
Upjohn, Hobart, 147
Urquhart, James B., 147

Vanderbilt, G. W., 133
Vaux, Calvert, 88
View of South Carolina (Drayton), 4

Wagner, Thomas M., 14
Walker, C. Irvine, 128
Walker, George Edward, 19, 20 31, 35, 45, 55, 75, 103
Walker, Nat Gaillard, 147
Wallace, William W., 85, 86
Walter, Thomas U., 145
Ward, John Quincy Adams, 126
Ware, William R., 139

Waring, George W., 102, 104
Washington, George, 6–8, 48
Watson, Tillman, 32, 102
Webb, T. L., 64
Weidenmann, Jacob, 88
Werner, Charles (Christopher), 17, 39, 40, 42, 91
Whaley, W. B. Smith, 104, 114, 131
White, E. R. J., 102
White, Edward Brickell, 14, 18, 19, 75
White, Edwin J., 104
White, Stanford, 126
Williams, John F., 34, 36, 60, 61, 66, 79, 80
Wilson, Charles Coker, 115, 116, 119, 121–23, 126, 127, *140*, 141, 143–46, 152
Wilson, John, 11, 14
Winn, Richard, 9
Wise, George M., 68

Young, Ammi B., 19